BETTER
LIVES
for Our Grandchildren

BETTER LIVES

for Our Grandchildren

*A Plane Crash Survivor's
Perspective on Politics and Life*

BILL ROBERTSON

BETTER LIVES for Our Grandchildren: A Plane Crash Survivor's Perspective on Politics and Life

Copyright ©2018 by Bill Robertson

Published by:
NoSmokeBlown
Wheaton, Illinois

ISBN: 978-0-9993777-0-3
eISBN: 978-0-9993777-1-0

Cover and Interior Design by GKS Creative

To Mom, who gave me so much.

The Greatest Generation Lost Mom Last Week

September 29, 2009

On September 24, 2009, the Greatest Generation lost another charter member: my mom.

Mom was born in 1915. She lived on a farm in Missouri and her dad died when she was eight. She had to go live with an older brother in Kansas City and finish high school there. She and Dad were married on New Year's Eve in 1935, during the Great Depression. They got on a train with all their worldly possessions and went to Michigan, where an uncle of Dad's knew of a job. The uncle told them they could stay with him, but the aunt said no, so they toughed it out like most people were doing in that era.

I was born less than a month after Pearl Harbor. Dad went off to the navy and was sent to the Pacific. Mom was home with a new baby and a job. Just like lots of young women are today who have husbands in Iraq or Afghanistan. Mom really understood these kids today. She worried about them.

Dad made it home and went into the construction business. They had two more kids and Mom did what she did best—be a mom.

As retirement approached, they started going to Florida during the winters. They bought a little place in rural Florida. Dad suffered a series of strokes and Mom took care of him until he died in 1981. Losing a dad at a young age, living through the Depression, praying through a war, raising three kids, getting them through college, and losing a husband would have broken many of our spirits.

Mom, who had never been on an airplane, flew off on a junket to Asia. Then she took another to the Holy Land; then one more, to Europe. She took up golf and played weekly with the neighbors. She started painting and did some pretty acceptable art. She walked two miles every day around her neighborhood and got to know everyone. She volunteered in the church nursery and taught Sunday school to the kids. Her motto: Dad died, I didn't, and I have to keep moving.

Finally, it was the car. She parked it herself, saying she shouldn't drive anymore. She did get a couple of speeding tickets, but that wasn't the problem. She knew it wasn't safe with her vision.

Then, she had to give up the house and go to assisted living. That was really tough. It was another chance to quit on life. To get bitter and blame God and life for all the setbacks. She coped, like her generation did so well. She became the queen of the assisted-living home. Still walked every day, finally with a cane, then a walker, then a scooter, then a wheelchair. She played bingo, played SkipBo, and was never in her room, always with people, always busy.

Then, it was time to move again to a place where she could receive more care. She had fallen a couple of times. Again, a tough move, but she coped. On the day she died, she played bingo, did her physical therapy, exercised, and had breakfast and lunch with her friends. Almost ninety-five and the lady was still going strong at the end.

Our country may be losing a lot with the passing of Mom's generation. She was steel on the inside when it came to dealing with adversity but lived believing if you put family first and shower them with love and kindness, it will be repaid. She was nice to people and people were nice to her. She knew the key to a long life was to keep moving and stay positive.

How do we replace good citizens like Mom?

Contents

Introduction

A Grandfather's Gift: This is my gift to my six grandchildren, who have given me so much in return.

Like most of my generation, we are late to new advances in the world of technology. I knew almost nothing about blogs. I began to read blogs. I began to research how one starts a blog.

This curiosity was prompted by my spending more time paying attention to the direction of our country. With two daughters, two sons-in-law, and six grandkids, this was a great concern. In 2007, I began to believe that my grandkids' generation would be the first to have a lower standard of living than their parents. When I would discuss this with friends and family, I would get the eye roll. I felt I needed a format to speak to a broad audience about these concerns.

I found a place called Squarespace and experimented with creating a blog. I titled it *Grandparents of America Awaken*. In January 2008, I began writing a daily blog expressing my beliefs regarding my vision of a declining future for my country. For the next five years, I wrote a daily entry. Then, with encouragement from my readers in lieu of ending it, I went to writing one entry every three days. Along the way, the title was changed to *NO SMOKE BLOWN*.

The content of these blogs is far too great to put in a book. So painstakingly, I have winnowed it down to a typical book size. What these blogs chronicle is the genesis for the election of one Donald J. Trump. The issues I identified are very close to the platform Mr. Trump presented to convince sufficient voters to give him the election. I am very proud of that.

You may ask why a successful sixty-five-year-old business-man would get involved in writing political blogs. I will try to answer that, as it is directly related to two separate epiphanies that shaped major changes in my life.

The first epiphany is about surviving a plane crash in 1989. I was a passenger on United Airlines Flight 232 that crashed on July 19, 1989, in Sioux City, Iowa. I was one of the 185 who survived a crash where 111 fellow passengers did not survive.*

The days and years that followed were not always easy. I was tested and found to have PTSD. They hooked me up to a machine and when I talked about the crash, everything went haywire. Naturally, everyone wanted to hear the story. Survivors were calling and asking me to join their groups. I received advice from a very wise man and declined.

As time passed, it got easier. Time does heal all wounds. But my perspective on life changed dramatically. I was a workaholic. Dedicated to climbing the corporate ladder. I was also an alcoholic and had given up drinking a month earlier. I managed to stick to that through all of this and have been sober and drink free for twenty-eight years. My family got me through the whole ordeal and we grew closer. I can never thank them enough for what they did for me.

My interest in work was diminished. I began to put more balance in my life. I determined that I was going to take early retirement at some point, which I did. Eight years later, at age fifty-six, I walked out the door. I was on four boards and was a VP of Marketing at Fortune 50 company and said goodbye to it all.

There is no question that the crash gave me the clarity to do this. Life is precious and when you get extra time, you value that time. Time to travel and spend time with the growing family and to chase new goals.

After the plane crash I made a bucket list. It started with achievements:

1. Sober six months
2. Married twenty-four years
3. Two beautiful children
4. Survived Flight 232
5. Network TV appearances (all three morning shows air my interview at airport leaving Sioux City that night)
6. Worth a million dollars
7. Played eighteen holes of golf with Neil Armstrong
8. Ran a marathon (Chicago 1980, in less than four hours)
9. Two holes in one (now six)
10. Broke 80 in golf (twenty times)
11. National Honor Society
12. Attended Harvard Business School (PMD36)
13. Lettered three sports in high school
14. Lettered one sport at university
15. Saved at least one life
16. Scuba dived
17. Skied Colorado
18. Rode a lap with Mario Andretti (Road America)

19. Met and spent time with Paul Newman
20. Spoke to an audience of over 1,000 (several times)
21. Traveled internationally
22. Nominated for class speaker (Harvard Business School)
23. Whitewater rafting (Snake River)
24. Saw two daughters graduate from college
25. Performed on stage in Vegas
26. President of a successful company
27. Stopped smoking
28. Soloed with a sailboat on Lake Michigan
29. Attended a World Series game
30. Played Augusta National

Those were the accomplishments in 1998. Here are the bucket list items that I have accomplished since:

31. Stay sober the rest of my life
32. Stay married to Susan (fifty-two years and counting)
33. Spend maximum time with family
34. Be a good grandfather
35. Leave something substantial to my heirs
36. Drive a racecar (have a valid racing license)
37. Be elected a VP in my company
38. Fly in a hot air balloon
39. Climb a mountain (Mt. Rainier)
40. Become very involved in a worthy charity event (American Dream Flight)
41. Build a retirement home (bought one, but did major renovations)
42. Meet a US President (the best, Reagan)
43. Meet Al Haynes, Captain of US Flight 232 (I didn't meet Al, but my whole family met Denny Fitch, the captain

who came forward into the cockpit and worked the pedals)

44. Teach a university class (did a seminar and taught a class for a professor friend of mine)
45. Work on values (work in progress)
46. Be a good friend to more friends
47. See my business unit that was losing money when I took it over make a minimum $10 million profit
48. Keep the extended family together (twenty-four of us in Florida every Thanksgiving for a week)
49. Build and appreciate an aquarium
50. Do something with kids (Dream Flight)
51. Be a better son to my mom
52. Counsel alcoholics (several employees and friends)
53. Help my children stay happy

There were fifty-six items on that bucket list in 1989, and twenty-seven will never happen. Like win a racquetball tournament, speak a foreign language, own my own business, certify as a scuba diver, get elected to public office, parakite, and get another degree. Some are remote, like attend a Cubs World Series—happened but I chose not to spend $2,000 to go. But one is becoming a reality: publish a book.

Many of the items on the list above will appear in the text or in a photograph. The list has kept me moving forward during retirement, and I would highly recommend making such a list.

And now to epiphany number two. When I was working, my focus was very much task related. I was so busy that my time for anything other than work was spent recharging my batteries. Sixty-hour workweeks were the norm. There was always a lot of travel and time away from family. Deciding to give that up and take my life in a different direction gave me time to look at the bigger picture. Not just loving and caring for family, but concern for their future when I'm no longer here.

It forced me to look at the world in general—and more specifically, our country. I could leave my family assets to help my heirs but if the country was in dire straits, assets are quickly devalued. l wanted a bully pulpit to try to change the direction of my country. When our debt reaches $20 trillion, we are in serious trouble.

So, I started writing blogs. I wrote a daily blog for years, thinking of my kids and grandkids. I pointed out the problems I saw and made efforts to suggest a fix. It's easy to criticize but not so easy to work on fixes. My subject matter was to address what a businessman saw going poorly for my grandkids in a country that I dearly love.

It's a lot of my heart in a lot of words and pages. It's a gift to my kids and grandkids. A piece of me that might have some value to them. My love for them is immense and if they get one millisecond of value from this, it's all worthwhile.

The blog may not have had a significant role in the recent election, but I had thousands of pages read and hundreds of thousands of hits and visits from all over the world.

That's my story, and I hope you will travel with me and learn something from my experiences. Read what helped me cope with the recovery from a massive tragedy I experienced. See how that gave me the time and interest to become a blogging grandfather—a hobby I would never have pursued without the benefit of a new perspective on how I wanted to live out my last years. So, here it is in all its unvarnished beauty. Seven years of an old man's wisdom.

To my grandchildren, let me start with a few of my ideas about living a rich life:

Love yourself. If you don't love yourself, you can't love others.
Dream big.
Believe you can do anything.
Never live in fear. Fear will paralyze you and restrict your quality of life.
Never envy what others have.
Make enough money to give you the freedom to live as big as your dreams require.
Build a great family—it will be your most valuable asset.
Love others without qualification.
Be giving to those who are in need.
Find your version of God and live by those rules.
Develop a great sense of humor.
Make good friends by being a good friend.
When things go wrong, make them right.
Find sunshine, not clouds.
Don't be a bully or a doormat.
Learn how to make others laugh.
Be energetic, and others will seek out you for that energy.
Learn to lead; the scenery changes only for the lead dog.
Learn to follow; we all have leaders.
Learn to listen; it's a skill you can develop.
Listen to our elders—they know more than your smartphone. They've lived longer, seen more, and possess wisdom you can't buy.
Tell the truth, even when it hurts.
If you dented a car in a parking lot and no one saw it, leave a note.
Be the better person in a conflict.

You have only so much time here, and low energy wastes
time.
People know whether you really care—you can't fake it.
Shallow people have shallow friends.
Take care of yourself. Don't be a burden.
If you gave less than your best, you will know who was
shortchanged.
What you do isn't what makes you tired—its what you didn't
do.

If you try to follow this path, when your time here is over
you will have many regrets—but fewer than most.

* If you want to read more details about the crash, please
see the Addendum on page 345.

2008

We Should Be Ashamed

January 27, 2008

We do not have one candidate running for president who is dealing with the key issues. Why? It is political suicide to tell us the truth. Why? We, as a nation, simply don't want to tackle the tough choices. Global warming takes precedence over becoming a third-rate nation. Heath Ledger's death takes our focus from dealing with no true energy policy to ensure we can maintain our economy and defend our nation. The fact that our grandchildren will be the first generation in this country to have a lower standard of living than their parents is something we don't want to hear.

We can't deal with the truth. Running out of gas in ten years is too difficult to think about. If you think we will run on ethanol and hydrogen, I've got some swampland I'd love to sell you. We want to be environmentalists, but we can't fathom giving up anything to accomplish that goal. But we have and we are. No new refineries in fifty years and not drilling in Alaska or offshore will be a very costly price to pay to be so concerned about our environment. Soon we will be 80% dependent on foreign energy sources. Tell me how we have any way to run this country, and defend it, if someone decides not to sell us crude or fuel. And someone will. They are just waiting until we get to that point. We would rather give money to other countries than build roads, improve the electrical grid, or maintain our infrastructure. Aren't we the big spenders?

If a business ran the way we are trying to run our country, it would have been bankrupt long ago. And we shareholders would be angry. We should be angry because that's how our country is run. But let's just put our heads in the sand and ignore the hard questions. It's easier than demanding our elected officials address them. If we don't require prioritizing the things that need to be fixed to keep our country viable, who will?

We have raised a generation of kids who demand instant gratification. The spin has been put on them their entire lives. Why would they suspect the United States is on the brink of becoming a third-rate nation? When China, Russia, and Canada are telling our grandkids how to live, will they be happy with what we did in the last twenty years? I think not.

Wake up, people. Tune out Al Gore and Michael Moore and demand someone tell us what we are going to do about our future. Not 200 years from now but ten years from now. Tradeoffs must be made. We can't satisfy everyone and do what is right. Sometimes those we are trying to satisfy are wrong. We need to spend our time and money here at home fixing the things that are destroying us. If we don't, we will suffer, and suffer greatly. We are teetering on the brink of self-destruction while we proudly try to solve the world's problems. Do we think others will step up and help us solve our problems when we hit the wall? I can hear the laughter now.

We are a country of fools led by idiots who pander to our inflated sense of importance. We had better find real leaders and listen to them. It's time to get our heads out of the sand and start rebuilding our country. We need to find answers to the things that will put our country out of business.

Here are a few things we can't afford: Foreign aid. We can't fix the world's financial problems. Troops overseas, anywhere. We can't be the world's policemen. The United Nations. Kick them out and let someone else pay their bills. The space program. Give me a break—it's a pork barrel now. Government should cut it to the bone. Farm subsidies. Eliminate them. Ethanol subsidies and medical malpractice. Put a lid on it. This will fix most of our health problems. Illegal aliens. Why is it so hard to enforce our laws?

How would we spend all that money? First, we must have an energy plan that will work. We need significant new sources of electrical energy. This means new nuclear plants, clean coal-fired plants, and more hydro generation. Cars and trucks that run on some electricity are the most viable options. We need to follow our neighbors to the north and get the oil shale option up and running and methanol from coal. The federal government must fast-track all of this. We need to drill in Alaska and offshore. We need new refineries. Again, this must be supported by the feds. No one in this country wants any of this in his backyard. Hence, no permits. Once we are so low on energy and everyone sees the need clearly, it will be too late. All of this has a long time line.

We need to fix our infrastructure. Road, bridges, electrical grid, railroads, and border protection are a few areas that have been neglected far too long. We need to upgrade education; we are falling behind. We need to create jobs for our poor. We need a strong defense, not to go off and fight others' wars but to protect ourselves if someone wants to attack us on our home soil.

In the past several decades, we have developed an appetite to take care of the world. Like the cobbler whose kids have no shoes, we have not taken care of ourselves. It's time to get our inflated egos in check and resign as the experts for everything the rest of the world wants. They hate us more and more each day for butting into their business. Let's make them happy and step aside. Let's focus on our own house before it collapses on us.

Fix the Blame—Don't Fix the Problem

January 31, 2008

When did this happen to us? When did we become obsessed as a country with fixing blame? Today, whenever anything goes wrong in government, business, or society, all efforts turn to finding the culprit or the scapegoat. The problem is left unsolved.

Let's take an example from each sector. The war in Iraq is going badly, and it's clearly Bush's fault. Let's spend all our time blaming W and no time suggesting solutions. The war in Iraq is going better, so let's forget Iraq and go to the economy. Who can we blame? Greenspan. He seems to be getting a lot of heat. Enron goes to pot, so let's wreck Arthur Andersen and just destroy a long-time successful company. They must have been at fault. They were the auditors and shredded files. Gas prices are high and the oil industry is setting prices illegally. Let's have another hearing in Washington. We've had, what, fifty since 1973? Has any hearing produced one barrel of oil or one indictment? No. But they make voters feel as though Washington is doing something.

How do you solve problems in this environment? Maybe you don't. What's being solved today—immigration, social security, energy, or health care? No, elected officials just point across the aisle and say they did it. Or they hunker down and hope no one is pointing at them. When a corporation gets to this point, one of three things happen: (1) they go away, (2) they go broke, get fixed, and go away, or (3) someone with a healthy culture takes them over. If the United States doesn't move on from the fun of fixing blame or the fear of getting blamed to the point of accepting accountability for making decisions, good or bad, and fixing the bad ones, we will continue to accumulate problems until they sink us.

Should Style Trump Substance?

February 6, 2008

We had eight years of Bill Clinton with style and no substance. We had eight years of George W. Bush with neither style nor substance. He mumbled and stumbled every time he needed to speak. He never got better. He did Dad's bidding and finished the job Dad left undone in

Iraq. That's it. No more. He hadn't insulted us enough, so he tried to lease key ports to Dubai. The day after he turned the House and Senate over to the Democrats, he fired Donald Rumsfeld. He increased the size of government, raised the deficit, and destroyed the dollar. Wow, George, that's quite a job. Wait . . . on the way out, let's wreck the economy.

Now, we have a love affair with Obama. Is it any wonder? The man can speak, answer questions, and look smooth in the process. This is another credit we can give W. We are so desperate as a country to have someone we can be proud of as president, we don't even care about experience, credibility, platform, or anything else that pertains to substance. We are willing to put a socialist in as president if he delivers good speeches.

Thanks to George, today I believe style does trump substance. We will elect Obama, then try to survive four years while government grows, taxes increase, health care is socialized, business is taxed for the good of illegal aliens, and all those wonderful dreams we had while intoxicated by Obama's charm are shattered as we see how really ill prepared he is for the job.

I was part of an organization where style trumped substance. It's gone—a $40 billion company, gone. All senior people were clones of the main man. None had ever achieved results. They just looked good trying. Diversity was more important than meeting profit goals.

Excuses were well explained. It's what happens when glib is God. We better strap it down. The United States may be headed for another four years of not accomplishing anything.

Cloistered Children

February 11, 2008

In three short generations, children in the United States have lost the option and will to play outside. My father spent his whole childhood outside, growing up on a farm. That carried over into his adult life. He was a contractor and spent most of his life outdoors. His only hobbies were hunting and fishing.

When I was four, my mother asked me to ride my bike to our downtown area and pay the bills by delivering checks. In the summer, I spent many days never coming home until the streetlights came on. My children spent less time outside, but we still felt safe letting them roam the neighborhood and create their own entertainment. When the weather was good, they were never in the house.

My grandchildren are rarely outside, except for organized activities. Statistics show today's kids in this country spend very little time outside the house. When they are outside, they are in their own yard. Outdoor activities are replaced by digital entertainment. Today, an adult minds children while they wait for the bus. My kids walked to school. What does this mean for the future?

Will we continue to grow perverts faster than the law can control? Will bankrupt family values create greater threats to the safety of our kids? Will my grandkids not know the joys of hiking, camping, fishing, and enjoying nature? Why protect the environment since the lack of law and order won't allow kids to enjoy it?

Why did this happen? I first point my finger at the ACLU. They work harder to protect the perverts than the law does to arrest them. Next, the judges are too soft, resorting to too many slaps on the wrist. Next, we seem to have money to police foreign nations, but no money for new jails. Family values come next. What type of home spawns child molesters, and worse, child killers? Why can't we restore our country to the type of land where we allow our kids to play outside? Why did we let Castro dump his prisons at our doorstep? Why didn't we ship their sorry asses back to Fidel with a few of our own?

Lethargy. We just resign ourselves to this. Why? This isn't even mentioned in Senator Obama's change plans. Why can't we be tough on crime here? Why should my adult children live in fear that something bad will happen to their kids if they are out of their sight?

This is a huge symptom of how sick this nation is. Where does the cure come from?

Haves and Have Nots

March 22, 2008

Why will my grandchildren have a lower standard of living than my kids? Basically, it boils down to this: Capitalists and conservatives have done the most to make this country what it is. Socialists and liberals have nipped away at progress and tried to destroy our nation's wealth and courage. Effectively, they have won. We are stopped dead in our tracks. We want to be a nation that doesn't reward hard work and success.

How did this happen? Simply, the "haves" and the "have nots."

Liberals have the ACLU. Conservatives have not.

Liberals have the Sierra Club, Greenpeace, and hundreds of on-call, out-of-work deadbeats who will show up anywhere, anytime, to protest any progress. Conservatives have not.

Liberals have Hollywood and the major networks to shape thoughts in the United States. Conservatives have not.

Liberals have 90% of the university professors preaching their political philosophy in the classroom. Conservatives have not.

Liberals have Jesse Jackson and Al Sharpton. Conservatives have not.

Liberals have Al Gore, who has sold climate change as a fact. Conservatives have not.

There is only one area where I see conservatives outgunning liberals: the NRA (pun intended). It shows an effective organization that has the funding and courage to take on anyone. This same plan, applied to all areas where the tide has turned, could reverse serious trends and get us back on a reasonable path.

Majority Rules

March 27, 2008

In a democracy, the majority should rule. But it doesn't in our democracy. In the United States, money rules. Washington is for sale. Open for business. Just contact your local lobbyist and lay some heavy coin on them. They will bring home the bacon. Do I have proof? You bet.

Farmers make up less than 1% of the US population. Food consumers comprise 100%. In a showdown in Congress, who wins? The 1%, of course. That 1% represents some big corporations, David Rockefeller, and Ted Turner. They put $80 million into the pot and bought a new farm support bill that will cost $260 billion in our tax dollars for the good of less than 1%. You can kiss their grits and step up and pay twice——once in taxes and again at the grocery.

A democrat from Wisconsin, Ron Kind, sponsored a measure that would have cut the subsidies by a paltry $10 billion. It was stomped on the House floor. Grain prices are at an all-time high. Global demand is doing that, and the same with crude oil. But the American taxpayer gets screwed on both deals. Corn is $5.52 a bushel, up from $2.20 in 2006. So, Congress adds to the farm bill so the small minority in the United States can benefit. You might just want to take a moment and pen a letter to your congressman and senator and see what kind of B.S. he feeds you about his position on this.

How can less than 1% of the population make such a difference? Less than 1% of the US population is considered militant environmentalists. They have more control than the farmer. They will destroy this country. Need I go on?

The minority is running this country. Washington cares not about you or your kids or grandkids. Unless you have a lobbyist, don't bother to think you are being represented. Of course, if the majority ever gets smart enough to throw out everyone who voted yes on the farm bill, we might just be heard. Stop the rape of the average citizen for the special interest groups. Make the majority heard and force our interests above all others.

Time to Reboot Washington

April 23, 2008

When your computer locks up and won't work, you reboot, right? It's time to reboot Washington.

In the business world, it's a given you can't delegate authority without accountability. In our country, we have done just that. If everything is W's fault, why not have a benevolent dictator and get rid of Congress and the Supremes? If they have nothing to do with the mess we are in, why have any of them? In the corporate world, heads would fall. There would be no bonuses paid and expenses would be pared to the bone. This is the model that has made this country work. Not the political model.

In history, most civilizations have lasted no more than 200 years. Apathy sets in. We need a new model, at all levels, for who represents us in Washington. No more attorneys. Attorneys are beavers who dam up the streams of progress. We need farmers, steel workers, firefighters, teachers, and a true cross section of our country.

If we are going to save this country, we need to get rid of the whole kit and caboodle. Everyone. We need to start over. Our elected officials go to Washington to get rich, not serve the country. Let's give them the reboot.

A Breath of Fresh Air

April 28, 2008

I left my Arizona home to return to Illinois for the summer. There are many things I will miss leaving Arizona and one big one is Sheriff Joe Arpaio. Sheriff Joe is the Sierra Club of politics. He's clean air in a cesspool of political scum.

There is no lack of clarity when Joe speaks. There is no smog, no dirty laundry, and no "for sale signs" on Joe's office. The liberal media is working full time to make Joe go away. They blast him day in and day out. The mayor of Phoenix is trying to get reelected by trashing Joe. What has Joe done to make everyone so mad? He's done his job, that's all.

Joe doesn't use a computer. He has a typewriter. He saves all the thousands of letters he receives and answers each one personally. He doesn't have a signature stamp. He's been the sheriff of Maricopa Country for sixteen years and will run again in November. Since he has an 80% approval rating, he will be reelected, despite all the efforts by the media to bring him down.

Joe arrests illegal aliens at the rate of 200–300 a day and puts them in jail for processing out of the country. It's the law in Arizona and Joe is just enforcing it. What do the Valley religious leaders, other law enforcement officers, Hispanic groups, civil rights leaders, the media, and Mayor of Phoenix want Joe to do? Stop enforcing the law like the rest of the country is doing.

Joe's response: "Everybody supports me. I've got thousands of letters from the public. They're my bosses. I do what the people want me to do. I'm elected. If you've got politicians who don't like what I'm doing, that's their problem. I serve the people; I don't serve mayors, bureaucrats, governors. I serve the people." Wow, what a novel concept. And you get an 80% approval rating for doing it.

Joe says if you cross the border, you committed a crime. You can get six months in prison. It's a federal offense. If we lock them up, they can't send money home. It's a hardship. They will think twice about coming back across. For most places in the United States, there's no penalty. Catch them, send them back, and they return in a week. If we want to stop the flow of illegals, start enforcing the laws on the books.

Here's my point. What if two-thirds of the elected officials in Washington had Joe's perspective? I serve the people. Not the people who are represented by lobbyists, not the high-profile people, but the real people back home. People who want our country to prosper and grow, not go backwards. People who will respect you if you do the right thing. People who will reelect you even if the media trash you day in and day out, because the people trust you to do the right thing. You always do. What if you answer your own mail? What if you spend enough time with the people to know what the people consider important?

The liberal media today believes they control this country. They can put someone out of office and they can put someone in. But they can't put Joe out and he doesn't need to pander to their liberal perspective to get in. They just can't believe it. They will never stop going after Joe at every level. He's one of their few failures. They control most of the candidates and incumbents much more than we do as citizens.

Joe has an 80% approval rating and Congress has 15%. Guys, we can learn from Joe.

McCain Can't Win

June 15, 2008

Senator John McCain has no chance in November. So why is he the Republican candidate? If the senator is the patriot I believe him to be, he should drop out of the race and let the party replace him at the convention. He is 6% behind and the worst is yet to come.

No one can run without a platform. His platform is to extend the Bush tax cuts and extend the Bush war. Obama says McCain will be four more years of Bush and he is correct. If you thought no one could have a career in politics and look worse behind a podium than George W. Bush, you haven't watched McCain. He hasn't mastered the teleprompter and Obama doesn't need one. When McCain stands behind the podium, he disappears. With no movement of the arms that were damaged so badly in the POW camp, you just have a head behind a podium stammering.

He has lost the far right in the party. He has lost those who believe we need to trash global warming and get about the business of using our resources to save our country. He has lost the anti-war people. Who does that leave? I'm not sure, but it won't add up to much.

How can a political party commit suicide? Easy. Just pick the wrong guy with the wrong platform and ideology to run for the top job when everyone else in the party is fighting for their political lives. Rep. John Boehner (R-OH) says, "The Democratic Majority's callous indifference as American families and small businesses struggle with $4 gasoline is both inexcusable and irresponsible. By flatly refusing to schedule votes on the

House GOP plan to help reduce fuel costs and achieve energy independence, the Democrats in control of Congress are proving themselves complicit in our nation's energy crisis, which is growing worse by the day on their watch." Rep. Mac Thornberry (R-TX) authored legislation called the No More Excuses Energy Act, H.R. 3089. Rep. Tim Walberg (R-MI) put forth a discharge petition to force a vote on this proposal.

Most Republican candidates are lining up strongly in favor of a platform for the party that pits them against the Democrats on energy issues. These candidates are far smarter than the man they picked to run for president, who is very much on the side of global warming. As the party distances itself from the man at the top of the ticket, who will support him?

I honestly thought Bush was the worst president since Carter. But now, I believe McCain has the potential to be worse yet. Bush has two major flaws. He can't speak and he is terminally stubborn. If he could speak, he would be stumping for domestic energy to help his party. He has nothing to lose. If he tried, he would just make it worse. His stubbornness was borne out when he held on to the idea of leasing our ports to Dubai until the heat was unbearable. Then, he hung with Rumsfeld until the party lost the majority in Congress. The Republicans up for election see that 57% of Americans want domestic energy production to begin now and that number will continue to grow. McCain, on the other hand, does not see this. Is he devoid of vision, or is he being led by elitists?

If Bush were to debate McCain, Bush would probably win. And in a stubbornness test, McCain would win.

You had better keep firing off letters to the Republican Committee, because McCain will take the horse Big Brown's failure to win the triple crown at the Belmont to a new level. He will set the record for the biggest loss in US election history.

Bad Decisions Equal Pain

June 16, 2008

Making bad decisions over time results in pain! If you marry the wrong person, you will endure a painful divorce or a bleak life. If you disdain education, you may face fewer quality job choices. If you abuse substances, you might lose your driving privileges or worse. Bad choices spell pain. The more bad choices you make, the more pain you will face.

Our leaders have been making bad decisions for a long time. First, we believe we will always be the world's leader. We feel entitled. The people today who are making bad decisions had nothing to do with making us the world's leader. But they can have a lot to do with causing us to lose the title. There are two paths they can take: one, a path of vision that corrects past errors and leads the way to making us stronger; or two, a path that weakens us and causes us to lose our edge and our spot at the top.

In business, you see company after company go down the wrong path, making the wrong decisions. There is a long list of well-known companies in the country that no longer exist: American Motors, Pan Am, Eastern Airlines, Arthur Andersen, and Enron, just to name a few.

Public confidence in this country is at a low. Citizens, you and I know we are on a bad path. We are feeling the pain. Have we made bad decisions that will make us a second-rate nation? Two out of five Americans believe we have. In a recent poll, that's the percentage of Americans who believe China will overtake us as the world power in five years or less.

What are the bad decisions causing us to feel we are on the road to pain? As the richest nation in the world, we believe we have endless spending limits. We give money to foreign countries, we fund a space program with no tangible goals, and we fight a war that may result in no gain and big losses for all. We put all our attention on a goal that may have no benefit—global warming—because a former vice president wrote a paper on it as a student at Harvard, and a majority of the media, most Democrats, all of Hollywood, and few misguided Republicans have bought into the myth.

What does all of this add up to? We have stopped making things in America. Manufacturing is at an all-time low. We have stepped up spending money we don't have. We are shipping dollars out of the country at a record rate. Between the war and the price of oil we import, we are destroying the value of our currency.

We want to be the world's buyer of products made elsewhere. To finance this, we have an investment economy. As the mortgage mess showed us, some of the basis for this investment is not sound. As the dollar falls, other countries investing in US companies are backing away. They smell pending trouble with our house of cards investment economy.

We ask the rest of the world to supply us with cheap energy by doing what we refuse to do here. Is that the epitome of arrogance or a symptom of ignorance? The other countries are on to us. We can count on less and less help with our future energy needs. Plus, we will have to use more and more deflated dollars to buy what scraps we get.

We are going to have pain. Lots of pain! Until we personally decide we need leaders who make better decisions, we will suffer. Even after we clean house, we will suffer until new leaders can fix the damage. It will not start for at least five years, because we have no one running for president who will fix it. Most of Congress will not. There will be lots and lots of pain and you might as well prepare yourself to endure it. It's time to teach your kids and grandkids to live a leaner, meaner lifestyle! Sorry, but the die was cast a long time ago. Bad decision piled on bad decision equals pain.

America Is Suffering a Stroke

August 5, 2008

Historians have said that prior world leaders have lost their way for a myriad of reasons. I think what we are witnessing right now is the primary reason. Our country is suffering a stroke.

When politicians of both parties abandon their grassroots dedication for personal greed, either bad things or not much of anything happens. Washington, D.C., is recession proof. Most politicians go to Washington for one of four reasons: First, for bigger and better things. Second, to grow wealthy. Third, to train to be a lobbyist where they can make millions. Fourth, to forge a lifelong career in power.

Special interest groups figure prominently in all these ambitions. They raise money for the next campaign. They point the politician toward personal wealth enhancement. They get the vote out to keep the candidate in office.

If there is no purging of the politicians, it's like your body gorging on animal fat. The main arteries that keep the life-blood flowing to keep our country healthy begin to clog. Ultimately, the country slows to a halt. Nothing gets done. This is where we are today. Special interests have clogged our arteries and we are stroking out.

The general public knows it, hence, the 9% approval rating. But it crosses party lines. Past purges have occurred when the public is mad at one party and puts the other in power. Today, the public is mad at the whole lot of them. If we could meet and pick our options, the most popular might be to end the two party-system. It might take a long time for this to happen. And, as sick as this country is, we could be in hospice when that happens.

We might have to settle for a marginal fix. A possible start is term limits. This would eliminate two of the four political ambitions. No one could go there for a career. And they probably can't steal enough in two terms to get stinking rich. Plus, the life of a lobbyist gets harder when they face change. This would be a good first step in unclogging the arteries and trying to fix our political mess.

Obama's Platform in Plain Terms

August 29, 2008

Vote for Obama and here's what you will get: you will have an energy policy that grows government and creates no energy; a cap and trade tax that will increase your gas prices and heating bills; a labor union policy that will unionize more businesses and send some out of the country or out of business; bigger government; lower stock prices; more taxes; and more regulation.

Basically you get Nancy Pelosi on crack.

Plus, you get no experience and no feel for the commander-in-chief part of the job.

Vote for Obama and you will get a new Bill of Rights. The government owes you health care. You are free to enter this country illegally with impunity. If you don't work, the government will provide for you. If you work hard and do succeed, you must pay the government so we can take care of all of the above. Exception: Obama chooses not to give any help to his own half-brother who lives in a hovel in Africa and exists on a dollar a day.

But you get a very good speaker. You get a man with a lot of style. You get diversity. You get a man who aspires to be the leader of the entire world. Lots of ambition, lots of arrogance, lots of ego.

The LPGA (Ladies Professional Golf Association) has a lot of diversity. So much so that it is the Asian tour in America. The only problem is the average US golf fan doesn't want to watch Asians play golf in America. So they are losing sponsors, getting no TV airtime, and will soon be no more. In desperation, they are stipulating you must speak English to play on the LPGA. Of course, the ACLU is all over that. Point, diversity.

When it comes to speaking, as a reader wrote this week, the empty drum makes a lot of noise.

Obama's Health Care

September 8, 2008

Our government, the same government that wants to fix health care, broke it.

To a large extent, the US government determines the number of doctors we produce every year. Obviously, the more doctors we have, the more competitive the business is and the lower costs become. How does the government peg the number of doctors? The funding from the government determines the number of medical residencies available. Prior to 1997, the government budgeted $11 billion annually to fund 100,000 residents at $110,000 per resident. To save money in 1997, that was capped at 80,000 new residents per year. So we created a shortage of doctors.

Now, Obama wants to make sure the 50 million uninsured people have medical insurance, with the same number of doctors. Gee, aren't most doctors pretty busy today? How do they take on another 50 million patients? Plus, many are approaching retirement age and the idea of more work for less money will push that decision up. Of the 50 million uninsured, over 10 million are here illegally. Another 20 million may already be qualified for Medicaid, but just don't bother to apply.

Remember when Jimmy Carter got in the oil business? He had the DOE setting allocations for everyone in the business. It raised prices and created false shortages. Reagan cancelled his policies the first month he was in office. Prices went down dramatically.

Here's how it works with Obama Medical: too many people seeking medical attention and too few doctors, nurses, and hospitals to provide the care.

Some bureaucrat will decide whether you get treatment—and then, when and where. Even if you want to pay for your treatment, you can't, as they have found in Canada. You just get your ass in line like all the illegals and deadbeats. Some ex-postal employee will decide your fate. Remember the Colorado governor, Lamm, who actually said the elderly have a duty to die rather than take medical care that could best be given to someone younger and more productive?

You want a reason not to vote for Obama? How about your life or that of your elderly parents or your children? I had to deal with those bureaucrats in the 1970s in the Department of Energy for allocations for gasoline. If you asked me to rate the top one hundred jerks I met in my business career, ninety-nine of them worked for the DOE—little gods who couldn't get hired to do anything else. Just think how big they would feel if they could deny you medical care you needed to stay alive.

Unless you are an illegal or a deadbeat, you probably don't want the government deciding your live-or-die future. You better give this hard thought in November.

Presidential Platform Needs to Trump the Candidates

October 3, 2008

In case you missed it, this country is in a big, big mess. It came a lot faster than I thought it would, and it's worse than you or I could ever believe. If someone doesn't turn the old Queen Mary, it will run aground. Options are getting to be fewer and fewer.

While the ship is sinking, Al Gore is on deck with a big fire hose putting water in as fast as he can. He suggested civil unrest to stop any further use of coal in this country. China is building coal-fired generators at a record pace. Let's export Al to China. Maybe he can whip up some unrest over there. He epitomizes the type of leadership we can't afford right now. The luxury of buying into bad ideas has passed for us. The Chinese would run him over with a bulldozer on day one.

Last Thursday, I predicted a 700-point Dow drop this Monday. A friend sent an email criticizing me for underestimating it by seventy-three points. We can't make a mistake in November. It's not about style verses substance. It's all about intent.

Here's my call. For a few reasons, I believe Obama will sink the ship. First, I believe Barack will raise corporate taxes. Facts show the countries that have reduced corporate taxes have the fastest rate of GDP growth. Do we want to reduce GDP in the face of a growing depression?

Next, I believe Obama will increase entitlements. I blame most of our economic woes on excessive entitlements.

Energy will be critical to growing and creating jobs. Obama is on the same page as Gore. He's says he isn't, but he will do nothing to increase domestic energy production except put a windfall profits tax on the oil industry and create a big government bureaucracy to achieve renewable energy. Nothing will come of this.

The costs of health care for everyone will be borne by business and those who have health care. More entitlements—more we can't afford.

Obama is against the First Amendment and that really scares me. His staff is trying to stop any ad that McCain runs that attacks him. He is a pretty sensitive guy when it comes to attacks. Ask Bill Clinton. Bill is still mad about the race card incident. While we don't have a free press, we still have free speech. The press looks for problems only with those they don't support. How else can you explain the mortgage mess and the lack of good investigative reporting leading up to the problem becoming public?

The liberal Democrats are up to their eyeballs in this mess and the media is giving them a pass. With the media in his pocket and his record of attacking any detractors, Obama is really a dangerous threat to the First Amendment. This at a time when the American people need real facts and solid journalism! All we stand to lose is everything.

George Bush will go down in history as the worst president of my lifetime. It's hard to be worse than Carter, but he has managed to do it. So much for an Ivy League education!

McCain is not going to be the solution, but Obama's platform just doesn't fit the times. Everything he wants to do will worsen an already bad economic climate. It just doesn't seem to be the time to try to make things worse.

Trust Will Determine the Election

October 19, 2008

When it gets right down to it, trust will decide who will be our next president. McCain must carry the Bush presidency on his back. It's a big, big burden. He may not be the man for the job.

Sometimes when you are as eloquent as Senator Obama, you do get people's trust. Most people in this country want someone who can stand up and speak and not embarrass us like President Bush has done. But too smooth is still too slick. Senator Obama can shed sticky material better than anyone I have seen in my lifetime. He does not always rely on truth to do that. For example, he refutes his connections to William Ayers with a quick and easy dismissal. He always mentions President Reagan's ambassador Annenberg as the money man. He doesn't accept any responsibility for the surge working. Using nice language every time, he refused to be indignant about the reference to McCain being a George Wallace. He dances around that!

If McCain has any chance whatsoever to win this, it will get down to the trust issue. Personally, I do not trust Obama. I believe he wants our country to go down the road of rampant socialism. With the leaders of the Democratic Party in power today—Reid and Pelosi—and with Joe Biden, he has all the tools he needs to make that happen.

Not that Bush and King Henry haven't already started that journey. King Henry being Paulson! When you call the banks in and tell them you are going to sell a percentage of yourselves to the government, you are starting to nationalize business.

More government, more taxes, less freedom, fewer personal choices, more labor unions, fewer jobs, higher capital gains taxes, more government jobs, and income redistribution. That's the choice.

You can put all the words you want to put around it, but if that's what you want, buy it. If you believe you won't get this, you will be very surprised. There are no surprises with Senator McCain. That trust gap will be the only lifeline McCain can hope to grab.

Stay tuned.

2009 Economic Surprise

October 22, 2008

If you buy the polls, it's all but over. When President Obama takes over in 2009, there will be some surprises. Here are my calls.

There are no windfall profits to tax with the crude price back down. Interest in offshore leases will be diminished. Hence, there will be no Obama energy strategy, since it was all based on windfall profits taxes. Sorry, you will have to pay money to foreign governments that hate us for four more years. If and when the global economy recovers, it will be worse for us next time the crude price runs up.

Obama will nationalize the auto industry much like Europe has done in the past. The fact that the government regulations here have caused much of the pain for the industry will prove the industry was smarter than the government. For example, all the US automakers have fuel-efficient cars they sell in other parts of the world. They can't sell them here due to minor regulatory differences. Would it not make sense to waive those now, rather than give money to the car manufacturers? No. That would require government to admit to their part of the problem. Obama will run the industry but it may take a few tax dollars to offset the losses. It will dwarf Amtrak in tax subsidies.

The airline industry may be next. Remember, President Obama will tell you what's best for you and the country. No need to ask.

The European economy will be worse than ours. It's strange that we are going to elect a president who wants to model us after Europe. Japan will be even worse. China will continue to grow, but at a somewhat slower rate than the 12% they have experienced.

The $500 and $1,000 refundable tax credit Obama used to buy the election will come due. In 2006, 220 million Americans were eligible to vote and 40% paid no taxes. This will jump to 49% with the tax credits. Plus, another 11% will pay less than the $1,000 tax credit. The plan to pay for this with tax increases for the 5% that now pay 60% of the taxes won't stretch. Thus, to pay for the votes he bought, he will need to lower that tax increase income level from $250,000 to $75,000. This will certainly capture a lot of college professors, media types, and small business people who believed that only the 5% in brackets over $250,000 would be punished. Surprise! Surprise! There is a certain justice in this. If he tries to get it all from the 5%, history has shown that group can be very creative. They will cut back investment, spending, and hiring, and even move, as California and New York have found. That will wreak havoc on the overall damaged economy.

Today's economy is much like a sewage disposal plant. It takes a lot of churning to get the bad stuff to come to the top. It's far from all there yet. As more and more surfaces between now and the crowing of the new king in January, more retirement accounts will be severely damaged, more jobs will be lost, and more tax dollars will be pledged to clean the new floating material at the sewage plant.

President Obama owes the environmentalists. Cap and trade will pass. It will increase every form of energy, including gasoline and heating oil, plus jet fuel. Europe is trying to take it out since the economic pressure to do so is mounting. While they take it out, we will put it in.

Day in and day out, President Obama and the media will lay this at the feet of the Bush administration. Meanwhile, the backup at the sewage disposal plant will begin to stink. People will become more and more upset with Congress and begin to refuse to breathe the rancid air.

There will be no stock market recovery until 2011, when President Obama loses the Democratic majority in Congress and much of the damage done is reversed.

The Victor's Spoils

November 7, 2008

We have a new president-elect. As someone who doesn't plan to move out of the country, it is important that I support the new president. It's the same for all of us. I pray he does what needs to be done to pull our country's fat out of the fire. Many have done much to give Senator Obama this opportunity. Some may still be celebrating today. For some of those who worked so hard to make this happen, there will be a price. This is not a negative attack on you or Senator Obama. This is just reality.

First, the group that did the most—mainstream media— you got the job done. Never before have I seen any group work so hard to accomplish a goal. You should be proud. But you have lost 48% of your customer base, or potential customer base, in the process. At some point, very soon, the big guys who control your budgets will say enough. The top guys and gals will be fired and replaced with people who do not have the same political ideology. Ultimately, you, too, will lose your job. As these businesses scramble to regain some lost revenue, you will find it hard to get employment in a place where you can pimp for your liberal causes. Sorry, but yours is a business and money rules. Don't worry. Your government will take care of you.

Hollywood, take your bow. You have wanted this for a long, long time. If you have been too enthusiastic and some people may choose not to see your movies, don't fret. When the economy picks up, your business will, too. Making good films might help. Keeping your politics to yourself might open your work up to people who don't think your eighty IQ points qualify you to tell us how to vote.

Oprah, you were doing damage control on your show today, trying to save the brand. You may find ratings down, too.

Walmart shoppers, clean up in aisle ten. I'm guessing that 90% of both the employees and shoppers at Walmart voted for Senator Obama. Here's your payoff. The labor bill, already passed in the House, will fly through the Senate and be signed into law by the new president. Walmart is the first target to use the card check program to unionize the company. Walmart will pass the costs on to consumers. Those of you who count on Walmart to stretch your tight budgets will not be able to buy as much. Those of you who work there may find stores closing and fewer places to work. Maybe this isn't the change you voted for. May be you should have asked more questions about what change means.

Government contractors, Barney Frank wants to cut the defense budget 25% for social programs. Sorry, you won't be able to sell as many $200 toilet seats.

New Yorkers, you did your part. But here's the bad news: as the country moves forward on social programs like the very ones that have put you in a big financial hole, there will not be any money from Washington to bail you out. You will probably have to keep moving out of the state like you have been doing. Hey, the weather is not that great there. Try Texas.

New England, you folks are at the wrong end of the energy pipeline. In fact, you have resisted any pipelines for years. So, you use heating oil and power that is pretty darned expensive. Wait until you start getting Henry Waxman's bills. It gets cold and dark up there in the winter. Texas might look good to you, too.

Ohio and Pennsylvania, the new president is on record saying he might just bankrupt the coal industry. That won't hurt your economy too much. You are big in mining but not that big. But the factories that close due to taxes, power costs, and unionization might hurt. There will be jobs working for the government. You can rebuild bridges or put up windmills. Plus, like most government workers, you don't even have to show up for work most of the time.

California: like New York, don't count on the feds to bail you out of your budget woes. As the feds are hard at work making the country more like California and New York, they will not have time or money for your problems.

Charities, you helped the new president. I had a nice African American lady ring my doorbell last night and ask me to donate to a charity. I responded by saying the new president was going to take more of my money for taxes and I was counting on him to handle my charitable giving from now on. She had a very strange response, and I plan to say this a lot in the next four years. Charities, you are going to get less and less, and many of you who work there are going to be dependent on charity.

Raise a glass to change. It's coming and it will be fun to watch. If your ox gets gored by the change, it's just part of the process. Sometimes change is painful. As the president-elect said in his victory speech, we will have to sacrifice. Elections don't come with warranties. It is buyer beware. If you bought and didn't think about what the product might do for you, beware. I'm just here to point out the fine print. I tried to read it before I bought. It's a good practice.

Life for Our Grandchildren

December 8, 2008

Why should we be concerned for the future of our grandchildren?

We've come a long way in three generations. My parent's generation lived on farms, or in small towns in small houses, or in big cities in small apartments. They grew up with the automobile. Very few people could afford to fly. Most who travelled out of the country did so in the military during WWII. Few went to college. Many or most worked with their hands. They also grew up without TV.

Our generation migrated to the suburbs. Land became important. We owned a lot with a lawn and a power mower. Many of us were the first of our families to graduate from college. We flew for business and pleasure. Most of us have traveled internationally. We may have worked for the same company for most of our careers. We worked hard and played hard, lived in the backyard and in front of the TV.

Many of us know how to do things around the house by ourselves, but may have chosen not to. We had it much better than our parents. We had Vietnam, the Cold War, and polio, but no Great Depression or world war.

Our kids went to college, married later, married often, bought bigger houses on bigger lots, and manage their careers by moving between companies. Both parents work, and day care is the order of the day. They had Desert Storm and now the Iraq War and Afghanistan. They had kids later than past generations. Their kids started flying as babies and families travelled. Life is big. Everything about it! The cars are big, kids are big, yards are big, and dreams are big. The computer is key to their lives. PAs, laptops, and desktops. Can't live without them!

Their kids, our grandkids, are just starting to grow up. Some are just reaching the teen years. How does their future look?

If you listen carefully to the people who are deciding their futures, we have made it impossible for them to move forward. They say we have poisoned the planet, grown obese, been too greedy, overextended our credit, become dependent on illegal immigrants to do our hard work, grown lazy, stopped making anything, overbought the world's energy, borrowed too much, and are the bane of the world.

So according to them, we have to stop driving, flying, living in houses over 1,000 square feet, eating, borrowing, having children, and making money, and we have to start feeding the world.

But I see no indication that any of "them," the ones who want to make this happen, plan to do any of this. It's do what I say is best for you, but don't ask me to do the same.

Look at the beltway around Washington: there is no recession there. Hollywood is fine. Politicians steal all they need to make sure they and the next three generations do fine. The wealthiest in America—Gates and Buffet—won't suffer.

The displaced in America, those whose voices are not heard because they feel it is a lost cause, might choose a different path. I don't plan to be silent because I owe it to my grandchildren to be a voice. I want to be louder than the fools who are taking us down a bad road. This is not a Democrat or Republican thing. This is an American thing.

By being silent, you condemn your grandchildren to make undue choices that fools are deciding. Do you want that to be your legacy to them?

Take a Brick Out, Put a Brick Back

December 24, 2008

As a business executive, I enjoyed working with and around a lot of talented people. There were two traits that I grew very intolerant toward. First was the employee who would come to me and say, "We have a problem." Early on, I loved these challenges. I could help my direct reports solve these problems and it made me feel good. Later in my career, I grew wiser. My response was always, "No, you have a problem. If I need to solve your problem, I don't need you. If I need to find someone else in our group to solve your problem, I don't need you. If you go away and solve your problem, I don't even know you had a problem." Usually, an employee came only once with the "we have a problem" story.

The second trait was the faultfinder. Every organization needs good faultfinders. But if all they do is find faults and never offer solutions, no organization needs them. Whenever an employee pointed out a fault, my response was "Take a brick out, put a brick back. I welcome your idea that we have a fault with something, but I don't want to hear the fault if you haven't thought about it long enough to come up with a possible fix."

Some commenters pointed out this blog only points out faults and offers no solutions. Pulling bricks out and not putting bricks back. There is some merit to that criticism. I have said from the beginning the premise of this blog is the theory that I believe my grandchildren will be the first generation in this country to have a lower standard of living than their parents. Further, I blame my generation for this. Lastly, I believe my generation has an obligation to put energy and resources into this before we depart this earth. I believe we have the talent and time now to make a difference.

Even with consensus science, like global warming, you must make a case for it to get consensus. If I see that one glacier fall one more time I will scream; so, most of this year, I'm making a case for my theory.

Today, I went back through the blogs to see if I have grossly violated my two pet peeves. First, am I bringing you, the readers, a problem and then saying "We have a problem"? Second, am I taking hundreds of bricks out and putting none back?

By my count, 95% of the entries have a problem and a possible solution. Perhaps the problem or the solution is not one a reader accepts, but they are there. The rest probably violate the brick out, brick back in principle. In my defense, remember my theory is not a rosy future for my grandchildren. If I thought that, I could go back to reading fiction and sleeping well at night.

My third great bit of wisdom is the mirror test. When business people have to make tough decisions, they often struggle with how the outcomes affect others. For me, the mirror test was the only answer to this. If I could face myself in the mirror with the decision, I was okay with it.

After rereading most of a year's work and giving it the three big litmus tests, I'm okay with where this blog has been and where it's going.

I set out to try to make more people think about what we might be doing to our kids and grandkids down the road without actions, past and present. My generation can dwarf most of the groups that make protests today. The hardcore environmentalists have hundreds of young deadbeats who can show up at a protest at a moment's notice. We have millions of retirees who can do the same.

My long-term goal is to get this generation to transform apathy into action. We have the anger; it's just a matter of organization until we make ourselves heard.

Why Christmas Is So Special to Me

December 25, 2008

One fine summer day in 1989, I was flying home to Chicago from a business trip in Denver. I landed in Iowa instead.

My heroes in life will always be the fine men in the cockpit who did a masterful job trying to land a DC-10 with no hydraulics. Just a big glider that could make only right turns.

Thanks to them, I've had almost twenty years since that day. That's twenty more than I thought I would have that day—years to watch my two daughters have children of their own.

My six grandkids are a big, big part of my life. Before that day, I might have put lots of things before family. After that day, never again. I retired early to make up for time I didn't spend with my kids when I was building my career.

So here's my Christmas gift to you: You make plans and God smiles. Tomorrow, you may step in front of a beer truck and be history. This Christmas season, most of us will be with family. Take a little time and look around and enjoy being a part of a family celebration.

If you are unhappy, chances are you are a big part of your own unhappiness. Stop making yourself unhappy and let the world back in.

I haven't had too many unhappy days in the past nineteen years. I haven't found too many things that beat me down. I know what a bad day really is. Many of you have no clue. I

have never forgotten some of the people who weren't as lucky as I was that day. Kids who didn't get the chance to live their lives.

Paying back is part of my deal when I walked out of that cornfield in 1989. Maybe reading this will help someone realize they have no reason to be unhappy.

I really don't like talking or writing about Flight 232. It does play a role in why I do this blog. My concern for the future of my grandchildren is genuine. When I started this blog in January of this year, things weren't all that bad. How fast that has changed.

We don't have enough heroes in the cockpit of this country. We really need to work on that.

2009

Economics 101 as I Remember

January 9, 2009

Here's what I retained from Economics 101. Mike O'Conner, my professor, would be proud.

Americans have stopped spending and started saving. I guess that should be a good thing, since banks would have more money to lend. But, the private sector has stopped investing. Demand is down and the economy is bad, so business is not expanding. Plus, banks have balance sheet problems, so they are not lending. This has caused a lot of savings to go to treasury notes, not into bank CD's.

Now, Professor O'Conner, you told me demand increase can come from consumption, exports, government, or investment. When our investments were wiped out by the housing market and the stock market, there were trillions lost. So, investment is not going to recover soon. Exports? Well, the world is consuming less, so this doesn't look too rosy. Consumption? The public is smarter than the government. We know excessive debt and spending put us where we are. We aren't going to go back there for a while. So, that leaves government.

Government spending does not create investment capital that creates new business, bigger business, and more goods to sell and export. It will be slow to develop new jobs, and the jobs it does develop will be short-term. When the government spending stops, the jobs go away.

The government says they have understated their unemployment forecasts. When haven't they understated them? They use voodoo economics to keep score on this critical factor of the health of our economy. They now say unemployment may hit 9% next year. I say we will break 10% in the first quarter. It may go higher before the year is out.

So, the only creation of demand in 2009 will be government. When the stimulus package is used primarily to bail out the states that put Obama in office, all state Medicare and Medicaid problems, pork barrel projects, earmarks (Obama, the king of earmarks, says no more earmarks), and other nonproductive projects, little will be done for infrastructure.

Basically, until you and I get our confidence back that we can invest in corporations, put money in banks, and buy things again, there will be no economic recovery. We will just move deeper and deeper into socialism; more and more dependent on central government; more and more like Cuba.

I'm not going to spend and I'm not going to invest in this climate. Until we throw the bums out of Washington and our state and local governments, and hire competent people to run the business of government, why should we spent and invest?

Obama's Blind Spot

January 12, 2009

President-elect Obama has a blind spot. Until he overcomes this shortcoming, it will make economic recovery impossible.

He will spend $700 billion in taxpayer dollars, debt, or newly printed greenbacks to create new jobs. Only a small part will be spent on energy and this will go toward "soft" technology. That decision, regardless of how prudently he monitors the spending of those dollars, will ensure we don't recover from the deep economic depression we are entering.

For years, California has been following the "soft" technology energy strategy espoused by one Amory Lovins, a crackpot darling of the environmental zealots. Obama is a fan of Lovins. Since 1976, Lovins has been saying the United States should never build another nuclear or coal power plant. He has gotten his way in California, and all over the United States, and stopped new nuclear plants.

California has driven consumption down to the best of all fifty states in electricity per capita. They have only built new cogeneration plants. Still, they have an energy shortage. They rely on neighboring states for 20% of their power demand. This, despite over one hundred windmill facilities, forty-three geothermal sites, the world's largest complement of solar-electric cells, and fifty-six more renewable-energy projects on the drawing boards. Lovins says the state is "freeloading" on the neighboring states.

The facts are in. It didn't work. Despite billions of dollars spent and all the ideas implemented, only small inroads have been made in the supply side. Meanwhile, old power plants go out of service or produce less. The "soft" energy technology doesn't keep up.

So, all the money Obama wants to spend from the $700 billion will go to "soft" technology, despite the lessons learned in California.

Ultimately, it's going to be coal or nuclear. And, clean coal. So clean it's not a threat. That's it. Make a choice. If the blind spot didn't exist, we could pick one or both or proceed to use the money to build things we need and work. But, we will continue to spend on things that are favorites of environmentalists, but not productive enough to offset lost production. Lovins wants us to live in a cave, and with Obama's help, he will get his crackpot wish. To my knowledge, no one voted for Lovins. Still, he exerts far too much influence on all of us.

Without this energy, there will be no job growth. The government money will be spent by the states to cover the deficits they have run up by spending amounts they may never have again for years. They refuse to make cuts and will keep their deficit spending going with the help of Obama.

Experts have tracked jobs with energy in America. Jobs go up when cheap energy is readily available. Jobs go down when energy gets tight and expensive. So, we bet on something that didn't work for the past twenty years in California. We lose time and money. And, we make the future worse than the past. We watch. We let it happen.

Our Grandchildren Will Get the Bills for Our Mistakes

January 24, 2009

The now generation couldn't wait. They had to have everything now. It was all pretty easy. Jobs to pick from, easy money to borrow, stock markets going up and up, home prices skyrocketing, and home equity loans easy to get.

We watched as they bought everything they could buy. America with 4% of the population consumed 20% of the world's GDP. We were the world's market.

The party's over; turn out the lights. We have hard choices to make. We can let all the excesses of the past fifteen years shake out and absorb the consequences of our spending binge, or we can postpone reality and delay the pain for the next generation to deal with.

The die is cast. Trillions of dollars of deficits as far as the eye can see. No one can say it better. Print it, or borrow it, or tax it, but don't face the music. Put it off for someone else, like my grandkids, to face.

Never, never deal with the hard choices when we can delay the pain. Create an energy plan that makes sense. Why? Let's get on with global warming. It doesn't make sense, but we feel good doing it. Until we run out of energy. Don't worry; my grandkids will deal with that. Fix social security or Medicare or Medicaid. Why? Let my grandkids worry about it. Fix our broken manufacturing economy. Why? It's impossible to make things and still take care of the environment. We'll just buy them from some other country that trashes their environment. What, no jobs here in America? Let our grandkids worry about that. Labor unions out of control. No problem. They gave us $400 million for the last election. Let's give them an easier way to penetrate more businesses. We'll call it card check. It will wreak havoc on the economy. No problem. Our grandkids will clean it up. Pension plans underfunded. No problem. They won't run dry until our grandkids go to draw on them.

Everyone is looking to the government to fix things. It will make government more powerful and the public less powerful. When government can't fix it, no problem. The grandkids will.

Someone needs to stop postponing the pain. I guess my kids need to do that. I will help, but until they see the light and realize they are destroying any chance my grandkids, their kids, have for a decent standard of living, I can't help.

Until anger replaces apathy, it will be business as usual. Do not, under any circumstances, take the hard road to problem solving. Always, always find the easy road and postpone the pain. It's going to get really ugly and there will be lots of anger. Some may be directed at the parents of the grandchildren for being the "now" generation and using up the American Dream, not preserving it for their kids.

This might result in the grandkids being the "tough" generation. The "tough" generation that shoulders responsibility for fixing problems, not shoving them aside. That's the only positive I have been able to find in this discouraging trend.

The Immigration Program in the United States Is an Embarrassment

March 3, 2009

Are you sleeping well these days? Please read *Immigration Chaos* by Nevelle W. Cramer. He spent twenty-six years in the Immigration and Naturalization Service. I'm sure he both over- and understates things, like most former employees are prone to do. What he describes is an organization that is totally incompetent from top to bottom. The larger the budget—and it's grown very large—the more agents they hire, which resulted in more illegals coming into this country. According to Mr. Cramer, it became worse when Homeland Security took over.

Janet Napolitano is the new head of Homeland Security. She made headlines last week when she failed to utter the words terrorist or terrorism once in her opening remarks to the confirmation committee. She's a piece of work. On July 2, 2007, as governor of Arizona, she signed into law House Bill 2779. This requires all employers to verify through Homeland Security the immigration status and Social Security numbers of all employees. You see, the voters in Arizona are tired of illegal immigrants. They are tired of the crime, the expense, and the jobs being taken from out-of-work citizens. They wanted action.

While governor, Napolitano "got it." She signed all the bills that were meant to control the illegal alien situation in Arizona. But, just as Cramer describes the INS, she wanted to appease the people, but not enforce the laws.

But Washington is now speaking. The director of Homeland Security has a priority: to have the most incompetent agency in Washington do the local enforcement because the local enforcer is doing it too well. She wants him to be as incompetent as she is. She is not going to protect our porous borders, stop the $24 billion in wages exported to Mexico last year, protect much-needed jobs here for American workers, or keep us from—God forbid—another terrorist attack. She is going to protect human rights, first and foremost. Isn't that the role of the ACLU?

She is soft on border protection, soft on crime, and believes terrorism isn't part of her job description. She is incompetent and not very smart. Is that the person we want running Homeland Security?

America With No Middle Class

March 9, 2009

What will we face in this country with no middle class? Like it or not, the ranks of the middle class in this country are shrinking. The middle class has always been made up of people who worked hard and achieved success. People who invested in stock for businesses that grew, paid dividends, and appreciated in value, like GE and GM. People who put money back into houses to add to their appreciation. People who ran successful businesses, hired people, and made them middle class. People who worked hard for large corporations and added to the success of their employers. People who bought things and made others successful. People who paid their taxes and gave to charity. People who put a premium on education so their children could achieve more than they achieved. People who had health insurance.

The rewards for this group today are few and far between. They have lost 60% of their investment values. They have lost 50% of their home values. They have lost their jobs. They can't spend and give to charity. They can't trust investing in corporations, since they have no trust the corporations will pay dividends or appreciate in value. People are losing hope. They are scared and angry.

Who is not part of the middle class? Those who have so much money they have no grasp of reality. They are committed to lofty goals like a pristine environment with no manufacturing, no drilling, and no concern about jobs since many have never had one. People who may want everything for everyone, but many do not make personal charitable donations of any magnitude. People who make laws, make movies, and make friends with others who are obscenely rich.

Then there are those who have tried to do better but struggle. Or, those who don't try but expect to be taken care of in the same way as the middle class. For want of a better term, this is the lower class. Some will move up, others never try.

We have a government now that has taken a head count. They feel they can stay in power without the middle class. They will always have the extreme rich vote. This group has had a guilt complex forever and, with no hitch to reality, they will support the idea that everyone else should be equal, excluding them, of course. The lower class is outnumbering the middle class. So, let's pull the middle class down and we will have a lock on the future. That's the current political end game.

Just a few more steps and the group in power will be there. Taxing the middle class will help. It will drive another stake in the perilous financial state they are suffering. Do card check. This union move will close some businesses, raise wages for the hourly worker, and drain some more profits from the middle class businesses. Put in cap and trade. This will tax everyone, but tax the middle class more since they are heavier energy users. Further, it will drive down the stock market, reduce corporate profits, and push more middle class voters into the lower class. Do universal health insurance. Fewer businesses will offer health insurance and everyone will be equal. That is, equally dependent on government.

As the middle class shrinks, America shrinks. We become poorer as a country. We need more money from taxes to cover the growing needs of a burgeoning lower class that is getting more and more help from the government.

Ultimately, we will become a country of few opportunities. That makes it self-fulfilling. There are few who can afford to try the American Dream again. They are too dependent on their government for everything. We will have regressed to a state where we can't turn it around.

I am not in favor of conspiracy theories. But, I believe when you elect a man president who was never properly vetted by a fawning media that let it happen, this is the risk you take.

If you are part of the middle class or aspire to be, you had better wake up and take heed. This is the master plan from Obama, Pelosi, Reid, Schumer, Durbin, and those in power. If successful, they will be in power forever.

When you have nothing left, no investments, no house, no job, no health care, and no prospects, you will vote for them. They are the only option for your survival, the survival of your kids and grandkids. Unless you move to a country that has not followed this path. Or, a country that did and is reverting to the formula that made this country so great.

Think about it hard, think about it every day, and then consider what you can do about it before it's too late. And too late is sooner than you think.

Engineering Socialism in America

March 20, 2009

To transition to total socialism, certain strategies must be created and implemented.

First, because America won't buy socialism by its given name, a substitute must be offered. In the 1930s, it was the Great Depression. All the social programs and government growth was to fix the economy. World War II created another opportunity to advance the cause. Now, it's Global Warming and the Environment.

Carol Browner is just the person to help it along. She was a card-carrying member of an International Socialist movement. It helps to have the media in your pocket, so they can spin the ideas into something more positive.

One by one, you must destroy the threats to becoming a socialist nation. Business is the biggest threat. Make all CEOs seem like bad guys. It translates into "Big business is bad. Big government is good." They take on big business and win.

Wealthy people with resources can cause trouble. Tax them. Take back some of their discretionary wealth. It makes it harder to use it to promote capitalism.

Dangle the carrots of a better life before the masses. Make it sound like there is no downside. Health care, housing, government jobs, no taxes, free education through college, everything a person needs can be provided by a government eager to help.

Find a clueless, dynamic leader who will push the buttons and let others push his buttons. Someone who has a long history of supporting socialist causes.

Keep the wounded opposition down. And, if possible, take them off the air (free choice bill). Tax environmental causes to provide more money and power to government (cap and trade). Strengthen the unions (card check). Reward the supporters and punish the detractors. Look where the stimulus money is being spent. Democratic areas get the rewards.

Now you have it. Central control. You have defeated all comers. Business is beaten into submission. And, taxed into destruction. The business of America is government, plain and simple. Everything revolves around central control. The government decides who gets jobs, who gets health care, who gets to pay no taxes, who keeps what they have, and who gives it up to the government.

If you don't think this is happening, you aren't paying attention. Every day, more Americans wake up and smell the coffee. Anger is building and it's building toward Washington. The clowns who are trying to take our country from us are not going to get it done without protest.

It's sleazy and getting worse. The idea put forth this week that veterans who need medical treatment from war wounds must have their personal health insurance pay first, not the government, is sleaze at its best. Every veteran in America who knows about this is incensed. It's another slap at their sacrifices by an ungrateful president. This is the kind of stuff that will grow into an ugliness none of us want to see. Get up and make your disgust known about this kind of stupidity.

Meanwhile, Obama goes on a fawning Leno show. That's a tough interview. Leno is still doing Bush jokes. Good luck with that prime-time show, Jay.

Worst States for Business Put Obama in Office

May 10, 2009

The CEOs choose the best and worst states for growth and business. No big surprises here. The states that put President Obama in office are at the very bottom. The five worst states for growth and business are: California (51st), New York (50th), Michigan (49th), New Jersey (48th), and Massachusetts (47th). Without these five states, Obama would not be president. The top five states are: Texas (1st), North Carolina (2nd), Florida (3rd), Georgia (4th), and Tennessee (5th). Florida is the only one that went for Obama.

Is there a message here? Our president wants to make the rest of the country like the five worst states. Residents and businesses are leaving these states. Unemployment is the highest in these states, as well. No surprise there, either. Texas wants to distance itself from the federal government. Business is good in Texas. They don't want the social disease that is killing the five worst states.

Many Americans see this coming. We are going to see an increase in states demanding their states' rights. Texas kicked this off. Now, Montana is following their lead. The CEOs graded all the states on three items: (1) taxation and regulation, (2) workforce quality, and (3) living environment. Citizens leaving these states are using the same criteria for leaving.

Soon the other states will find what it's like when entitlements exceed income. When regulations strangle businesses. When jobs go away. When special interests run the state to the detriment of the overall population. Who would want to move to Illinois? The state ranked 46th. The governor before Blagojevich is in prison and Blagojevich is headed there. The entire political system is corrupt. The public interest always comes after the opportunity to line political pockets. This is the state that brokered Obama into the presidency.

How much evidence do we need to realize we are on a path to destruction? How much money can government extract from productive people to support the bottom twenty states? How long will the top states continue to support the dogs?

It's all coming to a head. If Washington doesn't stop trying to make all of us like California, there will be a movement within the healthy states to bail from the United States. They won't take it much longer.

National Health Care Winners and Losers

June 19, 2009

I f you are on Medicare, you will be a big loser. President Obama says he will cut $600 billion from Medicare expenses. This will limit your ability to receive medical care. The very people who need medical care most. Where is AARP on this? You will find rationing for every medical need, including serious needs.

If you have a medical plan from your employer, you will be a big loser. Your benefit will be taxed, as well as your employer's contribution. Your next raise will reflect that employer's cost. Over time, your employer will drop your benefit and shift you to the national plan.

If you work for an employer who doesn't offer medical insurance, you may lose your job when your employer is faced with providing all employees medical insurance. You may have medical insurance, but no job. Today, you can go to an emergency room and receive treatment. Tomorrow, you will have to apply to a government employee and wait for your turn. You may have insurance under this plan, but you may die before you receive treatment.

If you are a gay partner of a federal government employee, you just hit the jackpot. You have the best medical insurance plan taxpayers can buy. But, when your partner must compete with the millions of new insurereds, you won't find your new plan to be so good. You will fall in line with all your new friends with national insurance.

However, as the proposal now stands, government employees will keep the insurance they have. Until this is changed, you should know the designers of the new plan want no part of the plan.

Certainly, there will be winners in all this. The biggest winners will be the people who never worked and never will. They could have insurance now with Medicaid, but most don't bother to sign up for the plan. They will now have health insurance. Others, who only work because of health insurance, can now stop working. If you are an illegal alien, you will have another reason to stay here and bring all your friends across the border with you.

But, using Canada and the United Kingdom as examples, we will all be losers. There is not enough supply to handle the expected new demand. Not enough doctors, nurses, and medical facilities. Health care will be rationed and Americans don't like to wait in line. The post office has cured all of us of that.

More doctors will retire, since their workload will go up and their income down. The quality of health care will go down. New drugs that might cure diseases will be fewer, since the government will regulate the prices.

This is part of the master plan. Level the playing field. Those who work hard and succeed and have assets have health care now, since they would have to put up assets to pay for health care if they didn't have insurance. Those who have no assets roll the dice, since health care providers just add the unpaid bills to your bill. Now, no one will be uninsured, but no one will receive quality health care. That pretty much levels the field.

Diversity at the University

July 14, 2009

Across the country, it has been so important to have diversity in the workplace. It should be particularly important at the university level. The young minds of our children and grandchildren are placed in the custody of the faculty during a critical time in their development. Does diversity include political affiliations? Evidently not.

Over the years, universities have been adding minorities and women to the rolls of their faculty, just like all business has done. We suspect it must be a lonely place for a conservative to work. And, it must be lonely for a conservative student to learn.

Dan Lawton, a journalism student at the University of Oregon, decided to do some research. He wrote an article for the school paper about this question. Dan's research showed there were one hundred and eleven registered Democrats and two Republicans in the schools of journalism, law, sociology, and economics. The Republicans were in the school of law and one was the university president. The president, Dave Frohnmayer, fostered a diversity plan in 2006. The plan was intended to help the "individual learn to question critically, think logically, and communicate clearly." It included political diversity as one of the elements to promote. Well, President Frohnmayer, you aren't going to like your grade on that mission.

More research showed 96% of political contributions went to Democrats in 2008; in 2004, 100% of political contributions went to Democrats. I guess the former president was a liberal.

So, the budding journalist published his story in the university paper. You can predict the outcome. He was vilified by the faculty. One professor confronted him, saying he was personally offended by the article. He said, "If you like conservatism, you can certainly attend the University of Texas and you can walk past the statue of Jefferson Davis every day on your way to class." Another stated, "You think you're so (expletive) cute with your little column. I read your piece and all you want is attention. You're just like Bill O'Reilly. You just want to get up on your (expletive) soapbox and have people look at you."

In this sea of liberalism that exists on every campus today, how does a student from a conservative family not get Stockholm syndrome? You know, the one where prisoners sympathize with their captors? If a university like Oregon really wanted to add political diversity to the faculty, how could they do that with tenure?

How did the conservatives in America let this happen? How do they fix the unfairness? Do you demand your kid's university of choice have political diversity? If you do, would that limit the choice to the University of Texas? I have a feeling if a student at the University of Texas did a similar piece of research, it might not be so different.

My Version of Health Care Reform
July 22, 2009

I believe we need health care reform in this country. I have a plan to improve health care.

First, we need tort reform. My research shows that tort reform could reduce medical expenses by $400 billion a year. Some states have already capped lawsuits. If $400 billion were taken out of the cost of health care, it would be a good start to add uninsured people to the rolls of insured.

Next, raise the budget for internships so we have more doctors and more competition. Start there, and provide more doctors to provide more health care before you juice up the demand for care without providers.

Put all government elected officials and employees who are on the blue-ribbon health care plan on the veterans' medical plan. This will accomplish two goals. One, the insurance for our heroes will get better. Two, the savings we accumulate will go into the pot to pay for more internships and provide insurance to more uninsured.

Eliminate fraud in Medicare and Medicaid. It is estimated that annual fraud runs as high as $10 billion dollars. Before you sell us the idea you can run health care in this country, fix the pieces you already mismanage. Reel in that money, tighten the system, and use the money to add people to the Medicaid roles.

Get serious about illegal aliens. They add billions to health care costs with unpaid visits to emergency rooms.

Offer tax breaks to small businesses not offering health care.

Encourage business to have wellness programs to reduce their health care expenses.

Offer tax incentives to the insurance companies to develop better databases to help patients and health care providers.

Give doctors tax incentives to do pro bono work on patients who can't afford health insurance.

Start with the savings from tort reform. That would reduce insurance premiums for all doctors. Require all doctors to rebate 50% of that savings to an uninsured patient fund. The money would go to states to fund uninsured patients' medical bills.

My Twin Granddaughters Would Have Died in Canada

July 27, 2009

I have nine-year-old identical twin granddaughters. They are great kids. Born three months prematurely, they weighed 1.9 pounds and 2.1 pounds. They spent three months in neonatal intensive care at Northwestern Memorial Hospital. The doctors and nurses brought them through with flying colors. It was a challenging time for my daughter, son-in-law, and our entire family. We worried until they were toddlers. We then knew they were not only perfectly normal in all respects, but even exceptional.

They are good students, average in size with their age peer group, very good athletes, and sweet little girls. They have the twin thing going which only twins, parents of twins, and grandparents of twins can ever understand. They are and always will be each other's best friend. What a treasure they are to all of us.

If my daughter and her husband were living in Canada, they would have died. The Canadian universal health care system has basically eliminated neonatal intensive care. I have done extensive research on this and preemies in Canada get an instant death sentence. It's far too expensive to save them. The bureaucrats who decide who lives and dies in the free health care world just can't, or won't, process the decisions fast enough to save them. If you are born too soon in Canada, it's just too bad. If you live too long in Canada, it's just too bad.

My daughter had good insurance through her employer and I'm sure the bill for two babies in neonatal intensive care was well over a million dollars. In my visits to the neonatal unit to see the twins, I saw lots of babies in the unit whose parents did not have adequate insurance. I could be wrong, but I would bet a lot that many of those babies were uninsured. But, Northwestern Memorial cared for them. And, in most cases, saved them. And, saved them without damage. I felt so strongly about the belief they were treating uninsured babies that my wife and I made a substantial donation to Northwestern to help them pay for those kids they treated.

The facts are facts. Mortality rates are higher in all types of illnesses in Canada. The numbers of doctors and nurses per capita are much lower in Canada than they are now in the United States. The fewer doctors and nurses per capita cannot treat the entire population of Canada.

In Canada, it is illegal to buy health care. That would move you ahead in line. You have to come to the United States to pay for health care, if you can't wait for treatment in Canada.

The time to get an appointment with a doctor in Canada has tripled since universal health care became law.

President Obama wants the government to run everything in your life. He wants the government to decide whether you get health care, the kind you get, and when you get the care. Too much demand and too few doctors and nurses, plus cost control, mandate bad health care. Free, but bad. In a move to include 46 million uninsured, Obama will destroy our health care system, add cost, reduce doctors' pay and caseloads, and give you or my twins a death sentence.

If it has not worked anywhere, why do it?

Stimulus Bill is Working

August 5, 2009

Finally, we get it. The stimulus bill is really working.

Who is benefiting from the $700 billion package? State and local government, that's who. So, your tax dollars are going from the federal government to some state and local governments to supplement the taxes you are not paying to them. You buy less, so less sales taxes. Your house is worth less, so less real estate tax revenue. State and local governments would never cut costs, so they need your money. Now, they just get it from Washington.

What are they doing with the money? They have hired more union workers. The Bureau of Labor Statistics shows 12,000 new employees added to the rolls of state and local governments.

And, they are passing out raises. Pay and benefits rose 4%. In the private sector it was 0.8%, the lowest since tracking started in 1980.

Other state and local spending was flat after adjusting for inflation. So, bottom line, state and local government income is down substantially. But, expenses have gone up. They have kept everything but employment costs flat and used federal money to add employees and pass out raises in a recession where the private sector has cut 1.3 million jobs and virtually cut raises.

So, stimulus funds let state and local government avoid making needed cuts. What will they do when the stimulus money dries up? They will raise taxes to recover the lost revenue from the feds.

Isn't all this reassuring?

The Goose and the Gander

August 8, 2009

Here are things I want to require all members of the House and Senate to do. This would be my employment contract for you, if I designed such a contract. It reflects the true value your jobs add to our nation. If we, the people, hired a professional human resources person to appraise and rate your jobs based on what you do, you would be a mid-level manager with little, if any, accountability. It would be very hard to set objectives for your annual appraisal. This employment contract is generous, based on how your jobs would measure versus a CEO or an executive VP in a large corporation:

1. Fly commercial air, just like you expect business executives to do. The auto industry was chastised by you for flying private aircraft to Washington to beg for money. Since all you do is beg for money, you don't get an exception. Spending $600 million for new private jets to fly you folks to your boondoggles is an insult to all voters. And, don't fly first class. Fly in the back and talk to the folks.

2. I expect you to take periodic drug tests, just like the majority of American workers must do. I suspect your percentage of drug use exceeds the statistical average of mainstream America. We really don't want you voting on multibillion-dollar proposals while high.

3. I expect you to take the heat. In my career as a business executive, I had to stand before groups of employees and explain why we were making decisions they didn't like. Or, dealers or jobbers who stood to make less money. Or, customers who were getting price increases they didn't like. But, never, ever did I stand in front of any of these groups without the facts. I was always prepared to handle most questions. Nor did I ever try to B.S. them. Since most of the town hall meetings I've seen in the last week deteriorated into chaos, you must not be experienced in delivering news people don't like. Most of you couldn't handle the questions or tried to B.S. the people. Some of you walked out. Who would walk out on a group of customers? You and only you. You don't see us as customers and that's the problem. Never has it been more obvious that you serve the president or lobbyists, not voters.

4. You should buy your own health care. We should not buy you Cadillac insurance. If you want it, you pay for it. If you want to try no health care, gamble. Use after-tax dollars to buy whatever type health care you need. Don't use my tax dollars to buy the best.

5. Close the perks in Washington. The barbershop, the gym, and all the other crap. If you need a haircut, go to the nearest barbershop and talk to the folks. Join a gym with your money. No cars with drivers; drive your own Smart car to show your environmental supporters how green you are. No shoeshines. Nothing. Cut it to the bone. You are failing just like AIG and you neither deserve, nor should get, any bonus treatment. You aren't all that special. Most of you are just attorneys who couldn't make it in the real world. You are mid-level employees of the people. Giving up the frills will help you remember who you are, who you work for, and who pays you.

6. You get a four-week vacation. That's it. The rest of the time, you are in Washington. If you own a home back home and want to keep it, fine, but you won't be there much. Move your family to Washington. That's how it would work in the private sector. Hit your office forty-eight weeks a year. If you want to come home and talk to the folks, rent a room. A nice conference room. That's how the private sector does meetings. Campaign during your four-week vacation.

7. You get a yearly expense account. The same amount for all, representatives and senators, no difference. Do all the traveling you want within budget. That's how the private sector does it. Remember, it will be audited. Don't cheat—you could be fired. When times

are tough, like they are now, expense budgets will be cut. So, make it work.

8. Effective 2010, your budget for staff will be cut by 50%. That's what the private sector has been doing for the past two years. It will be zero-based budgeting tied to the GDP. If the GDP goes up, your staff budget will go up on an index basis. If it goes down, yours will go down further.

9. Mandatory retirement is age sixty-five. Go play golf with your lobbyist friends. There is a reason why the private sector has a mandatory retirement age. We get old and set in our ways. It's time to move on and let the younger people take over.

10. You will show your daily schedule on your web page. If you meet with a lobbyist, it will be on your schedule. Since you will be working a real work year under this plan, you might find it a challenge to fill forty-eight weeks with meaningful work.

11. You have two years to make the post office and Amtrak profitable. If you fail, you resign. It's on your watch. Plus, it might dampen your interest in taking over every business in this country. See, that's how it works in the private sector. Get it done or get out.

Since all of you know so much about how to run businesses like the auto industry, health care, the post office, Amtrak, and banks, we think you need to have an employment contract that replicates the type of contract a mid-level executive has in the private sector. The accountability will be good for you and better for us. You might even find satisfaction in achieving something. Most of us who have worked with accountability have found that satisfaction.

60,000 AARP Members Can't Be Wrong

August 18, 2009

So far, 60,000 AARP members have cancelled membership since the AARP backed Obamacare. These wise seniors realize the proposed health care reform will be financed on the backs of the elderly. How many more cancelations will be needed before the management is changed?

Will it take all 40 million to cancel to get their attention? Go to the AARP website and look at the backgrounds of the management and the board of directors. It will tell you all you need to know.

The CEO is A. Barry Rand, who distinguished himself as a leader of social change in some of our nation's largest corporate and educational institutions. An African American who has pushed social change is not going to put AARP members before Obama.

The President, Jennie Chin Hansen, hails from San Francisco. She, too, is strong on liberal causes. I will give you 10,000 to one odds she voted for Obama.

The rest of the board is comprised of the likes of Hubert Humphrey III. I guess we know his ideology. Then, there are six professors. Since 80% of professors in the United States are liberal, we can gauge their posture.

Here's a flash to all AARP members: you might as well have the board of directors of *The New York Times* as your AARP board. Until now, it might not have made a difference.

But here, they disenfranchise you for their ideology. They cannot support your wishes to have Medicare as you have known it. They must support their president and their party. That comes first. It's the same with your elected officials. They are supposed to support you. But, they put special interests and their political futures first.

I'll bet you didn't know AARP made Harry Belafonte the "Man of the Year." Harry is the man who said, "Bin Laden didn't come from the 'abstract.' He came from somewhere, and if you look where you'll see America's hand of villainy." He proclaimed Colin Powell and Condoleezza Rice are "slaves with the privilege of living in the house of the master, exactly the way the master intended to have you serve him." I don't need any AARP hotel discounts enough to support these people who support everything I detest.

This board and this leadership will not get the message until the cancellations hit 5 million. Alternative groups have had 70,000 new members since all this started. There are choices. One is American Seniors Association. If you send a torn AARP card, they will give you free membership for a year. You can enroll online at their website Americanseniors. org. If you want betrayal, stay with the AARP. But, if you resent this, quit.

Been to Europe Lately?

September 6, 2009

Left wing elitists, like Obama and his administration, envy Europe. Have you been there lately?

I have traveled extensively in Europe. Recently, I

stayed with friends in the country in the United Kingdom. While I have always enjoyed my travel in Europe, I never once thought it would be a better place to live than America. I'm always happy when I board the plane to come home.

The rustic lifestyle just doesn't compare to home. The little cars, the little houses, the tiny pubs with bad food make me miss my country. High taxes keep Europe behind our many privileges. Poor teeth, stemming from poor dental programs, you don't ever want to snap off a tooth in the United Kingdom.

What, exactly, makes progressive liberals feel we should emulate them? Only one thing comes to mind: the government control they have is much greater than ours. Countries smaller than most of our states, speaking different languages and with different cultures, have little in common. Big government is the one common element—dependence on government.

Europeans feel we are lacking in culture because most of us are not bilingual and they are. Big deal. Our kids learn how to create things like small businesses. We survive with less help from our government. We are more independent. Our states and our constitution made us less dependent on a central government. It has made us unique and more successful. Why should we give that up and become less successful?

Without us, most of them would be speaking German. Without our aid and help through the years, many of them would be in far worse shape than they are. What right do they have to be arrogant and look down their noses at us? Because they want us to be like them, less successful?

To me, if you think life in Europe is more exciting, more culturally fulfilling, and better than ours, move there. Buy yourself a car that won't hold all your family and friends, move into a house so small the rats are hunchbacked, pay the government 80 percent in taxes, and get little back for your money.

Otherwise, thank your lucky stars you live in America. Resist with all your being any politician who wants to deal you the hand dealt to your European friends. And, don't wish it on your children and grandchildren.

Everything the Obama administration wants is dealing you and your progeny that hand. Stop it before it's too late.

A Lifetime in a Hope Chest

September 30, 2009

My mom was a member of the Greatest Generation. She kept a hope chest all her life. I remember poking around in there a bit as a kid, but most of the contents were pretty boring.

After she died, we celebrated her life and then reconvened at my sister's house. We gathered in shifts to sift through the contents of the hope chest.

It was like reviewing her ninety-five years of life, plus that of three generations of family before her. What she considered a key event in her life, or that of her family, went into the chest.

Her birth certificate, her marriage license, our old report cards, my ROTC brass, old newspaper clippings of my high school sports career, a newspaper article where my brother and a friend went into a house on fire and got some kids out when they were only kids themselves, and pictures, pictures, and more pictures. Pictures going back to the 1800s.

Letters my Dad wrote to her when he was in the navy in WWII. The letter he got from Admiral Forestall for serving his country in time of war.

Every family member received a chance to pick out the items they wanted to keep. It was like a huge scrapbook in a big box. There was a lot of teasing about some things that may have been serious twenty, thirty, or forty years ago but were pretty funny today.

As I was watching and picking through Mom's life, it occurred to me it was the end of an era. With electronic communications, fifty years from now there won't be hundreds of letters in a hope chest.

One of my grandkids said she was going to start a hope chest. She found the idea very exciting. Like many ideas, it is easy to wish for, but hard to do. It takes a lot of dedication to keep pouring your life into a box and to haul the box from place to place for seventy years.

Life got more and more complex and sophisticated over those seventy years, but there were items in that chest about my three-year-old grandchild. So, Mom still found a way to keep the hope in the hope chest alive.

I don't know how often she opened the chest and looked at the things she found important in her life. I never asked. My guess, it was often.

Funny how small things in a box add up to the history of a life where most hopes were met and dreams fulfilled. It kind of makes one wonder if all the technology we have today is better than a box full of memories that get a little yellow, smell a little musty, but are so tangible, like a letter or a picture or a piece of ROTC brass.

I am pleased the idea of a hope chest still appeals to my thirteen-year-old granddaughter. This is a story about real hope, not Obama hope.

My Grandchildren Count

October 2, 2009

The future for my grandchildren, my kids, and your kids matters. It is far more important than the current crop of politicians in Washington getting reelected. Your voice and mine are the only things standing between the irrational spending in Washington today.

We can and must be heard. You can't keep thinking and believing your voice doesn't count. When you protest, and are called radicals, you can't be deterred.

Look at the competition. Organizations like the ACLU, ACORN, the SEIU, the ardent environmentalists, the labor unions, the media, Hollywood, and others raise millions of dollars to push agendas that will ensure my grandchildren and yours will be the first generation in this country to have a poorer standard of living than their predecessors. They can be defeated. Accountability must be made a part of serving in office in Washington.

We have more than enough energy here, choose not to tap those resources, and yet sit by and watch while we send billions of dollars to foreign countries. We watch while politicians shut down manufacturing here on a planned basis. Manufacturing is a dirty word. We watch while a bloated stimulus bill, which in truth is earmarked for reelection, fails. We watch while cash for clunkers moves normal demand for car sales forward and dries up sales for the next four months. We watch while our government, which can't run anything, tries to run car companies and wants to run your health care.

We watch while we are lied to daily. We see Chicago, which has a major financial problem, blow $100 million on a failed Olympics bid to bolster the ego of Mayor Daley.

We see tax dollars go to ACORN. We see Washington destroy the housing market with Freddie and Fannie and let Barney Frank, Chris Dodd, and Dick Durbin lie about it. Then, they let the FHA go about the same practices, knowing the same problem is coming down the road. The same three culprits will lie again.

The educational system here is failing. But, the teacher's union is more important than fixing a broken system.

How much more do you plan to watch before you get mad enough to get involved? They are your kids and grandkids we are putting the screws to, and they will pay the price for our silence.

Marketing Socialism in America

October 14, 2009

This is a marketing exercise. As a retired marketing executive, if someone brought this product, socialism, to me and asked me how to sell the product to the majority of Americans, I would set the marketing strategy like this.

First, we should assess the competition. Capitalism is the competition. How do we take market share from capitalism? Capitalism has been the product of choice for America since the constitution framed the country with those freedoms. It's an enormous challenge to take the country from capitalism.

The alternative product, socialism, has a bad track record. It will be hard to get a majority of the public to buy the product. Statistics show only 35% of the buyers (voters) are liberals, or those who favor socialism. There is a sizable block of independents who may lean toward capitalism but could be convinced to buy the new product. This is the target market.

How do we gain share? We must create an economic disaster. Grow unemployment, destroy manufacturing, and increase government spending to show how much we can help those we disabled. The more people we make dependent on government spending, the more we gain.

Advertising is important. Since we own the media, this works in our favor. We just feed them the right lines and they provide billions in free media time for socialism.

Rebrand the product. Socialism as a brand will never sell here. We will call it change and hope.

Next, work on the so-called thought leaders: educators, Hollywood, the arts, those who can influence children, university students, and those who don't think for themselves. We have that now.

We must gain control of the levers that determine the direction the country takes. We have that now. We need a great communicator who can convince the buyers that socialism (hope and change) is a better product than free enterprise and capitalism. Remember, we can't call it socialism. Again, we have that now.

Now start pulling the levers. Regulation. Don't let the free enterprise system work. Don't let entrepreneurs do their thing. Regulate them. No drilling, no nuclear, no auto industry without the heavy hand of regulation. No mining, no heavy production, no chemical business: regulate, regulate, regulate. Wreak havoc on the financial sector, the one growing area of the GDP.

Create the nanny state. Get more and more Americans dependent on government. Grow government jobs. Increase government spending. Redistribute the wealth. Get the whole country dependent on the government for health care.

Blame all the fallout of this on capitalism. Deflect the true causes, since we have the media to help.

We have it. Despite long odds, we can turn this Queen Mary on a dime. Keep pulling the right levers. Just keep a wary eye on those damned independents. They can still upset our apple cart. **If they vote us out before we get everything in such a deplorable state that they need us, we're home free.**

There you have it. A foolproof marketing strategy to make the United States a socialist country.

Are you buying?

Spinning Ft. Hood

November 6, 2009

Last night, mainstream media began spinning the incident at Ft. Hood. Only Charlie Gibson dared mention that the shooter was a Muslim. Most news coverage that addressed this little tidbit claimed he was a recent convert to Islam.

He is a lifelong Muslim. He had been harassed by his fellow soldiers due to his religious beliefs. Sure, most majors in the military get harassed. Prior to the incident, he was seen on a security camera at a 7-Eleven in traditional Muslim robes.

Almost no one dares mention the fact that he was yelling *Allahu Akbar*, meaning God (Allah) is great, while he was killing fellow soldiers at close range.

The media, the government, and the Muslim community can spin this any way they wish, but this was a one-man jihad evolving from religious fervor. Christians don't go on killing sprees due to Christianity. Jews don't kill and wound nearly fifty people due to religion. Mormons don't. But Muslims do.

This was planned in advance. Maj. Nidal Malik Hasan was giving away furniture. He was sending goodbye notes. He had an agenda. He punished America and his fellow soldiers for waging war against Allah. Someone actually noticed him trying to convert patients to the Muslim religion. Any private psychiatrist would lose their license for that. He had become a religious fanatic. To a religion that seemingly encourages this kind of behavior.

Personally, I don't care what his family has to say to justify his actions. The media spin is the poor man was distraught about being deployed to Iraq or Afghanistan. This man should be totally accountable for his actions without lame excuses. He should be sent directly to Gitmo. But, no, Gitmo detainees with the same ideas about their religion (kill Americans) will be brought here to wage that war just like Maj. Hasan did.

Other religions don't have a core group of people with a burning desire to kill another large group of people. Muslims do. President Obama said he "gets it." Well, he doesn't "get this" for sure.

People in jobs where they are expected to protect Americans better get it, too. Remember, the London subway bombings were engineered by well-respected Muslim doctors. This was an act of terrorism, pure and simple, brought about by a Muslim fanatic who wanted to kill Americans in the name of Allah.

Do we want to live in a country where suicide bombings are commonplace? If not, we had better start looking at fanatical Muslims who are so dedicated to the Muslim sect that fosters jihad, or we will be there before we know.

The ACLU, the media, the far left, the excessively politically correct, and the current administration had better stop trying to protect these individuals living in our midst. They are at war with us. We need to be more vigilant.

Health Care Reform Facts

November 14, 2009

Since 2003, the cost of health insurance has risen nearly three times faster for individual plan holders than group plans. Under the Senate bill, plans costing more than $8,000 for individuals and $21,000 for a family would pay a 40% excise tax on the excess amount. The average premium is $13,375 for a family policy.

Texas Governor Perry notes that after Texas passed tort reform in 2003, malpractice insurance rates fell 27% and the number of doctors applying to practice in Texas rose by 57%.

Malpractice lawsuits fell 41%, as well. The same Democrats who claim health care reform will reduce the deficit reject the assertions that tort reform could also reduce the deficit by $54 billion. All those campaign contributions from the trial attorneys must distort their logic. I reject the first claim and believe the number on the second is grossly understated.

Remember that doctors go to college plus medical school. We expect them to be available 24/7, 365 days a year, and be perfect all the time. To assume we can cut pay, get the best and brightest, and pay them much less is ridiculous.

There are other questionable premises of the reform bills. Extending coverage to 25 million uninsured shifts treatment from the emergency rooms to cheaper preventive care. But, the uninsured consume 45% less health care than those who are insured. Increased use from newly insured may cut those expected cost reductions and increase costs. Plus, zero increase in doctors and hospitals will stress the system.

Digitizing medical records will cost billions but save much more, per the Democrats. This is refuted by none other than Harvard Medical School. Plus, the projected cost to do the project is likely far greater and will take much longer than projected.

Here's another broken campaign promise by Obama. He said he was opposed to a tax on benefits. But, the excise tax on Cadillac plans is just that.

There is a serious lack of competition between insurers in most areas of the country. Democrats are opposed to letting consumers buy insurance across state lines. How limited is the competition? In 96% of the Metropolitan Statistical Areas, one insurer has at least 30% market share and in 64%, one insurer has at least 50%. The much-maligned oil industry, for example, has no one with over 8% market share. This is a serious problem and one that will not be solved by any health care reform bill unless the feds go in the business.

It could be solved by letting competition exist across state lines. Employers could shop across the country for the best prices. But, the Democrats want more central government control. They fear their lock on using interstate commerce laws might weaken that hold and open up states' rights to all kinds of issues that threaten central control.

Wouldn't it be nice if your media and your elected officials shared some of this with you?

Obama Grades Himself B Plus

December 18, 2009

In his hourly TV show, the narcissist, unlikeable, insufferable, egotistical Barack Obama gave himself a B plus for his year as president. Mr. President, that's exactly why, in the private sector, most of us had to endure an annual performance review. Some annual performance reviews are made up of a 360-degree feedback. You are receiving this in the form of a job satisfaction approval. It's from your 300 million bosses. You also get one from the Congress. It's called zero votes on any of your proposals to Congress by the other party.

Mr. President, based on campaign promises, the feedback poll on job performance, and the complete lack of any supporters on the other side of the aisle, you get a D minus. We would fire you but we can't. Not yet. Next year, we can fire some of your fellow democrats in Congress. And we will. Actually, you deserve an F. But, you do read that teleprompter well. Being fair, we gave you credit for your only job skill for the job we hired you to do.

Typically, we consider this your job performance warning letter. Because your friends in the ACLU, and fellow Democrats, have worked tirelessly for the past twenty years to make it almost impossible to fire anyone for poor performance, we must follow the rules set down by Human Resources. Hence, you get the performance warning letter.

It's always better for someone with a performance this bad to resign. Better for all concerned, but we know you won't do that.

Here are some requirements to get your performance above minimum standards in the next six months, or we will be pressing harder for the resignation:

- You must close Gitmo as promised, without spending a dime.
- You must get your job approval rating above 55% and keep it there.
- You must get unemployment to the 8.6% you promised in early 2009.
- You must stay within your budget. You budget should be no more than you spent in 2009, since it was a record spending year for the country.
- You must get Republican support of some kind for your proposals or change your proposals.

Your TV time will be cut from a minimum of one hour per day in 2009 to no more than one hour a week. When you use that hour, cut the verbosity and get to the chase. No more teleprompters in 2010. This skill has been demonstrated. Now, we want to see if you can speak from the heart.

No more visits from Andy Stern to the White House. You work for us, not Andy Stern and the SEIU. The time you wasted with him is demonstrated in your dismal performance for 2009.

No more boondoggles in 2010. No more trips to get the 2016 Olympic Games or trips to Copenhagen to endorse voodoo science—Al Gore was there already. And, no more date nights in NYC with Michelle.

Finally, Mr. President, and read this carefully: no more blame games. One time blaming George Bush for something and you are fired. This also holds true for the Fat Cat bankers, Wall Street crooks, etc. President Truman laid it out how your jobs works. The buck stops with you. Man up, and start taking responsibility for your unacceptable performance in 2009. Only then can you hope to improve enough to dodge the performance review warning letter we just put in your file.

2010

We Elected a Community Organizer as President—We Got What We Deserved

January 1, 2010

First act: close Gitmo. It still isn't closed. He sends Gitmo prisoners to Yemen. We find Yemen is a hot bed for Al-Qaeda. Someone there recruits a man to try to blow up a plane over Detroit. Some seventy-two hours later, the community organizer realizes he needs to say something to the community he is organizing. He says it's an isolated incident. After counseling from inept staff, he says it's a breakdown of human and system errors. This may be one of the few true statements he has made since becoming president. He was right. It was a breakdown of leadership. His leadership.

It started with him naming Eric Holder Attorney General. Holder's last job was defending Al-Qaeda prisoners. He's still on that job. Then, we got Janet Napolitano. The "system worked," Janet. All this results in the man who tried to blow up the plane being lawyered up in Detroit instead of being interrogated at Gitmo to tell us where the next attack will be.

Our president named a record number of tax cheats to high positions. Some left, but some remain. Tim Geithner, running our economy without supervision, is throwing our tax dollars at every old friend from Wall Street. This is without any endorsement from Congress or the American people.

He passed the biggest earmark deal in history. Promising it would reduce unemployment to 8%, it rose to 10.2%. Now, the state unemployment coffers are empty and will need billions more in 2010.

He took over GM and Chrysler and benefited the UAW. Now, he needs to give a few more billion to GMAC and, under pressure, is backing off closing smaller dealerships. This was critical to making GM and Chrysler succeed.

Obama kowtowed to the Muslim world. In his inflated egotistical opinion, he just knew they would love him like the old community in Chicago did. Sorry, Mr. President, but they are still very much at war with us, despite your delusions.

He gave us cash for clunkers and pay your neighbor's mortgage programs. Buy cars and pay mortgages for others. Spread the wealth.

He tried to give us cap and tax: a plan to raise all energy costs in the country with zero global results. Town hall meetings and the polls scared the daylights out of Congress and this will not happen, despite the best efforts of Obama.

He is trying to give us health care reform and will probably succeed. The same government that can't run Medicare, Medicaid, veterans' insurance, and Native American medical plans will run everything.

He has created record deficits, spending and debt "as far as the eye can see," to quote him. He has broken every campaign promise, except one: to fundamentally change America forever. Partisan government has never been worse. There are more lobbyists than we have ever seen in government jobs. There have been more earmarks than ever. He has the lowest job approval rating seen since polls started. He grades himself a B plus.

He puts no skin in any game. He wants health care reform. Not a specific kind of reform, just any kind. He wants Gitmo closed, but has no plan. He's flying at 40,000 feet above everything he gets involved in and depends on the famous teleprompter to save him. He appears on TV daily, or more often, and says nothing.

A leader needs to be judged by his results, not his words. Mr. President, your results are not good. Your words are ringing hollow. We see you for what you are. You are a man with a plan to make America like France or Detroit.

We became unlike France because of our freedom and liberty and our capitalist economy. Detroit became Detroit because of entitlements and dependence on handouts from government.

Even Jimmy Carter didn't have your track record at this point in his presidency. It's hard to believe we could elect someone worse than Carter. But we have. Wake up, Mr. President—we get it. And, the majority of us don't like it.

Global Warming and Prohibition

January 4, 2010

Today's *Wall Street Journal* ran an article about the history of Prohibition in the United States. Cited in the article was a reference to a prominent Yale economist, Irving Fisher, who predicted a ban on alcohol would guarantee a 20% rise in industrial productivity. He cited "scientific tests" that proved alcohol diminished a worker's efficiency by as much as 30%.

A very militant anti-alcohol group called the Anti-Saloon League (ASL) were adamant the country needed to outlaw alcohol. It was a small but effective group, numbering some 20,000. Passed and signed into law in 1919 by President Wilson, it cost the Democrats the majority in Congress as angry Americans voted for Republicans.

Only a few would suggest that Prohibition, the law for thirteen years, was successful. It created a disdain for the law and received some share of the blame for the Great Depression. It created anger for politicians who felt they knew what was best for the public. It was a fraud, an abject failure, and ended with a repeal of the Eighteenth Amendment to the Constitution.

It was a bad idea, supported by a small minority. It cost thousands of jobs and accomplished nothing. Supported by experts and science, none of the so-called scientific predictions came to pass.

Now, in 2010, we have Al Gore, with his so-called science, his bevy of heavy believers, and his cause, global warming. Al wants all of us to sacrifice for his cause. Sacrifice lifestyles and jobs, pay more for gasoline and utilities, and bet the farm on the fact that it will be better for America based on his great wisdom.

The guy who gave us Prohibition was the foremost economist in America at the time, Irving Fisher. Al Gore is the foremost snake oil salesman in American history.

One guy with credentials gave America thirteen years of unrest and constant issues with enforcing the law. The other guy, with zero credentials, but soon with a billion dollars, wants to give us several years of heavy sacrifice with what may be zero reason and no results.

Will global warming be our version of Prohibition?

Government Cheese and Cheesy Government

February 2, 2010

My parents were young adults in the Great Depression. They shared with me the horrors of being poor and the scarcity of jobs during this dark time in America. They talked about government cheese and peanut butter handed out to hungry people in need. The government cheese wasn't smelly cheese, but American cheese as we know it today. It was a good idea in times when good ideas were few.

Today we have food stamps. The poor and needy can go to the store and get more than cheese and peanut butter. But today, we have cheesy politicians still passing out ideas that take the cheese from the people and transfer it to the government to waste in ideas no one could ever imagine.

The classic example is the idea Obama and Holder had, to try five terrorists in federal court in NYC. Estimates of the cost were

$400 million to $2 billion. That's a lot of cheese. Who benefits? Not the American people or the taxpayers. Who benefits is the ACLU, the far left, the president (who is still trying to damage the Bush reputation), a loony attorney general who wants to represent terrorists, and, most important, the terrorists themselves. New York City has thrown them out. Did they throw in the towel on a bad idea and say they were wrong? No. They are looking for another city or village to take them.

This is cheesy politics at the absolute worst. It's spending millions of dollars in a time of deficits and budget issues to further the beliefs of a few supporters. We have come a long way from the days of government cheese to a time when cheesy politicians are trying to give our liberties and our country away. Not to the poor and needy, but to the ACLU.

I've had enough of the cheesy politicians who care not one whit about what we want—the Obamas and the Holders, who put ideology above common sense and prudent government.

Have you?

My State of the Union Address

February 11, 2010

There is some good news. Corporate profits are up. Almost 80% of S&P 500 companies are beating earnings forecasts. And, 70% are beating revenue forecasts. Until recently, the stock market has reflected this, as investors received a large piece of their losses back.

The recent market setbacks are government driven. The

token freeze on nondiscretionary, non-security spending was put together with higher taxes on wealthy Americans, reduced itemized deductions, a "financial crisis responsibility fee" paid by banks, higher taxes on companies doing business outside the United States, higher carried interest taxes on private equity, and higher taxes on oil and gas firms. Most of these taxes will be passed back to consumers.

What does all this do? It discourages hiring. The auto industry is working off inventory. But, the government bashing of Toyota will cut sales for Toyota. Hence, jobs may be cut there. No one is buying, and Chrysler and GM are still getting a cold shoulder. If Ford doesn't pick up the slack for Toyota, we can blame overzealous government actions against Toyota for more job losses. The higher minimum wage isn't helping.

China may already be the number one economy in the world. They are the world's largest exporter, have the second largest economy, the second largest stock market, and the largest car market. They are doing everything they can to be smart. We, on the other hand, are doing everything we can to grow government.

The receipts for the federal government are 15% of GDP. Next year, they are expected to recover to the average of the past sixty years. Expenditures, however, are 25% of GDP, higher by 6% than the average over the same period. This spells enormous problems down the road.

In 2016, defense spending will be 19% of total government spending. Discretionary spending will be 10%. The balance, mandatory will be 71%. This is Medicare, Medicaid, Social Security, and much higher benefits for federal employees, compared to the private sector. At some point, soon, mandatory spending will have to be addressed. Not by increasing it by health care reform and growing government, but by reducing it by cutting government pay and benefits and cutting entitlements. How can any responsible leader look at this and recommend more entitlements and bigger government? Only a community organizer could do that.

That's my state of the union message. The economy should grow this year if government doesn't get involved. Taxes will go up dramatically and hiring will not. China has probably surpassed us as the world's economic power. They have a strategy to grow their economy and increase employment in the private sector, where the average wage is still $2,400 per year. We have a strategy to grow government and entitlements, when we can't afford those we have. If they haven't surpassed us already, they soon will.

It's the Supply Problem in Health Care, Stupid

March 11, 2010

Have you heard either side discuss the supply side of rising health care costs?

I have a dentist friend. Several years back there were too many dentists. To find and keep patients, they were forced to be competitive by cutting prices. They clamped down on the supply. They cut the number of admissions to dental schools, cut the number of dental schools, and solved their problem.

Unless the number of doctors is increased significantly, there will be cost increases and insurance premium increases.

If health care reform goes through, there will be rationing. Not one health care reform bill or discussion addresses this.

Here's a copy of a blog entry on my old blog, *Grandparents of America Awaken*, dated March 6, 2008. This should really get your blood pressure up.

Root of the Problem: Supply and Demand

March 6, 2008

Health care: hot topic on the campaign trail. Our government wants to get more involved in health care. Some want all health care to be free in this country. What got us to this point?

My theory—just a theory: supply and demand. There are too few doctors. Carl Getto is chairman of the Council on Graduate Medical Education. This is a panel Congress created to recommend how many doctors the nation needs. The debate is over how many.

Getto's advocacy of more doctors is remarkable because his advisory committee and the predecessor have been instrumental since the 1980s in efforts to restrict the supply of new physicians. In a new study sent to Congress, the council reverses that policy and recommends training 3,000 more doctors a year in US medical schools.

The production of new doctors has changed little since 1985. Today, new physicians roughly equal the number of doctors retiring. Within a decade, baby boom doctors licensed in the '60s, '70s, and '80s will retire in large numbers that will outstrip the 25,000 new doctors produced every year.

The effective number of physicians will fall even more, because doctors work shorter hours today. The public expects good health care but we aren't producing enough physicians to provide it. Why?

Congress controls the supply of physicians by how much federal funding it provides for medical residencies—the graduate training required of all doctors. The government spends about $11 billion annually on 100,000 medical residents, or roughly $110,000 per resident. In 1997, to save money, Congress capped the number of residents that Medicare will pay for at about 80,000 a year.

Surprise, surprise, the same body that is going to fix the problem caused a big part of the problem. By erring on the side of less, we have too few doctors, and the prospect for fixing that in the short term is not bright.

But, get this: we have a glut of attorneys. Too many attorneys, not enough work, so let's sue the doctors. Here's the picture. We have a shortage of doctors. And the doctors we do have work five months a year to pay their malpractice policy because too many attorneys are suing them.

Here's my health policy: Remove the government from the business of deciding how many doctors we need in this country. Let the marketplace decide. Let the insurance companies establish the funding for residencies. Cap the malpractice payments and shrink the population of attorneys, or allow them to find more productive work. Doctors would only have to work two months a year to pay the malpractice policies. We need more competition between doctors and lower costs for treatments. And, lower costs for insurance. Eliminate the red tape, and costs are reduced even more. Maybe, just maybe, health insurance can be affordable.

Isn't it strange? Almost every major problem we have in the country can be traced back to government involvement. Do you really want more?

Federal Government to Control All Student Loans

March 16, 2010

Here we go again. Fannie and Freddie, chapter III. The Congress, led by Barney Frank, Chris Dodd, and Dick Durbin, want all Americans to own a home. So, they loosen up Freddie and Fannie to insure any warm body who wants a mortgage gets one. Banks can't write mortgages fast enough. Down comes the house of cards and the perpetrators are all pointing fingers at everyone but themselves. Barney Frank even sounds more like Elmer Fudd when he's accused of playing any role whatsoever in this. Documentation or not, Barney is 100% innocent of any involvement in this debacle.

Now enter Barack and Arne. Obama and Arne Duncan, Secretary of Education, have shoved through a bill that will make it illegal for any private institution to make a federally guaranteed student loan. Coincidentally, *The Arizona Republic* ran an article that student loan defaults are at an all-time high. So, just as the business of student loans hits bottom, the federal government has set up a single loaner system. Perfect timing.

The ban that passed the house has $67 billion in savings but $77 billion in new spending. Plus, the data used by the CBO doesn't recognize the new spike in past due loans.

The Feds want the banks to process the loans. Guess why? Because no one can get through the red tape it takes to get a loan directly from the government. How's that health care takeover looking to you? May be worse than you know, since the scumbags may use reconciliation to pass this because, like health care, they can't get it through the Senate.

According to the CBO, many colleges oppose the federal plan because the feds don't make the same effort to prevent defaults that private lenders do. Students have more loans through the private options because with the government plan, they will be juniors before they can complete the paperwork and get approval.

The Obama promise is: anyone who wants to go to college can. Another given entitlement in America. But, even before he and Arne open the floodgates, the default rate in student loans is soaring.

Blatant Media Bias

May 4, 2010

If you think there is not a liberal media bias in this country, pay attention to the reporting of Arizona Bill 1070, the bill that makes illegal, illegal. Seventy percent of the population of Arizona approves the bill. A majority of the people in the United States approves the bill. The Rasmussen poll says 50%, and even a liberal poll (Gallup), gives a slight majority to those in favor. If public opinion means anything, one would presume the national and local media would give credence to the popularity of the bill, then give way to journalistic objectivity and present both sides of the issue.

Local media devotes a minimum of 90% of their coverage to those against the bill. Generally, at the end of ten minutes of celebrities protesting, students protesting, boycotts of business, and Sharpton coming to Arizona, they do say a majority of Arizonans favor the bill. This is a ten-second sound bite. National news is even worse.

Now, as many as eleven states are in the process of passing something akin to the Arizona bill. Still, the media rails on about the injustices of the bill. The different factions are suing to have it thrown out of court. Suddenly, the president seems to step back from his initial criticism of the bill. His people must be reading the polls.

This is a replay of Obamacare. After hammering the public for months with favorable treatment of the bill, the media failed to get a majority of the public to favor the bill. It must be very frustrating for the liberal media to see their inability to sway pubic opinion. This week, the founder of CNN said the network has become a joke. Guess the public agrees, since no one watches it anymore.

I truly believe the country is not listening to the media anymore. They are talking to themselves and their fellow liberal followers. This spells financial disaster for many of them. Tuned out and turned off, they are bleeding red ink.

I am truly heartened to see so many Americans becoming aware that they can't trust mainstream media, national or local, to deliver news. They deliver their ideology with some news sprinkled in to give it flavor.

Despite all the efforts by the media, the Arizona problem is not going away. The majority of Americans want something done about illegal aliens. Please note I did not use the politically correct term, immigrants. And, the folks in Washington are about to deliver the same thing the media is trying to sell. Something the public is not going to buy. Enough is enough, and we have had enough. Enforce our laws and protect our border; that's what we hired you to do.

Losing Touch With America

June 6, 2010

Every day, I realize I am losing touch with my country. Here are some of the reasons I feel that way.

A very large youth soccer group in upstate New York announced a new rule. To keep from embarrassing the children who lose self-esteem when they lose by a lot, they will absolutely prevent that from ever happening. No, it's not the slaughter rule from my children's generation. It's even more creative. Any team that takes more than a five-goal lead over an opponent automatically loses. That's a lesson all kids should learn. It's a big step into the brave new world of Obama socialism.

At least four politicians have been exposed for embellishing their resumes. With my parent's generation, men like my dad would never discuss their experience in WWII. Now, we have aspirants for important jobs who were never part of WWII lying about this. It's always been said the third generation will destroy a family business. I truly hope they were wrong, but there seems to be very little integrity in politics today.

A kid is told a rosary can't be worn to school. He's told it is a gang symbol.

We have good laws regarding immigration to this country. We choose not to enforce them. When a state chooses to enforce the very same laws set by the federal government, the federal government turns on that state. Why don't we turn on the federal government for not enforcing the laws we pay them to enforce?

We have an administration that tries to bribe candidates to drop out of races so their preferred candidate has no competition. No one cares.

I have a president who illegally took over the car companies. No one cares. A government that can't run anything is trying to run everything. No one cares. Now, that same president attacks BP for paying dividends to shareholders while fighting an oil spill and watching the stock price go down. With ample cash flow to pay claims and bills for the cleanup, what business is it of the president if the company pays dividends? Is this president a socialist, a communist, or a fascist? He sure hates capitalism and corporations.

Union memberships have been going down, but union power is up. How does that happen?

Walmart supports cap and trade and health care reform. What would Sam Walton say? Is this a bribe to get the SEIU off their backs? Sam came from my dad's Greatest Generation. The current CEO is from the new generation—no integrity.

AARP supports health care reform. It will injure most of

their members. They have lost thousands of members. Why did they do this? Because their board is composed of flaming liberals and they just can't help themselves.

Obama has added $5 trillion to the deficit, and the current congress is still passing spending bills. We have two wars, a leak in the Gulf, and we are going broke, and what is my senator working on? The esteemed liberal idiot, Dick Durbin, is proposing pet store reform. He wants to make sure no one buys a puppy that has problems. Way to go, Dick.

We passed a health care bill modeled after Canada's health care system, or that of Massachusetts, or Greece, you pick. All three are going broke. Who let this happen?

Somehow, all of this goes back to that soccer rule. We are making America into a country that can't compete on any front. We can't stand to win, and we can't stand to lose. An ump blows a call in a perfect game and apologizes, and the majority of the people want the pitcher to get his perfect game. Tell that to Harvey Haddix. He pitched eleven perfect innings and lost the game in the twelfth. No perfect game, according to baseball. Harvey took it like a man.

Life is tough. The men who went off to fight in WWII learned that at an early age. The men who went off to Vietnam got a tougher lesson. Too many people back here did not appreciate their sacrifices. Today, everyone wants a mulligan. Do something that doesn't work out and ask for a second chance. Go to rehab and discuss their upbringing; blame the boss, blame the government, blame someone. Do not, under any circumstances, do what the ump in Detroit did, and say "I blew it." I hope none of those soccer kids in Upstate New York ever become umpires.

Things You Might Not Know About China

June 11, 2010

China is growing as we shrink. They are fast becoming the new world power. When our grandkids are adults, they will wonder why we watched while China took our place at the head of the table. What will we tell them?

If you don't buy this idea, please educate yourself about what is really going on with China. Here are some starter facts.

By 2015, the year our debt is projected to be $20 trillion, a figure just released this week, China will be part of the middle-class growth in Asia. This will make the Asian nations' middle class the same or more than the population of the middle class in Europe and North America. This has not happened for 300 years. Chinese middle-class consumption will surpass that of the United States in a few years.

China is already the world's largest car market. In 2004, GM sold one car in China for every ten in the United States. That ratio for GM is now 1:1. China is the world's biggest cell phone market.

The Chinese express train from Wuhan to Guangzhou will run at 320 kmh. This covers the distance from Chicago to Washington, D.C., in less than three hours. China plans to build 16,000 km of high-speed trains, with four north–south corridors, four east–west corridors, and nineteen inner-city lines. One-quarter of this is done. Meanwhile, we give billions to ethanol producers to produce profits for ethanol producers.

Since 1990, Chinese retail sales have grown at a pace 4–5% faster than inflation. Household consumption is growing at a rate of 8–16% a year. Two-car families are skyrocketing. Sales of luxury goods are growing faster than anywhere in the world. And, companies doing business in China are making money. Reports say 75% have equal or higher margins than their average worldwide operations.

If I were the CEO of America and I looked at this data about a competitor, China, I would know we were doomed. The competitor is beating us in every area. Why? The management in China doesn't worry about the feelings of 2% of the population. They don't have to jump through bureaucratic hoops to build something, go through endless environmental studies, or fight every bit of progress in the courts, and because they build most of the progress themselves, they don't tax themselves to death.

You don't need a crystal ball to see where this goes. I'll bet your perspective is obsolete. And you, like me, don't give China credit for all the progress they've made. My suggestion is to pay attention. They are the new big dog.

Anyone Can Have a Bad Century

June 27, 2010

Look at the Chicago Cubs. The last time they were in the World Series was 1908. A bad century. Was it a money issue, bad management, or the hex of the goat? In over one hundred years, one might assume there would be a confluence of luck that would negate the money, management, and maybe the hex. After all, the hex of the Bambino finally left and let the Red Sox win a World Series.

Look at the Blackhawks. After years of bad management by Bill Wirtz, he died and his son, Rocky, took over. Immediately, the team got better, the fans came back, and they won the Stanley Cup this year. Look at the Bulls. They made one good trade for Michael Jordan, and won six championships. Even the White Sox lined up the cherries on the slot machine and won a World Series. The way they are playing now, they may win another this year.

Meanwhile, the Cubs's new owners are redecorating the restrooms at the park. And, trying to force the City of Mesa, Arizona, to build them a new stadium with taxpayer money by threatening to move spring training to Florida where the new owners winter.

The truth of the matter is the owners of the Cubs, past and present, don't care about winning. Especially if winning means spending money. They have the best little bar ever built on the north side of Chicago. People go there to get sunshine and drink beer, and a ball game breaks out. They will get their 3 million fans this year, despite a bad team and total disregard for the fans. It's been a bad century for the fans but not for the owners.

Where am I going with this? Our politicians are setting up a bad century for our kids and grandkids, and, like Cubs fans, we just keep buying.

Obama is in Toronto with the elf, Geithner, dodging riots and trying to convince the G-20 attendees to keep spending. They, on the other hand, are trying to tell Obama to stop spending. We've tried your strategy for fifty years and it doesn't work. Why are you putting in place our losing strategy?

In a ranking of political units likely to default on debt, Illinois ranks just behind Iraq and just ahead of California. Why? They can't stop spending, and they just keep borrowing to put off spending cuts. Pension obligations is the major factor.

If we don't get Democrats out of control in Congress in the fall and vote Obama out of office in 2012, we will be like the Cubs: headed for a bad century. Illinois must be the least intelligent state in the country, but now it's looking terrible compared to the worst countries in rest of the world. Thank God for Greece. The same corrupt people have been running the state for years. Governors come and go, from office to jail. Obama came from Illinois. He wants to make America like Illinois. It's all he knows.

Greece has already defaulted, for all practical purposes. They were bailed out by Europe and Obama. Next on the default probability list is: Venezuela, 58.05%; Argentina, 48.15%, Pakistan, 38.80%; Ukraine, 35.69%, Iraq; 29.29%, Dubai, 29.20%; then Illinois, 27.35% and California, 27.00%.

Back to the Cubs. If you have fans who support you regardless of what you do (voters) and management that understands this and is indifferent to their actions (politicians), you have the potential for a century of failure. Illinois, California, and the United States are in this situation. Illinois is teetering on the brink. There has been no balanced budget for nine years. They just keep borrowing.

So, if you keep watching while your elected officials screw up the future, you may be destined to find out what Cubs fans already know: anyone can have a bad century. It might take that long or longer to fix what's happening right now.

Independence Day

July 4, 2010

We celebrate this day because a group of brave people decided they couldn't accept the tyranny of King George. He simply took what he wanted from this country without discussion or debate. Those who emigrated here from England had to give whatever he asked. They received nothing from England. It was a one-way street. They wanted distance from the king. They left England because they yearned for a better life. They sought freedom and opportunity.

One of the founders, the one who wrote most of the Declaration of Independence, Thomas Jefferson, warned that it was a natural occurrence for government to grow and seek more and more power over the people

As I look back over my lifetime, every year the government has regulated more and more and taken liberty after liberty. This has occurred at every level. Federal, state, local, and in some cases, even a homeowners' association. Gun laws are put in and more people are murdered. Obesity laws against fast food restaurants, people get fatter. Cameras everywhere and crime goes up.

Elected officials are beginning to behave more and more like King George. A manager at a frozen custard shop in Wisconsin suggests to Biden that he should reduce taxes. Biden calls him a smart-ass. A young man tries to ask a congressman a question and gets physically abused. Who the hell do these people who live at the public trough think they are? Pelosi spends millions of our tax dollars flying back and forth to California, renting expensive office space, and believes she is entitled.

They are all becoming King Georges, and we let it happen. Their public behavior is despicable. They behave like spoiled professional athletes who constantly embarrass their teams. But, the athletes get suspended. The politicians go on with the behavior.

President Reagan said about the economy and the federal government: "If it moves, tax it, if it keeps moving, regulate it, if it stops moving, subsidize it." This is not just true about the economy. It's true about most everything today.

So, when you put your flag out on July 4, 2010, pause and remember you have work to do. We need to stop the Obama version of hope and change dead in its tracks and replace it with the hope and change Jefferson and Reagan gave us.

Why Stan Is My Friend

July 27, 2010

In an era where the governor of Illinois will find out next week whether he will join the previous governor in prison, it's hard to find anyone who has credibility. Our president tells us we can keep our doctor under his health care bill, but he knows, and many of us know, we may lose our doctor. Charlie Rangel is going to trial for ethics violations. Mark Kirk, Republican candidate for the Obama senate seat, tells tall tales about his military career and even an ordeal on a sailboat in Lake Michigan when he was a kid. His Democratic opponent made loans to gangsters and broke his bank. Some great choices on that ticket.

Where have all the honorable people gone? Who stands for anything today? Whose word is worth anything or whose handshake is good enough to take to the bank?

All my life I have tried to avoid people like Rob Blagojevich, Mark Kirk, Barack Obama, Charlie Rangel, and people like them. I'm proud I have friends like Stan.

Stan was playing in a golf tournament. They were giving away a car for a hole in one. When Stan got to that hole, he asked his caddie, "You want to risk your tip on me making this shot?" The caddie said, "My car is a piece of crap. Sure, I'll do it." Stan requested his six iron. The caddie said, "I'll give you a five iron." Stan knocked the shot in the hole and turned to the caddie and said, "Son, you just won a new jeep."

How many politicians do you think would have kept their deal with the caddie? Probably not many.

It makes me proud to be a friend of Stan's. I just wish we had more Stans in this world today.

We Won the War

August 23, 2010

The troops are coming home. It should be the most significant news of the decade. We won the war in Iraq. Mission accomplished. Yet, the mainstream media have stones in their mouths. There is token coverage of the big event. Why?

Admitting you were wrong seems impossible in this country these days. When it took years to achieve a victory, you should celebrate. Over 20 million Iraqis have freedom from Hussein. They have some semblance of democracy in a country that has never experienced such freedom. Thousands of brave young Americans made this possible at a huge sacrifice. But, being wrong trumps reporting good news.

We have had VJ Day, VE Day, and celebrations for Desert Storm. But, no VIQ Day. The silence is deafening. No parades, no celebrations, no national pride. Yet, the silence speaks volumes about the cancer that is eating away at this country.

Mainstream America is proud. That probably constitutes 70% or more of the public in this country. The 30% who suppress the celebrations are the people still smoking pot and wearing beads. Not overtly, but in their hearts. They hate this country as it is and as it was. None of them fought in Iraq or had sons or daughters who fought there. They are teaching in universities, smug in Hollywood, behind cameras at ABC, NBC, CBS, or worse, MSNBC. They work for *The New York Times*, run unions, or work for Obama. Or, they are Obama, who was taking credit but giving little to the ones who made it happen.

The true heroes who made this happen deserve more. They deserve a parade. They deserve a monument. They deserve the full spotlight of the mainstream media for days and weeks. They deserve the gratitude of a nation that should be proud of them and proud of what they did for a country that is far, far better for their efforts: Iraq.

Their work was monumental in the annals of our history. They resurrected a fallen nation. They eradicated an evil that mirrored that of Hitler. They trained a million Iraqi soldiers to defend their country from future perils. They trained thousands of Iraqi police to help the soldiers protect their citizens. They rebuilt a country. We spent billions in the effort.

If you have any doubts about the corrupt media in our country, just think about their response to this victory. They are incapable of doing one positive thing to laud the outcome. It isn't in their nature. It's against their ideology. They have lost all objectivity to report fairly on the events of the day. They want to spoon-feed you their versions of the world.

No ticker tape parades in Times Square. No pictures of a sailor kissing a nurse. Your president is so tired and stressed from two weeks of fundraising for his party, he takes a ten-day vacation in Nantucket. How many days did the military in Iraq get off between fighting and R&R. How many tours of duty did some do in Iraq?

If you still watch your evening news from the major networks, think about this: Can you really trust they are giving you the news fair and unbalanced?

Dr. Michael Burry

September 14, 2010

I'm reading a book by Michael Lewis titled *The Big Short*. It's about the housing bubble and the key players who participated in the great Ponzi scheme that was the mortgage bond business.

I have always wondered who saw it coming. According to Lewis, he could only find six people in the world who clearly saw it coming.

The first was Dr. Michael Burry. Dr. Burry never really practiced medicine. He suffers from Asperger's Syndrome, a form of autism and fear of people, so he didn't like dealing with patients. He quit medicine and became a money manager. His fund, Scion, was very successful. No point in trying to invest in it. He has closed the fund.

He saw the housing bubble coming. But, there was no way to benefit from that information, since he couldn't short the bond market. He convinced Goldman Sachs to create a credit default swap on the mortgage bond market. Goldman, in turn, convinced AIG to create and sell the product.

Burry made roughly $600 million buying swaps and betting the housing market would collapse. A few others made even more.

Burry discovered the fallibility of the mortgage bond business by simply looking at the products they contained and studying the underlying mortgages. He saw the default rate rising dramatically and the whole house of cards was being kept up by new money coming in. These mortgages were shakier than the ones defaulting. The rating agencies that were paid to see this did not see the problem. The highly paid Wall Street analysts did not see it coming. Even the CEOs of the big banks that lost billions did not see it coming. Yet, one former doctor who never took an economics or accounting course could see the problems by simply doing his homework.

Lewis, Burry, and the others who comment on the housing debacle don't see the Wall Street players as greedy, as much as they see them ignorant. Few do any real research and most research is done with a herd mentality. The young Turks get paid far too much money for far too little value.

Goldman, however, with help from Burry, saw it coming. They used AIG as their dupe. They sold credit default swaps underwritten by AIG to Burry and others. They bought swaps. Since credit default swaps are a zero-sum game, AIG ate all the losses until you, the taxpayer, bailed them out. They were the casino, and the casino made billions in bad bets. The Goldman people are running much of your national economy. The Goldman alumni are too numerous to mention in the Obama circle, with Tim Geithner being the highest profile. Before him, Hank Paulson, the guy who said AIG was too big to fail.

Goldman took money from the casino. First, in commissions, by acting as the middleman in selling swaps. Then by buying swaps themselves. They took AIG down. Then used their insiders to save them.

Sadly, when the damage was all done, the same people who created the mess were paid again to clean it up. Since they knew more about the mess than anyone, they got the job. Nice work—screw millions, create bank bailouts, rake in taxpayer money to patch it up, then get paid more to peddle what's worth anything in the debris.

Dr. Burry and Michael Lewis appeared on *Sixty Minutes*. It's worth fifteen minutes to watch the tape. Makes you wonder whether you will ever invest a dime with anyone purporting to be a money manager.

There is Such a Thing as a Free Lunch

September 28, 2010

All my life I've believed there is no free lunch. Now, I know there is. The Wall Street bankers ate one on you and me. I hope you enjoyed buying as much as I.

The so-called housing bubble was just a Ponzi scheme. Here's how it worked, in words even I can understand: First, you needed a tight inventory for houses on the market, then low interest rates. Then, you needed a new plan. Years ago, your bank gave you a mortgage and they held that mortgage until you sold the house, paid the mortgage, or refinanced the loan. Under the new plan, the mortgage was sold immediately. These mortgages were packaged into subprime bonds. But, there was a problem with that: these subprime mortgages were too easy to identify in those bonds. So, Wall Street invented a CDO: a collateralized debt obligation. In a CDO, no one knew what was in there.

Next, you needed the two main bond rating agencies in your pocket: Moody's and Standard & Poor's. They were still giving these crap CDOs an A rating a month before the lid blew off and after 20% of the mortgages in the CDO had defaulted. Everyone at high levels in these two companies should be in jail. No, they got a free lunch.

As a small minority of investors began to see the problems with subprime mortgages, you need to keep the lid on. So, go to some Wall Street firms with subprime intelligence and get them to issue insurance on the CDOs and mortgage bonds. Called credit default swaps, for a small insurance premium, you were paid if the bonds failed.

The big seller of credit default swaps: AIG. They got a free lunch. A few Wall Street firms, like Goldman Sachs (no surprise), held bonds and owned swaps.

So, as all of this is blowing and going, Wall Street made billions selling CDOs around the world. Local banks made millions selling mortgages, and mortgage brokers made billions finding suckers to get mortgages. And, the employees at the Wall Street firms made millions in bonus money for selling CDOs. All the risk was in the hands of the bondholders and with the government (Freddie, Fannie, and FHA).

When Hank Paulson sold Bush on the bailouts (Obama, too—he was there, remember?), he bought all the lunches with your tax dollars. Being an old Goldman guy, he looked after his friends. You and I are still paying for the free lunches. Freddie, Fannie, and the FHA are far from done. They will need to keep tapping your tax dollars for years to pay for the carnage they still hold from the bad mortgages. They are essentially landlords for millions of houses. Keeping the grass cut, etc. They are thinking about renting some. They are parceling out the foreclosures to keep from creating a panic. How well does the company that runs the post office do in the real estate business? We can only wait for the large exposé telling us they are paying $1,000 a week to have grass cut.

Our gift to Wall Street is the gift that just keeps giving. They all received the free lunch, but keep coming back for more. And, with the help of our government, we just keep buying. How dumb are we?

41 Million Americans on Food Stamps

October 8, 2010

Arecord 41 million Americans are now on food stamps. Unemployment is holding firm or moving up. There is some evidence the Obama crew, true to Chicago dirty tricks, may be adding the people who check you in at the election polling place to the unemployment rolls. Meanwhile, Nancy Pelosi, reflecting the politics of her district in San Francisco, says we get the biggest bang for our buck from food stamps and unemployment insurance.

And you wonder why the Democrats have problems. The best thing we have going for us now in this country is food stamps and unemployment insurance.

Once, we had businesses that were growing and hiring. Once, we had ideas that blossomed into new businesses. Once, we had a construction worker who became a contractor and hired twenty people.

Now, we have a government that spends so poorly the best thing they can hang their hat on is food stamps. I guess it's better than a stimulus package that doesn't work. It's better than wasted pork. It's better than giving our money to lobbyists and consultants in the Beltway. It's better than fraud. It's better than the post office or Amtrak. It's better than flying Pelosi back and forth to California on a plane that can accommodate 150 people. It's better than flying Obama around the country to campaign for soon-to-be losers. It's better than wasting money on Obamacare for another 15,000 IRS workers. It's better than giving Congress another pay raise.

When you look at the whole food chain, you can agree

with Ms. Speaker, Pelosi. But, you go pretty far down that food chain to find that list. It's better than a drilling moratorium in the Gulf that creates another 60,000 well-paid workers to be put on food stamps and unemployment.

How bad is it in Washington when the third person in line for the presidency says the best bang for the buck is food stamps?

Obamacare Was One Big Lie

October 9, 2010

It's tough to respect a pitchman who knowingly sells a defective product. He can't sell the product with fact, so he just lies about the product. No problem; make the sale and move on.

It may work for the door-to-door guy who never comes back. But, it's tough for the president of the United States to get away with. When your favorite part of the job is appearing on camera, you are there a lot. When you have a product that most people don't want to buy, you have to put a dress on a pig.

In this case, the brand of the product is your name: Obamacare. No one calls it Health Care Reform anymore. It's Obamacare.

The product was designed by a cast of minor bureaucrats and stitched together in a hurry. The CEO (Obama) wanted it done and off to market now. No quality testing. The CEO never looked at the product. He just hawked it to the market.

The board of directors (Congress) never looked at the product. They just approved going forward with the thing based on the CEO's recommendation.

To date, there are 114,000 waiver requests from different companies and political entities who say they can't comply with the demands of the product. It's just the tip of the iceberg. Many are unions who will get their waivers rubber-stamped.

The insurance companies who are supposed to deliver the product say it will cost a lot more to deliver. The health secretary says, baloney, eat the excess cost. Corporations and small businesses see this as an opportunity to get out of the insurance business. Just tell the employees to buy from the government. Give them the prior cost of the insurance in the paycheck and let them buy through the exchange.

The Big Salesman said too many times to count, "Let me make this clear: if you like your present insurance, you can keep it." How do you keep it if your employer drops you? And, remember this one: "If you like your present doctor, you can keep your doctor." How do you keep him or her if you have to go through the government for your insurance and the government tells you which doctors you can choose?

Obamacare is one giant dog's breakfast put together by fools working against an impossible time line, passed by bigger fools who will be voted out of office for doing it, and sold by the biggest fool: a puppet who just reads the script.

Remember the Troops

October 25, 2010

A while back, I was at the airport waiting for a plane. The gate representative for the airline announced the plane we would be flying had arrived at the gate and it was filled with many military personnel. As they deplaned, everyone in the gate area stood and applauded. The young people in uniform seemed embarrassed.

How often do we think about the sacrifices our military are making every day? How much do we see from the media about their heroics? We see more about Lindsay Lohan than our true heroes. Woodward wrote about how Obama is playing politics with the war in Afghanistan. He's playing politics with those who are doing a job most of us would prefer not to do.

Sometimes it takes a little thing to remind us how much our priorities are confused. I read about a young man from my town in Illinois who received the Medal of Honor post-humously. Saving many of his fellow marines, he gave his life with the greatest of courage. Sometimes it takes a story about a company coming home and watching the families meet them. We should get a daily dose of reminders from our media. We don't and we won't. There are few patriots working for the media. They are anti-war and can't get past that. I can tolerate anti-war, but not anti-warrior. If you don't like the war, go after Obama like you went after Bush. But, give the troops their due.

Sometimes a reminder comes from a place you would never expect to see. Would you ever think the band Kiss would be out there entertaining the troops? This week they were.

The Only Patriots Left in America Are the Military

November 13, 2010

'm writing this on Veterans Day. There is more than the normal amount of media attention to the holiday this year. At least in the media I read, watch, and listen to this day. It's good to see. No one makes more sacrifices than our people who have served, and are now serving, in the military. Including their families.

In contrast, the deficit commission President Obama put together reported their ideas for cutting the deficit. The outcry was deafening.

We have become a sniveling nation that refuses to make any sacrifice. Jesse Jackson warned the country about repealing Obamacare. The Democrats, led by the wicked witch from the west and Dickie Durbin, the dolt from my home state, rant on about not touching Social Security even though the proposal is seventy-five years out. The Republicans rant about cutting defense spending.

How do you cut the deficit when one party won't touch entitlements and the other won't do anything to increase revenue? You won't, and that's the plain truth. Look at Greece, France, and the United Kingdom, where people have taken to the streets over cuts in entitlements.

Sadly, we live in a country where we can send brave man and women off to war and expect them to make huge sacrifices. But we stay home and watch while our country goes broke and care nothing about our future generations.

Who will have the courage to cut 25% of the federal workforce? To simplify taxes? To stop the green energy crap that sucks up money with zero benefits? To divest of the post office, Amtrak, Freddie, Fannie, GM, and Chrysler? To face the Social Security issue? To repeal the Obamacare that is grossly underbudgeted and will make another mess we can't afford? Who will face the people stirred up by politicians, unions, the George Soros radicals, and those who are being asked to make sacrifices, large and small?

The reality is no one will do it. We no longer have the mettle in this country to sacrifice. Only the troops do. We need to take a lesson from them and make this a patriotic issue, not a political issue. Only then might we move forward.

The TSA Exemplifies Government Today

November 28, 2010

The country is up in arms over the TSA. Body scans and junk touching is their solution to air travel security. They tell us there is no other choice. Just suck it up and deal with it. It's for your own good.

The head of the TSA, John Pistole, is a marginal manager, at best. He wants to unionize the TSA. It seems to me to be a questionable goal. The average TSA employee is as marginal as Pistole. If unionized, we couldn't fire them. They would be overpaid for the job and still lack the qualifications we need. His boss, Janet Napolitano, is an embarrassment to Obama. She's lurching from one disaster to another. If someone puts a bomb in a shoe, we all take our shoes off. If someone puts a bomb in his underwear, we all let the TSA probe our junk. We spend billions for body scanners, all for illusionary security.

The TSA hires the wrong people. Diversity seems to be job one. Not background and ability. TSA employees are under trained and under motivated.

We refuse to pay special attention to those who might warrant special attention. So, the entire population, including my four-year-old granddaughter, must pay a price for that. We are traveling to Florida for Thanksgiving. My daughter, mother of the four-year-old, is very nervous that her daughter might be subject to a pat down. She has been told, since she could walk, not to let strangers touch her. She might freak. If she doesn't, my daughter might.

The shoe bomber and the underwear bomber did enough to warrant special attention. These were last minute deals: one-way tickets bought with cash. They should have been stopped at the ticket counter. But, they weren't. The 9/11 terrorists proceeded through security without a problem.

We can't use common sense in this country. No, we have come too far for that. The public must pay for inept management and poor judgment at the Department of Homeland Security and the TSA. We must pay for bad decisions by Obama in placing incompetent people in change. We must tolerate their telling us that hiring the right people, training them well, screening unusual behavior at the ticket counter, and not screening suspicious people can't be done.

The TSA needs to be restaffed by military veterans. They must be retrained to recognize suspicious behavior and react to that. Better screening of pre-travel arrangements must occur. Better no-fly lists must be made. Good judgment must occur.

But, no, we get the post office running our national security. We, the voters, deserve better and we need to demand better.

The Working Man's Enemy List

December 23, 2010

Why are we becoming a country that makes nothing? Why are manufacturing jobs moving elsewhere? Jobs that the so-called working man needs. Here's my enemy list for the working man:

1. Al Gore and the environmentalists. They had a grand vision of this country being smokeless. They attack all manufacturing plants, all smoke stacks, and all forms of energy needed to run manufacturing. They are winning. Jobs are being lost to their crusades.
2. Tax policy in this country. When manufacturing plants have one of the highest income tax rates of anywhere in the world, it makes it hard to compete.
3. Labor unions. Their greed and work rules destroyed the auto industry. They have run other industries out of the country.
4. Government regulation. No country in the world regulates industry more than the United States. Regulations cost money. Money that piles on labor costs, tax bills, regulatory costs, energy costs, and other disadvantages placed on US manufacturing.

5. Free trade. It's hard to compete with China when a worker there makes a dollar a day. We hope that China will be a market for US products. And, that we can stem the imports from there that cost less due to cheap labor, less regulation, lower taxes, and cheap energy. Sorry, working man; you will never win on this playing field.

6. The idea that finance will replace manufacturing in this country and growth will balance out the jobs lost by manufacturing. That happened. Then the housing bubble hit and wiped out the jobs in finance. Plus, financial institutions don't hire working men—or few, at best. We were going to retrain the workforce and integrate them into finance. Never happened.

7. Education and training. Our failing educational system produces far too many high school dropouts. Most manufacturing hires came from high school graduates who got some technical training to work in manufacturing. We have too few technical job training sites because there are too few jobs for those graduates to get.

So, working man with no job and no prospects, look around. The enemies are mostly those you see as friends. Your government, especially Democrats who purport to be on your side, is supporting most of the actions on the enemy list. Overzealous environmental regulation, regulation in general, labor unions, China, the educational status quo, high taxes on business, and Wall Street are your enemies.

Wake up. The Democrats have done far more than the Republicans to limit your job prospects.

Revenge of the Hicks

December 24, 2010

Elitists like President Obama often speak unkindly of rural Americans. Clutching their bibles and guns, per Obama. While Obama and his elitist progressives work to destroy our country, scoffing and apologizing about our greatness in the world, I think of my upbringing. Raised in a small town in Michigan by Depression-era parents, I was trained to be a survivor. Both my parents grew up on farms in Missouri. My dad was a building contractor. I was the first college graduate in my family.

I worked construction from the time I was fourteen and could do most jobs on a construction site. Had I not gone to college, I could have gotten a job on any construction crew in the country. I could pour cement, weld, lay brick, do carpentry work, put on a roof, do plumbing, and read blueprints. I could drive a tractor, a dump truck, a forklift, an overhead crane, and most anything that had an engine. I raised pigs and turned them into bacon. I hunted and fished. After school and sports practice, I would often go to the creek behind my house and catch some trout for dinner. I could shoot and dress game.

If the economy went to hell or I chose not to finish college, I had a lot of fallbacks to get by in this world. Some of my high school friends went that route. They spent their lives doing what I did before college. They brought up their kids to do that, too. Their kids are bringing up their kids that way. Obama would call them hicks. I call them prepared to get by in the world that may be coming their way, thanks to Obama and the politicians.

If the American dream explodes as a majority of Americans believe it will, who wins? Those elitist Ivy League educated attorneys and bankers or my high school friends' kids and their grandkids?

I have traveled extensively in this country, visiting every state except Alaska, which I plan to visit. My observations would make me believe the folks in rural America will make it if the country fails. They will use their bibles and guns for reinforcement. Their faith will help them face hard times. The guns will protect what they have when the folks from urban America try to take what they have when those urban folks have nothing.

The best insurance for hard times is an ability to survive on your own. To grow food, raise animals for food, build what you need to build for shelter, hunt and fish, can what you grow, and to have good neighbors for a support system.

If the hard times come, it will be the revenge of the hicks. They will survive.

Enough With the Emotional Appeals

December 29, 2010

The largest regret from Obama in his parting Christmas vacation press conference was not getting the Dream Act approved before he left.

This crystallizes everything that's wrong in Washington and is at the core of what's putting this country into bankruptcy today. You pick one single issue from a huge problem.

Then, you bang away at the issue using an emotional appeal to create a wedge, allowing you to overlook the bigger issues. He went on to say it's not the fault of a child who was brought into this country illegally. That child, should he choose to go to college or enter the military, should be forgiven for what his parents did: bring him into the country illegally.

It's like going to the doctor for a physical and finding you have a tumor and need a knee replacement. If the Doctor said we are going to replace the knee so you can be mobile for your cancer treatments, what would you say?

The tumor in Obama's case is the still-unsecured border. The tumor is growing and it's costing the country billions we can't afford. It's causing states along the border to try to fix the problem Obama won't address. He is attacking them for trying to do the right thing. He's telling the country our number one problem on illegal immigration is whether we should do something for a few thousand children of illegals who choose to go to college or enter the military. In his eyes, I guess, this solves the border problem and fixes the issue of millions of illegals who are here consuming billions in tax dollars.

The lapdog media eats this up like a dog bone. No one ever asks our president how doing this will solve the bigger problems. Why does the president, and all politicians in general, keep diverting our attention from the big issues by throwing us a bone that appeals to our emotions? Simple: we eat the bones. Until we as voters stop eating dog treats, we will never force the politicians to face the big issues.

It will be very hard to fix the problems the voters asked to get fixed in November. The opposition, supported by the media, will find the emotional soft spot on every change. The opposition will put forth a knee replacement in lieu of cancer surgery for every solution.

It's the political version of bait and switch. As a nation that loves reality TV, we will buy the knee replacements. As the tumors grow, we will wonder what is killing us.

New Year's Resolutions for Congress

December 31, 2010

First and foremost, they must delouse Congress. The spelling difference between louse and Pelosi is just three letters. Pelosi has increased the deficit by $3 trillion on her watch. She is proud of this, along with the fact that the latest rating for Congress is 13% and dropping. She made the New Deal look like child's play. With help from Obama the last two years, she has pushed this country to the brink of European socialism. So much so that she woke up a sleeping public and got many of her fellow Democrats thrown out of office in November. She and the Democrats are unrepentant about any of this, and the party showed that by keeping her in power.

Every effort must be made to revoke Obamacare. Obama will veto an outright revocation, but that should happen. As the year unfolds and the truth about the program emerges, it will become a political embarrassment to Obama and the Democrats. If it becomes reality, any chance of avoiding European socialism will be lost. It's the whole enchilada. Once thirty million voters get free medical care, it's over. This will be difficult, since the liberal media will not report fairly the ugly underbelly as it's exposed in reality and in hearings. It's a huge job and must be done.

Real spending cuts must happen. It will mean putting thousands, if not millions, of government workers out of a job. Workers might be a kind term. Pay cuts for government workers must happen. Benefit changes and pension reform need to be done, also.

Income tax reform must happen. A simple tax code is long overdue.

Work on sealing the borders is a priority. A plan to deal with illegal aliens, changed to illegal immigrants, now trying to be changed to undocumented workers, is next. Round them up and ship them home. Simple as that.

Slashing the regulatory power of government agencies running wild under Obama has to happen. The EPA is the worst. They are implementing cap and trade under the noses of Congress. Stop them: the FCC (internet regulation), the Department of Agriculture (hybrid seed regulation), and all the other job killers Obama has put in place. Strip the Department of Education of as much power as possible. They are just an arm of the NEA right now. Push it back to the states. Get real education reform, despite the unions.

Pass a resolution that no states will be bailed out by the federal government. Let California and Illinois file bankruptcy. It will finally force change.

Last, but not least, hear the voters from last November. Do not stray from the mission. Overturn as much of the mischief of Pelosi, Reid, and Obama as fast as you can. Be good to businesses, especially small businesses. Jobs will come from there.

2011

Birthday Wishes

January 3, 2011

Today, I celebrate my sixty-ninth birthday. I am a son of parents of the Greatest Generation. It is with great regret that I feel my generation has not measured up to the standard set by our parents.

We have watched as inadequate leadership mortgaged the futures of our children and grandchildren. Those leaders have led for the moment, poll by poll, never addressing the impact of their decisions on our next generations.

Politicians call Social Security the third rail of politics. Touch it and you are fried. There seem to be a lot of third rails these days—energy, for one. We keep trying to avoid the truth that we need all forms of energy to survive and prosper as a nation and for national security. We get sucked into lofty goals, like saving the planet, when we need to save the country.

It's an extensive list of things that need to be addressed for the long term: illegal immigration, excessive spending, excessive government, incompetent government, etc.

My birthday wish is our generation will see the errors of our ways and step up to the plate. We need to work to get leaders at all levels of government with vision and courage to do the right thing for our kids and grandkids. If we don't, they face a far worse future than we did. Our greed and apathy have made this a fact.

I am only guardedly optimistic we can rise to that challenge. We have not proven we can take on these large issues of the future. We are watchers and not doers. It would be nice to get this birthday wish, but its a big one and may be more than we are willing to do at this point in our lives.

Arizona in Mourning

January 10, 2011

An unbalanced young gunman shot twenty people at a political rally in Tucson. Six people died. Four heroes kept it from becoming worse. A seventy-four-year-old woman stepped in as the shooter was trying to load a fresh clip. Two men jumped on the shooter and a third helped hold him down. A medical intern certainly saved Rep. Gabrielle Giffords with his aid. It is a tragedy and Arizona is in mourning for the dead and wounded. It's another senseless sign of our troubled times.

Led by Pima County Sheriff, Clarence Dupnik, the news immediately politicized the event. He attacked the amount of vitriol in political rhetoric, suggesting that may have contributed to this violence. I feel Sheriff Dupnik is setting the same example he is blaming for the tragedy.

Dupnik's comments lit up the media in Arizona and they

jumped on the political aspect of the tirade. The national media soon followed. It's the same media that said we need to take pause after the Ft. Hood shooting, and not make this a political/religious issue.

No one really knows the shooter's motives for doing what he did. If it were pure politics, it seems he would have stopped after shooting the congresswoman. For all the sheriff knows, he just looked for a crowd.

I believe it is truly classless for Sheriff Dupnik to use this tragedy to stump for his personal political beliefs. He would be better served by investigating the crime and recognizing the citizens who did such a heroic job of mitigating the damage. Evidently, there was no police presence at the scene.

Local media, now national media, even suggest it could be Tea Party motivated. It shows the sad state of communications in this country and how far the media has sunk from their job of journalistic reporting. The media and the sheriff treat this like a TV reality show.

To the sheriff's position on guns, if the young man who helped subdue the suspect had arrived five minutes sooner, he might have reduced the carnage. He was carrying a 9mm handgun, legal in Arizona.

Some reasonable journalist wrote, "This is a rush to see who can be wrong first." Isn't that the truth.

Tucson Heroes: It's Time to Exit the Stage

January 14, 2011

I n 1989, I was involved in a major tragedy. An airplane crash killed over one hundred of my fellow passengers and left another hundred hospitalized. I flew home that night and woke to find media trucks all over my street. I declined to give but one interview. It was with Elizabeth Vargas. The phone rang and Oprah wanted me to be on her show. I declined. Some were trying to put the hero label on me for helping to carry an invalid nun from the wreckage and out of the cornfield.

I had an epiphany. The wife and two children of an employee of the company I worked for were lost in the crash. I did not know them, but I thought about the surviving husband a lot. It struck me that I would not want to see the survivors and knighted heroes paraded on the TV while I was trying to get through my personal grief and figure out how to survive without my entire family.

It struck me that I owed it to the families of those who did not survive to never be seen on TV or in any media by those families. I did not want to parade myself in front of them as a survivor of something that killed their loved ones.

While I give all the heroes of the Tucson shooting their due, I find the one who was the first responder gets the most credit from me. It's the man who hit the shooter with the chair. I have searched and can't find if he ever came forward to take credit. If that's true, he is my hero. It took me a day or two to put together the need to keep my face out of the media in respect for those who lost loved ones. He seemed to do it in minutes.

I have been hounded by the media for over twenty years. On anniversaries, when there are other plane crashes, and when a fellow survivor dies. I have never responded with an interview or anything but a polite thank you, but I don't do comments or interviews. You heroes of Tucson, you will see the same. My advice: hunker down and be a silent hero. It's better for those who lost family and friends.

"Investing in America" Truth

February 4, 2011

The president said we need to invest in education, infrastructure, green energy, and health care.

Here's the real data—increases in budgets between 2008 and 2010:

Education: up 116%
Transportation: up 40%
Transit spending: up 60%
Department of Energy: up 81%
Housing: up 84%

Before Obama, Bush added 32% to infrastructure, education, and R&D budgets. Bush signed a $284 billion highway bill.

Have you seen a jump in jobs from this Obama strategy? Why would you go back to failed efforts and make this the centerpiece of your big State of the Union Address?

Here's the Obama history: Create a hostile business climate like the one that ruined California; bigger government like the one that ruined the Soviet Union; green energy like the one that ruined Spain; an unprofitable infrastructure like the one that ruined Japan; gin up a huge national debt like the one that ruined Greece; and have a big socialized medicine plan like the one that ruined Massachusetts.

It's simple. Pick any loser and Obama is for it and will spend every dollar he can to support that loser.

One Obama Comment Says It All

February 19, 2011

Suddenly, new Republican governors in Wisconsin, Florida, and Michigan are joining Chris Christie and Mitch Daniels in getting their state budgets under control before their states become Illinois and California.

In Wisconsin, Governor Scott Walker has proposed severe changes in public employee unions. A vote was to be heard this week. The response was teachers vacating classrooms for public protests. Fourteen Democratic legislators went into hiding to prevent a quorum.

The governors from these three states have one thing in common. They came from the world of business, not politics. In Wisconsin, union employees were asked to pay 5.8% of their pension contributions and 12.6% of their health care up from an average of 6%. This is far below the average paid by the private sector and would avoid the loss of 5,500 state jobs and 5,000 local jobs. He, Walker, would promise no layoffs or furloughs for the 170,000 public employees.

Similar bills are pending in Arizona, Indiana, Iowa, Michigan, New Hampshire, New Jersey, and New Mexico, with another sixteen states debating such changes. Wisconsin is facing a $3.6 billion budget deficit in the next budget year. Many of the governors in these states were put in office to do just that.

President Obama's response in a speech in Wisconsin: "This is an attack on the unions."

There you have it folks—a president who will destroy state budgets, force state bankruptcies, destroy the futures for coming generations, let teachers flee the classroom, and promote deficits to protect his union vote. It's his entire outlook on the economic future for this country, in a nutshell. Protect the unions and push the problem down the road for future generations of politicians to solve.

It's time for the Obama economic policy to go away. It's time to put business people with courage into public office across the country.

A Tale of Two Cities

March 18, 2011

I own two houses, one in Illinois and one in Arizona.

Both have lower assessments than they had two years ago. The housing values have gone down on both places. No surprise. That's where the similarities end.

In Illinois, despite the lower assessed value, the tax bill is up 5%. In Arizona, the tax bill is down 25%.

So, in one state and county, the homeowner, despite losing value in an asset, is expected to pay more for government spending. In the other, the politicians have made adjustments for less revenue and did not offset voter net worth loss with spending increases.

Where will housing values recover? In Illinois, with more and more homeowners seeing home values go below the mortgage amount, the politicians don't see a reason to keep more homeowners from walking away from those houses. They will see increased foreclosures as increased real estate taxes add another reason to pack it in. In Arizona, the politicians are tightening their belts to keep home ownership woes from getting worse.

The state of Illinois is trying to keep from going bankrupt by raising taxes. The state of Arizona is trying to balance a budget by cutting expenses.

Does common sense tell you this is a microcosm of the country? Democrats believe we need to keep spending and raise taxes to fix our broken economy. Republicans believe we need to lower taxes and cut expenses to get our economy back on track.

It's very simple when it gets right down to your property taxes. Do you believe it's fair to watch the value of your house go down 40% and have your property taxes go up?

Pipelines Are Just Too Scary

March 22, 2011

D id you know the first pipeline was built in the United States in 1865? The first pipeline was only 6 km long. But in 1875, pipelines started their real role in America. Due largely to pipelines, we have the most sophisticated and efficient hydrocarbon distribution system in the world. Pipelines save you hundreds of dollars every year on your gasoline and natural gas or heating oil bills.

When the Trans-Alaskan pipeline was proposed across Alaska in 1970, the critics came out of the woodwork. To us, they said, pipelines are evil. You can have leaks, explosions, block the migration paths of caribou, melt the permafrost, etc. Somehow, despite the delays due to lawsuits, environmental impact studies, political haymaking, and God knows what else, the pipeline began operation in 1977. Since then, it has brought 16 billion barrels of oil from the North Slope that we would not have had.

A new pipeline is being proposed. Dubbed the Keystone line, it would bring 500,000 barrels a day from the Canadian tar sands to the Gulf Coast refineries. Declining production from Mexico and Venezuela make this a pressing need.

Do-gooders in the Obama administration don't like the

idea of Canadian tar oil. They think it's America's respon-
sibility to stop this practice, not purchase the end product.
To stop this project, they cite the recent pipeline problem in
Michigan with a line that is forty-two years old.

They want you to believe pipelines are truly scary things.
Gee, how many Americans have died since 1865 from pipelines? More kids have died in unsafe cribs than deaths from
pipelines.

If you are afraid of pipelines, you are truly paranoid and
might want to seek professional help. If you believe we in
America should stop buying from our main oil supplier
because we don't approve of tar sand oil extraction, then
move to Canada and vote for people who agree with you.

There is absolutely no common sense being applied to this
project. And, the Canadians don't need us to do this. They
can simply ship to the West and sell to China. Of course,
China is building pipelines wherever they need them, signing
contracts with countries like Canada to buy their crude oil on
a long-term basis, and seem to think it's Canada's business if
they want all that revenue and all those jobs that come from
sand extraction.

Who is really calling the shots here? How is it that no one
cares if this high-priority project gets delayed indefinitely—
and maybe, just maybe, China ends up with the oil?

I care and it's Obama's fault. Plain and simple. If he wants
you to have energy for the next twenty years, he needs to
move this forward. He can't and he won't. So, vote for someone who will.

Obama Wants to Unionize the TSA

April 07, 2011

Even as we watch states like Wisconsin try to get out from under a union situation they can't afford, our president wants to unionize the TSA. Public unions get what they want because politicians buy their votes with your tax dollars. There is no limit to what they will pay for those votes. While cities and states try to get out from under this crushing problem, hundreds of TSA workers are voting to pick a union to give them the same benefits we can't afford. And this is with the overwhelming blessing of Obama and his liberal associates.

Candidate Obama sent a letter to the American Federation of Government Employees head, John Gage, stating it was a top priority to give the TSA collective bargaining rights. After closing Gitmo, of course.

Well, it's finally time to provide that kickback to union bosses by Obama. The TSA started because of 9/11. Since inception, tests have shown it's flawed. Now, Obama wants to give them union protection to maintain and grow those flaws. Plus, let's make sure they can't have competition from the private sector.

Isn't this president a prize?

Give the Man His Due

May 3, 2011

I admire the way President Obama continued to pursue Bin Laden. I believe the method approved for the attack was perfect. I thought the speech he made announcing the event was just right; measured and solemn. This was very well done, Mr. President.

I have been, and will continue to be, a staunch critic of yours, Mr. President. I do not have one iota of bitterness about your moment of triumph. Some of your critics seem to resent the great deed you engineered. I do not.

Does this crowning achievement of your short presidency mean I will forgive and forget and vote for you in 2012? Absolutely not. I do not endorse your politics or your policies. I do not believe your leadership stands the test of the challenges of this country. I don't trust your integrity. I will work my hardest to see you become a one-term president.

That said, without qualification, on the matter of the long-awaited justice you brought to us with the death of this generation's version of Hitler, I say: Well done, Mr. President.

Let's Tax This Group of Rich Americans

June 4, 2011

Obama's solution to the debt ceiling, the deficit, and excess government spending and regulation is to raise taxes on the rich. Don't cut spending, downsize government, and

roll back regulation. Just tax the rich. That will fix everything. It will fix the housing market (how?). It will fix unemployment (how?). It will fix the budget, even though statistics
show if they took all the money his so-called rich have, it
wouldn't put a dent in the budget problem.

Well, not to be outdone by Obama, I have a tax solution
to the budget problem. And, I think mine will fix many problems.

Let's tax campaign contributions. It would work like this.
You pay a flat tax on campaign contributions you spend
during an election cycle, an election cycle as defined by the
period from your last election to the current one for incumbents. All others, it's between the time you announced for
office until the election.

Let's not be greedy like Obama wants to be with the rich
and collect over 50%; we'll just take 35%. Now, all you
democrats who like estate taxes so much, line up and support this. With estate taxes, it's pure double taxation and you
don't mind that a bit. The estate paid income taxes, capital gains taxes, interest income taxes, and dividend taxes on
everything in the estate once. You still think it's fair to grab
another 50% when the estate is probated? With campaign
contributions, the politician paid no taxes and really didn't
do anything to earn the money, so why worry about taking a
mere 35% for government spending?

When the campaign is over, win or lose, whatever is left
over goes to the government. Right—100%—all of it. Any
politician in the country holding campaign funds in trust will
have to give all those funds over to Uncle Sam. Now. Local,
state, and federal.

You see, we have no idea how many billions in campaign
dollars are just sitting around like cash in the bank for the

person whose trust controls that money. Need a new car, just dip into the funds. Want a new yacht, just dip in. On your last term in office, campaign hard and spend little. Those funds will be part of the retirement. Along with the generous retirement taxpayers provide and the medical plan that is the envy of the world.

You see, this is even better than term limits. The playing field gets leveled every election. No one is sitting on millions they can use to ensure they will win every election. Everybody starts fund raising at the same time. And, if you raise a lot, you will pay more back in taxes. Again, leveling the playing field.

Since President Obama and Democrats like taxing the rich so much, let's tax the political rich. If we did this, we would probably make more the first year than if he got his tax increase on everyone who makes over $200,000. Just think, 35% on all that dormant campaign money lying around the country being used by rich politicians for cars and yachts.

You Can Keep Your Doctor with Obamacare

June 10, 2011

This week, the above statement President Obama made time and time again while pimping for his great accomplishment, the abortive Obamacare, was found to be just another Obama lie.

When it comes to business and the private sector, give the president credit. He is always wrong. He is clueless about how the private sector in this country works. McKinsey, a consulting firm I have worked with extensively, did a survey to confirm what all of us who spent time in any business executive suite already knew: you won't have health insurance from your employer under Obamacare.

Businesses, large and small, didn't choose to be the supplier of health insurance to employees. It became a competitive necessity. For years, employers have struggled to find a way to keep these costs down. The have instituted wellness plans. They have studied the competitive labor market to find ways to cut costs. They have cut benefits to employees. They have cut benefits to retirees.

Now Obama has given them an out. Just pay the $2,000 annual fine and don't be in the health insurance business. Let the employees find their own health insurance.

According to McKinsey, only seventy-eight million Americans now insured by employers will get alternative insurance. Gee, if it affected only seventy-eight million Americans, was it really an important lie Obama was telling? Or, did he even know, or care? Was he just reading the teleprompter? If you gave him a test on Obamacare, could he pass? Did he have meaningful debates with the lackeys who designed Obamacare? Was the constitutionality of it ever questioned like it is being questioned in a courtroom in Atlanta? Did they think thousands of waivers would be needed to keep big employers like McDonald's from dropping their low-cost coverage?

McKinsey's study showed that many employers who don't opt for the $2,000 fine will opt for the subsidized coverage—subsidized by your tax dollars—driving up the cost of

Obamacare, as originally estimated, by billions. Meanwhile, the prime minister of the United Kingdom is trying to cut back their universal health care because the country can't afford it any longer.

It's time to get rid of Obamacare. We can have health care reform, but a version that is truthful about the outcomes, both for the public and the budget. Get a clean piece of paper and start again.

Lack of Independence Day

July 4, 2011

Every year, it seems like it gets harder to celebrate Independence Day.

This is the last year I will be able to buy the light bulbs I prefer to use. Next year, unless the Republicans muster up some courage, I will buy bulbs that look like the cones I used to buy as a kid at the Zesto Drive-In. Chock full of mercury, I have to call HAZMAT if I break one. They cost more, provide poorer light, take longer to warm up, and last far less longer than promised. Why don't I have a choice of the light bulbs I use? Why do I, and millions of other Americans, have to stock our basements with bulbs to exercise our rights as Americans?

Why do I have to buy gasoline with ethanol in it while third world countries have starving people? It is to create a summer blend to reduce emissions in warmer weather. But, knock sensors on cars have prevented that for twenty years.

So, it's to keep or get votes in farm states. It doesn't save any foreign oil purchases and it adds carbon to the environment. I'm doing this to help fat cat corporate farmers? Why is this different than corporate jets?

I am thankful this Fourth of July that I don't live in San Francisco. They are banning circumcision. How bad is that? Plus, the whole state has banned charcoal grills, a Fourth of July tradition for us die-hard purists. Now they are trying to ban the sale of pets. For the Jewish population, pet lovers, and traditional grillers, where is their freedom? Who decides what is banned and not banned in the City by the Bay?

We have the Feds banning everything they can ban and mandating what they like. We have states picking up the slack and banning more and mandating more. We have the cities jumping in on the act. And, in some cases, you have the worst threat to freedom: homeowners' associations and their Covenants, Conditions, and Restrictions. They tell you what color you can paint your house, whether you can park a car overnight in your own driveway, and what bushes you can plant in your yard.

Combine all this help we get and it's a tsunami of insults to our way of living. It's no longer the land of the free and the home of the brave.

It's the land where the few decide what we need and force us to like it. Isn't that why our forefathers left England to begin with?

Obama's Leadership Style

July 7, 2011

I've been a student of leadership styles for the past forty years. It has taken a while, but I believe I finally have a handle on the Obama leadership style. I'm struggling for a label, but have ultimately settled on: demagogic/attacking. I've seen it before.

With this style, the leader does basically nothing and hopes all will go well. Generally, the leader has one person that he/she relies on for advice. In the case of Obama, it's Valerie Jarrett. This type of leader is humorless, arrogant, sensitive about criticism, and has an aura of being in complete control. All of these are necessary to pull it off—to offer little, if any, leadership while appearing to be involved.

People with this type of leadership can go far until they are Peter-Principled to a point where the visibility is too sharp and the responsibility too much. When things start going wrong at this level, the fallback is to attack/blame, thus the label, demagogic/attacking.

The first step in defending failure is to find straw men to blame. George W. Bush, for example. He is to blame for the economy. But, the blaming must be attacking, not just finger pointing. It must be done with soaring oratory. The teleprompter needs to be smoking. Ultimately, so many things go wrong for this style of leader that he/she can't find enough straw men and spew enough vitriol often enough to cover the problems. That's where Obama is right now.

His game on the debt ceiling is not working. Not yet, at least. Enough Americans have watched him try to raise the debt ceiling by $2 trillion with every intention of spending that, submit a budget that went down in flames in the senate by a vote of 97–0, and try to convince the public that changing depreciation of corporate jets will work and spending can go on. He then attacks Congress for not working while he offers no solutions, except tax increases on the very rich, which really means anyone making over $250,000 a year. Most small business people fall into that category.

The worst president in my lifetime, Jimmy Carter, was a micromanager. He had to have his fingers in everything. And, he was ineffective. So, while touching everything, he screwed everything up.

Obama touches nothing. He is in the stands watching the game and writing his critique of the players on the field. Like most Monday-morning quarterbacks, he is really good at finding the flaws. He feels no responsibility for the outcome of the game. He has no intention of getting in the game. But, because he is responsible for the outcome of the game, he must have excuses for the losses. Find the ones to blame, strike out at the losers who are causing his criticism, and deflect blame.

This leadership style is worse than Carter's. In Jimmy's case, he at least worked. He tried, he was involved, too involved, and he cared. With the Obama style, you play golf, raise money, campaign, travel, tweet on Twitter, make speeches, and watch. You have no plan, no strategy, no interest, and no involvement.

But, you do have a lengthy list of people you attack when it all goes south. It's going south fast, Mr. President. You may want to take a break from golf or fundraising and polish up that list.

Epitome of Washington Ignorance and Arrogance

July 17, 2011

Want yet another example of what little respect our president and Congress have for our tax dollars? When you listen to the huge struggles about downsizing the federal government, keep this in mind.

Bush put together the 2007 energy bill. It was indicative of his lack of courage. But, in fairness, if he mentioned anything that involved hydrocarbons, the Democrats and the press pointed out he was an ex-oilman and Cheney worked for Halliburton. Hence, they are playing to the oil industry. We aren't smart enough to think for ourselves, so we just listened and didn't challenge. In his nothing of an energy bill, there was a lot about ethanol, which shows you that Bush was never really an oil man and he was just pandering to environmentalists.

Mandates for ethanol were big in that bill. But, Bush was big on cellulosic ethanol. It was to be made from switchgrass, wood, or whatever some flimflam artist was selling to Washington and being covered extensively on the major media news. That was 2007 and the EPA set the standard for 6 million gallons of this big solution to our energy dependence in year 2011, with that amount going up dramatically in subsequent years.

How many gallons have been produced to blend in 2011? Zero—that's it, zero. I tried to find how many millions of dollars the government has given to scammers who said they would produce this snake oil, but it's a closely guarded secret. Rest assured, it's lots of millions.

So, naturally, Obama, Lisa Jackson (EPA), and good old Dr. Chu, head of the DOE, are pulling this plan, right? After all, it was a Bush mess, so Obama can blame him for this.

No, of course, our government doesn't acknowledge a bad idea and drop the mandate. Our government just says refiners must buy cellulosic credits. They must pay $1.13 a gallon for a product that can't be produced. Of course, that money will be passed back in the pump price of gasoline and the revenue handed out to more failing scam artists who promise to make stuff that no one has made.

But, certainly the EPA will fix this for 2012. Sure they have; they are raising the mandate to some number between 3.55 million and 15.7 million gallons. Is this a tax on the middle class? Of course, the EPA gives billions in budgeted assistance to failed enterprises that never make viable energies, but we guess those billions aren't enough. So, if the EPA keeps raising the quota for this junk, they collect from refiners and it's off-book revenue. It can be used to raise Lisa Jackson's expense account or her salary, or just squandered.

If you are one of the 15% of Americans who think Congress is doing a good job, please read this again, one more time, before you respond to another poll.

When Faced With Accountability, Teachers Cheat

July 18, 2011

No surprise. The chosen few who never need to account for performance grow comfortable not performing. Rate busters on the union assembly lines are quickly brought into compliance. Slow it down; don't make us look bad. Government workers, if they ever had to perform to any standard, would fold like a cheap suit.

The very curve that educators perfected over time exists in any group of people. Jack Welch of GE broke it into four categories. He graded his people on these curves. First, there were the top performers who met all the goals and did it the right way. Next were the ones who met all the goals but left problems behind: morale problems, customer problems, budget problems, etc. Then came the ones who didn't meet goals, but did it the right way. With groups two and three, more training and help was provided.

Finally, there was the fourth group, those who neither met goals nor did things the right way. This group was sent packing to become teachers, government employees, politicians, or union employees. He said this group was 15–20% every year, year in and year out. It's the same as 15% of any class on the curve that flunked the test.

If a high-performing corporation like GE under Welch must weed out 15% a year, what would that curve look like in education? It looks like it must be a very high percentage if you look at teachers' response to accountability. They have been trying to block the accountability tests for years. Now that accountability exists, they don't seem to want to teach harder and help students improve their test scores. They just rig the scores. They are very creative in their methods to rig results.

So far, it's been uncovered in a small number of school systems where the accountability was put into effect. But, trust me, this is just the beginning. In business, I dealt with people who just can't get the job done but can find creative ways to hide the results or excuse away incompetence. The teaching cadre in the United States is rife with incompetence and indolence. One can't be fixed, one can. But it's hard to go back to work after skating for years.

Want proof? Just look at the US student test scores versus other countries.

Want your kids educated? You better think hard about what Governor Walker did in Wisconsin. In Wisconsin, the teacher of the year was let go when jobs were cut because she didn't have seniority. Her job was kept by someone who probably falls into Jack Welch's bottom 15%. Until the teacher's union is broken, this is what you get.

Since the United States rates so low in the world on average standardized test score comparisons, the people responsible to the students and parents to make these scores higher must be fraught with underperformers. Once accountability is put in place, those facts will be obvious. No wonder the union and the teachers don't want this. Also, no wonder, when faced with getting fired because the facts are clear a teacher is not teaching, that teacher opts to cheat. No wonder, when a whole school system, like Atlanta, is going to fail, the system cheats. Once accountability is put in place, hundreds of superintendents, principals, and teachers will be out of work.

Tough deal, but the alternative is to keep under educating our kids and grandkids.

America Has Tipped

July 28, 2011

It may be too late for our great country.

Fifty percent of Americans pay no taxes. Twenty percent of US males under forty don't work. Eighty million checks are mailed out by the US Treasury each month. And, 131 million Americans voted in the 2008 election. You do the math.

Obama and the left now own the country. They control the media and the votes. They have enough voters dependent on the government to win the elections.

We are hanging by a thread as a country. The American Dream has become "doing nothing and getting paid not to do it." Too much is broken.

When I started this blog on January 20, 2008, I feared for my kids and grandkids. I had been saying for years that my grandkids would be the first generation in this country to have a poorer standard of living than their parents. Now, I have no doubts. Sure, this country has been through tough times before. The Civil War, the Great Depression, WWI and WWII, and other bad times. But, this may be the worst.

We have outspent our future. We have mortgaged our greatness. We have tried to raise everyone's standard of living with government checks. Want a glimpse of our future? Look at Detroit. Billions have been poured into Detroit to save the city. It didn't work. Central planning has never worked for any country. It isn't working for ours. The Great Society was the start of it all. Now we have the Not-So-Great Society.

We have a government that works only for votes. Not for doing the right things.

We have a spending problem. We have a jobs problem. We have economic problems at every level in this country. Some are being solved, but not at the national level.

The next election is the last great hope and it looks bleak. The free enterprise system is under attack in Washington. And, it's losing. It's not called the free enterprise system. It's called billionaires, millionaires, corporate jets, and evil corporations. Those who pay taxes and create jobs are greedy and need to give more to the government so we can have 20% of the males under forty not working, so we can send out 80 million government checks every month, and most important, so we can assure Obama, Reid, Durbin, and Pelosi keep their jobs forever.

If you care about any of this, you had better get active. The next election in 2012 is about saving the country. Plain and simple.

Don't Count Obama Out in 2012

September 8, 2011

It's a funny thing about presidential elections. Despite poll numbers that would suggest Obama is done in 2012, despite a double dip recession, despite 10% unemployment, despite speech after speech that changes nothing, and despite being the worst president since Jimmy Carter, Obama may get another term.

It's all in the math. Obama will have 175 electoral votes in his pocket before the polls open. He will have California, Connecticut, Delaware, Hawaii, Illinois, Maryland, Massachusetts, New Jersey, New York, Rhode Island, Vermont, Washington state and Washington, D.C. Most of these states are in worse shape than the country and are getting worse. But, they continue to elect state governments that maintain the destructive Obama doctrine. New Jersey is the exception. Obama needs only eighty-five more electoral votes to win the second term.

He has a large pool of states to draw from. Michigan, New Mexico, Pennsylvania, Minnesota, Oregon, Maine, and Wisconsin hold seventy-two votes. If they all go his way, he's in. Wisconsin and Pennsylvania might not go for Obama this time.

Seven swing states will tell the story: Colorado, Florida, Iowa, Nevada, New Hampshire, Ohio, and Virginia. This group has eighty-six votes. Before they are tallied, it would seem the count would be Obama 247 and the Republican candidate 206. To win, the Republican candidate must get Florida (29), Ohio (18), and Virginia (13), plus Colorado (9) or a combination of wins in the other states to reach 270.

This assumes none of the true-blue states are fed up with Obama, which is highly unlikely. So, Obama needs to focus on the seven swing states, plus Pennsylvania, Wisconsin, North Carolina, and New Mexico, to win. Note Colorado and New Mexico have large Hispanic populations. Obama did the amnesty program last month. Do you get it now?

With 175 electoral votes in his pocket from states that endorse Obama, it's an enormous hill for the Republicans to climb.

The electoral data were provided by Larry Sabato in a *Wall Street Journal* article dated September 6, 2011.

Close the Post Office

September 10, 2011

For the past thirty days, I've gone through my mail to see what, if anything, I had to have that day. There was nothing.

Let's assume, for discussion, that UPS or Federal Express brought me a box on Monday and a box on Friday with all my mail. Would that be a problem? And, I had an inventory of boxes with prepaid postage that I could use for my outgoing mail. Would that be a problem? NO.

We used to have a pony express. We don't have that anymore. More cost-effective ways to deliver mail came along. Now, we have the internet and it's displacing the post office. Why do we hang onto a government-owned and -operated system that has become passé? Why do we throw tax money away trying to keep it going? Why does the media go to some remote post office in Idaho to interview people who say they enjoy the social aspect of having a post office?

I love my mailman, Miguel. He takes very good care of my mail. But, I haven't seen Miguel in three months. Every day, I have a new mail person. Sometimes they deliver my mail at 10:00 a.m., something Miguel never did, but sometimes it comes at 5:30 p.m. Miguel hasn't worked a full work year in five years. See, he's disabled because of a back problem on the job. In the real world, Miguel's disability pay would have run out months ago, but not in the world of our federal government.

It all gets down to this, as the postmaster general is finding out: union jobs and minority jobs. He, the postmaster, has proposed huge cutbacks. But, they, the liberals in Congress, are fighting this. They say they will come up with the money to avoid this happening.

It's this simple. Put the business up for sale. Let the private sector figure out a way to deliver mail and make a profit. Shipping three days of mail in a box makes economic sense. It's being done every day. The government can pick up a few billion for selling the business, and the buyers can figure out a way to make a profit. The buyers will need to hire employees and we, the customers and creditors, can adapt to a different delivery schedule and system. Who loses? You tell me.

Social Security Is a Ponzi Scheme

September 15, 2011

I knew a man who ran a Ponzi scheme. It was small when compared to Bernie Madoff; only about $15 million. He took in many of his lifelong friends. I had the pleasure of hearing his pitch and rejected the opportunity to invest with him. When questioned by a nervous investor, he would put them on his life insurance policy as a beneficiary. But, insurance companies notify people when they are put on, but not when they are taken off. He would put them on, then take them off and put his wife back on. He shot himself when it crumbled. It crumbled when the new money was slower coming in than interest to investors could be paid back.

Social Security is different than this man's Ponzi scheme. You could choose not to give this man money but you have no choice about contributing to Social Security.

It is a well-known fact that those who are paying in today have almost no chance of getting 100% of the money back when they retire. That's a Ponzi scheme. There would be enough there to handle those of us drawing Social Security and those paying in for the future, except for one small problem. The government, like this man, tapped the funds. The government put IOUs in the fund from the Treasury.

Now the Treasury is broke. To pay the IOUs, the Treasury would have to borrow money or print money. We have over-borrowed and show little chance of being able to borrow more to pay these IOUs. If we printed that much money, the dollar would drop like a rock.

Those who attack Rick Perry for his position on Social Security just choose to put the problem on the back burner. Changes must be made in Social Security to keep the house of cards from falling. One change would be to start paying the Social Security Trust back for the money stolen by the government. Cut expenses elsewhere and start putting the stolen money back in the pot. Invest the money in the pot. And, lower the expectations of the younger payers. If they know they will get less from Social Security, they will know to save and invest more for their retirement.

Calling it a Ponzi scheme does not mean eliminating Social Security. It means facing the truth. It means addressing a problem, not ignoring a future mess.

Home Already

October 13, 2011

Less than forty-eight hours after I was rolled into surgery for a knee replacement, I was back home.

It was routine, as knee replacements go, except for the "audible," per the surgeon. The surgeon and the representative from Zimmer, the knee manufacturer, talked. As they both revisited the historical profiles of the x-rays and the first look at the mess of a knee, they realized there were virtually no ligaments to hold the new knee in place. So, the rep grabbed a different model and they put that one in. It has more capacity to find surface areas to grip and relies less on ligaments to hold it in place.

Will audibles be allowed under Obamacare? Will a shorter stay be an option? Most people I talked to said no to both. Like most things government, there will be hard and fast rules. You get the off-the-shelf model knee and you stay the time the rules require you to stay.

Good judgment always seems like a positive to me. I was permitted to go home early because I am in good physical shape, can tolerate pain, and was driven to do so. I received a more complex knee based on need. One saved money and one cost more. On balance, the savings was greater than the cost increase.

One of these days, knee replacements will be outpatient procedures. I'm glad I did mine before that becomes practice.

Who's Running the Railroad?

October 20, 2011

Amtrak says it all about our government today.

According to *The Wall Street Journal*, Amtrak announced a milestone. They carried a record 30 million passengers last year. But, despite record traffic, they hit a near record loss, requiring $560 million in tax dollars from millionaires and billionaires to cover that loss.

Who got fired? Nobody. Who got called on the carpet? Nobody. Who cares? Nobody?

The $560 million operating loss for 2011 is just the tip of the iceberg. They received an early $1 billion in capital subsidies, $52 million in debt restructuring relief, and access to a $562 million low-interest loan with the Department of Transportation. Building on this success, Obama and Ray LaHood want $117 billion over the next two years to build twenty bullet trains.

Why do we tolerate this? Who says, enough? When do we stop it and drop it? Sell the assets and get out of the rail transportation business. Why do we want to expand a losing business?

The answer to this is the answer to all things that are wrong in Washington. Zero accountability. No one is responsible for making a profit from Amtrak. If they were, significant changes would have been instituted years ago.

Bus companies are running most of the same routes as Amtrak and making money. Their rates are much lower and they still make money. We don't need to provide rail transportation as a competitive alternative to the airlines and bus lines. It's not an obligation.

Who in government will step up to the plate and say, that's it, we don't run a national railroad anymore in this country?

Iraq Troop Withdrawal

October 24, 2011

We fought and appeared to win a war in Iraq. A dictator who killed thousands of his people was deposed. A country in an area that is critical to us was free to put in a new government that could be friendly to us. Lives were lost and billions spent to accomplish this.

But, we have a president who opposed this war from the beginning. He opposed the surge that allowed our military personnel to overthrow the insurgents and save more American lives. Therefore, he can't support our victory in word or deed. It's a burr under his saddle. To coddle his far-left friends and show he kept at least one campaign promise, he's bringing all the troops home by the end of this year.

I have listed (below) our troop population around the world. Does it make sense to you that we would have 40,000 troops in South Korea and zero in Iraq? Or, 75,000 troops in Germany and zero in Iraq? I challenge the need for troops everywhere but Iraq. If this president wants to keep our gains in Iraq, he should acknowledge that we no longer need troops in Germany and shift them to Iraq.

You can make a case for troop drawdown in Iraq, but you can't make a case for keeping troops all over the world—everywhere but Iraq. Unless you just don't care about all the fine work our troops did in Iraq, the Iraqi people, the threat of Iran, or any of the obvious reasons to keep troops there. You care only about your next election.

There are 6,000 military bases and/or military warehouses located in the United States (See Wikipedia, February 2007).

Total military personnel is in the order of 1.4 million, of which 1,168,195 are in the United States and US overseas territories.

Taking figures from the same source, there are 325,000 US military personnel in foreign countries:

800 in Africa
97,000 in Asia (excluding the Middle East and Central Asia)
40,258 in South Korea
40,045 in Japan
491 at the Diego Garcia Base in the Indian Ocean
100 in the Philippines
196 in Singapore
113 in Thailand
200 in Australia
16,601 afloat

In Europe, there are 116,000 US military personnel, including 75,603 who are stationed in Germany.

But, there will be none in Iraq.

Need a Little Humor?

October 26, 2011

Two pieces of news struck me as some well-needed humor this week.

Fist, in a press announcement, Joe Biden says he won't rule out a run for the presidency in 2016. If you had any doubts as to the cluelessness of Washington, this tidbit from the most clueless of all should clear that up for you. A man who is hitting on two of eight cylinders thinks this country might elect him president when he is seventy-six years old and hitting on no cylinders. Is there no end to the egocentric idiocy of politicians like Joe?

Google CEO Eric Schmidt is called into a Congressional hearing about fair competition. Get this: a company that gives their product away is grilled by Congress. Does Congress want Google to pay people to use their product?

It irritated Schmidt, a big Obama supporter, and he gave an interview where he blasted the administration. Basically, he said lobbyists for companies who don't hit the top of the Google search list want regulations to get them to the top. Schmidt, who must be naive, has just realized that companies use regulations to succeed.

He should read the history of Archer Daniels Midland. They have used the ethanol regulation to make billions in the past thirty years. And, they kept it going despite the groundswell to end it. Hiding behind the Corn Growers Association, ADM has increased the mandatory requirements for ethanol every few years with every administration. They have kept the tariff on imported ethanol and piped billions from the taxpayer to ethanol producers like them.

Here's the bad news, Mr. Schmidt. Free may not be good enough. You may have to stay free but move favored contributors to politicians up the list to the top of your search engines. That's how business is done in Washington.

What's your vote? Biden for president or free isn't good enough?

No Pain, No Gain

October 30, 2011

I injured my knee wrestling in college. For fifty years, I've lived with knee problems. Until the last few years, the knee didn't inhibit my activities. In 1980, I ran the Chicago marathon and climbed Mt. Rainier a few years later. I jogged until six years ago, when my doctor said it was time to stop. Then, I walked on the treadmill with elevation to keep my aerobic conditioning. But, finally it was cortisone shots three times a year to keep going. I still walked three miles a day, but some days it was slow and I paid for it with pain. This year it was time for a new knee. I had the surgery October 11th.

Going through rehab is no fun. Anyone who tells you otherwise is not telling the truth. But, living with some degree of pain for fifty years made the rehab seem a little easier. Plus, being in decent shape from working with personal trainers three days a week, every week.

The process made me think of our country. This country is like my knee: in bad shape, in pain, but taking the equivalent of cortisone shots. This country is borrowing money, running up the debt, and avoiding the real solution: major surgery and painful rehab.

Those who commit to the rehab and take the pain, recover and are almost as good as new. Those who don't, and avoid the pain, limp worse and never get back to near normal. They trade a month of avoiding agony for a lifetime of disability.

If everyone in this country won't decide to take some pain, we will have a lifetime of agony. We have pain now, just like I did for years, but we are not opting for the surgery.

This country needs major surgery and a period of painful rehab to get back on our feet.

Yesterday, I walked five miles on the new knee. The pain was less than with the old knee at three miles. I have a long way to go. More rehab, more ice, more pain, and pushing and pushing even harder. But, I know from that walk I'm already better than I have been for the last five years.

Until most Americans realize that getting out of the mess we're in can't be pain-free, we will limp and get worse. When we are ready to face it and find a leader or leaders who will do the surgery, we can begin the healing process. Let's hope it happens sooner rather than later.

The Difference Between Government and Business

November 2, 2011

Abusiness allocates capital based on some value-added formula. Various projects must compete for scarce capital based on the present value return of each investment over time. The projects that give the best return receive the capital. Those that don't get scrapped or delayed.

We have a so-called Super Committee supposedly working to reduce costs. If they fail, costs will be automatically cut beginning in 2013. Why 2013? Because there is a big election in 2012. It appears the Super Committee may fail. We had our credit rating cut for the first time in our country's history. We have no surplus cash flow until the budget is cut or revenue is increased. We must borrow to meet current needs.

A business, faced with this problem, goes about cutting expenses. When expenses are cut or revenue raised and cash flow is positive, capital budgets are resumed. Until then, only maintenance is done. Especially if the business can't really borrow more without further credit downgrades. Assets are sold, business lines cut, unprofitable businesses eliminated, personnel reduced, and all the stops are pulled out. Without capital infusions, the business will die.

We have our president standing before bridges all over the country telling us that businesses are losing billions because those bridges need to be built or rebuilt. What happened to the no-shovel-ready projects joke? Factually, shovel ready is not going to happen in this country. Every project the president is standing by needs an environmental impact study.

Those studies take months, if not years. In many cases, they don't happen because the cost to meet the environmental requirements make the project too expensive.

A local community near me needed a traffic light. There were too many accidents. It took six months, an environmental study that cost $30,000, and a "meet the union rate clause" to get the traffic light.

President Obama would not last six months as a CEO of any corporation of any size. Yet, we tolerate him as the CEO of the biggest corporation in the world.

Merry Christmas

December 24, 2011

Wishing you a Merry Christmas may be politically incorrect in some circles, but in my circle of friends and family it is very appropriate. I'm spending the next two days with family celebrating the birth of Jesus.

Sue and I say the vows in Three Rivers, Michigan, on August 21, 1965.

Knock off an item from the bucket list: drive a race car.

Another bucket list item: on the Swilcan Bridge in St. Andrews,
Scotland, on the Old Course with Bob and Terry (friends).

Plane crash site. I was in the section that traveled from black smudge impact on the runway to cornfield.

Family on beach at Siesta Key, Florida—a tradition that started Thanksgiving 1989 after the plane crash and has continued every year since to give thanks for our good fortune.

Sue and our daughters having lunch.

Renewing our vows on our fiftieth anniversary at Walloon Lake in Petoskey, Michigan, with the family for a week.

Reliving the glory days: Brian (son-in-law),
Lisa (daughter), and me.

Staying strong: lifting ninety-pound dumbbells
with trainer, Gary, in April 2017.

Grandkids last Christmas in the back yard.

2012

A Long Ten Months

January 2, 2012

As we enter 2012, there is little about 2011 we can look back and celebrate. Even though the voters gave the Republicans the House, Obama was successful in keeping his drive to make America Europe moving forward. Now he begins his war on success in earnest.

He is pitting the country against one another. Trying to get more and more voters dependent on the government to survive. If he wins four more years, there is little hope for having a country that celebrates success. Whether it's individual success or business success, it's what has made us a great nation.

The irony of making us Europe seems to escape the president and those who embrace class warfare. Trying to emulate a broken model defies common sense. But, common sense is rare in Washington these days.

So, it's with trepidation that we begin 2012. Unless we stop Obama in the November election, it's a dismal future we face. With no way to stop his march, he will be free to step up the pace. It's downright scary.

I started this blog at the end of the Bush era because I

feared for the futures of my grandkids. Now, I'm terrified. They work hard in school, they have big plans, and they may face a world that doesn't reward hard work and big plans.

All we can do is pray and work for a change and a better future for all.

January 3 Is a Big Day

January 3, 2012

Not because it's my birthday, but because January 3rd marks the end of the Iowa primaries. This is the best example of our need for election reform we will ever see. It is weeks of nothing but the Iowa caucuses on TV, polls showing Iowans shuffle the deck with the Republican candidates, and candidates going back and forth across the state. Millions of dollars are spent in campaign ads. Millions of network dollars are expended covering this campaign.

For what? It is estimated that 150,000 people will cast votes. How absurd is that? How dumb has this country become? It's not like Iowa predicts the primary outcome. If you watched every televised hour of this, you would probably have seen everyone who will cast a vote.

There has to be a better way to nominate a presidential candidate. The rest of the country has to take a position that we've had enough of this. It reminds me of the monarchy in the United Kingdom; something that has long ago outlived its usefulness. Get real, America. Enough is enough.

I love Iowa and Iowans. They are hard-working, honest people. It is Middle America at its best.

On my birthday, I won't be celebrating my birthday, but the end of the Iowa primaries.

Suddenly Obama's Natural Gas

January 25, 2012

I'm writing this before the eagerly anticipated State of the Union lie-fest on January 24. Amazing, the man who has no less than eight departments and agencies eyeing fracking, the process that has liberated untapped gas, with the intent to add regulations. No new natural gas is being produced on any public lands. No permits have been issued. The oil and gas industry doing the job on natural gas complain about the roadblocks the Obama administration has put up to delay drilling.

The oil industry has made the natural gas boom without one ounce of assistance or encouragement from the government. The natural gas price is so low, two things are about to happen. First, export terminals are about to export surplus gas in the form of liquefied natural gas. Second, the industry is cutting capital budgets to drill more in the United States.

Obama has never once pushed for CNG (compressed natural gas) as a replacement for gasoline. T. Boone Pickens spent millions doing that. Obama wants electric cars. But does that make sense if we are going to export natural gas?

Natural gas is saving Obama's bacon with his closing of

coal-fired power plants. Without it, we would face power price increases and possible brownouts. Coal mines are closing. Obama is putting another industry in the unemployment line.

Now that homeowners see their heating bills go down, Obama detects another opportunity to take credit for something he had nothing to do with. You will see Obama's unabashed arrogance. He will stake his claim to the development of new natural gas in this country. This man has absolutely no shame.

If you are dumb enough to let him get away with it, you'll get him for another four years. Obama never learned the lesson my dad taught me, "If you blow your own horn too much, someone will use it for a funnel." In the case of Obama, the horn is so big it will take a fire hose.

Why College Tuition Grows So Fast

January 29, 2012

Here are the tuition facts for Arizona State University: Fifty percent of students pay zero. Another 11% pay less than half. The remaining 39% pay full price. Does this remind you of income tax percentages in the United States?

President Obama is basing his 2012 campaign on fair share/fair shake. Who gets a fair shake at ASU? It's certainly not the 39% paying almost 100% of the revenue for the university. As more free rides are passed out, tuition increases dramatically, to cover the freebies.

Obama feels the rich need to pay more taxes. But, just like ASU, 50% pay zero taxes. And, also like ASU, 30% pay almost 100%. It seems like income redistribution always falls into the same pattern, whether it's a country or a university.

Then the inevitable happens. ASU must cut tuition or enrollment drops off. Cutting expenses is out of the question. You can't stop giving away the store to those with a free ride. There aren't enough students who can or would pay full price.

Obama wants to raise government spending, and help those with a free ride even more. To do that, he has to increase taxes. But those paying seventy percent of taxes now don't see that as fair. He knows there aren't enough to tax if he took 100% to cover his spending. But, it makes a good story. Now Obama is addressing the tuition increase problem. We can all guess the outcome of his price controls on tuition. Obama is not satisfied with fifty percent getting a free ride; he wants more who can't pay to go to college. At the same time, he wants to forgive student loans and lower tuition. Let's see, I'm going to increase the number of free students, give away loan debt, and reduce revenue for colleges and universities. Want more proof Obama lives in Fantasyland?

ASU is in a bad place. Obama will put America in that same bad place. When half the people are getting free rides, it's hard to make ends meet.

Obama Kisses the Catholic Vote Goodbye

February 5, 2012

What prompted President Obama to pick a fight with Catholics? What can he possibly gain from what he did?

He signed off on a Health and Human Services ruling that says under Obamacare, Catholic institutions, including charities, hospitals, and schools, will be required by law to provide and pay for insurance coverage that includes contraceptives, abortion-inducing drugs, and sterilization procedures. If they do not, they will face fines in the millions of dollars. Or, they can just close. Some are already suggesting they will.

Now we can add the Catholic vote to the Jewish vote Obama has given up. His positions on Israel have cost him dearly with Jews in America. Remember the Anthony Wiener replacement vote where a Republican replaced Wiener in a democratic Jewish district for the first time since Franklin Roosevelt was president? Add to that a little-known statistic: for the first time in twenty-two years, more women voters chose Republican candidates (49%) over Democrat candidates (48%) in the 2010 midterm elections. In 2008, women favored Obama by a 56%–43% margin.

Then you have Wall Street. Obama conned the Wall Street crowd into believing he was on their team in the 2008 campaign. Now they know him for what he really is: a man who will say anything and do what he chooses. Cross off their contributions for this campaign.

It's starting to pile up on this president. You can't wipe your feet on people and expect them to support you, even if the mirror tells you every day the seas will part for you. Next time you are in Hawaii, stroll down to the beach and give it a shot.

Cliff Notes on Obama's Budget

February 18, 2012

When you are royalty, you should not be asked to produce a budget. Obama really hasn't since he has been in office. The Senate has never passed an Obama administration budget.

But this is an election year. So, why not publish a nice wish list for the ignorant voters who might like this fiction and vote for me? It's hundreds of pages long so no one will read it. It's ridiculous, so no Congress will pass it. It is just hundreds of pages of campaign strategy. As your king, I owe you nothing. That's what I gave you: nothing.

Here are the key data from that bogus budget:

Federal debt is now $16 trillion. It would increase to $26 trillion over ten years.

The cost of servicing the national debt is now $225 billion. It would go up to $850 billion in 2022.

The federal debt is 100% of annual GDP.

Federal spending is $3.8 trillion. It would go to $5.8 trillion in 2022.

Obama hired a debt commission. He ignored what they

brought him. Here are some differences between what they recommended and Obama's proposed budget:

- Debt commission brought spending to 21.6% of GDP by 2015. Under Obama, it remains at 22.8% in 2022.
- Debt commission comparison between 2013 and 2020 would trim $2 trillion in annual deficits vs. Obama plan.

No right-minded politician would approve the Obama budget. It's a straw man to blame Republicans again. But, Republicans didn't name a debt commission to get spending under control—Obama did. Republicans didn't ignore all the recommendations to fix our coming financial crisis—Obama did.

Steve Jobs, Corporate America, and the Federal Government

March 11, 2012

I've just wrapped up reading the biography, *Steve Jobs*. It's a pretty remarkable read. The author exposes Steve for the genius and character he was.

Apple's success is tied to Jobs himself. Until the cancer took him out, he was very much in control of everything that happened at both Apple and Pixar, until he sold Pixar to Disney. Steve was a control freak who needed to be involved in every detail of every project. He had zero political correctness and less diversity. He didn't delegate and had horrible people skills. He broke every rule ever taught by any business school. Any corporation of any size in this country would have fired him. Apple fired him.

When Apple brought him back, it was out of desperation. The buttoned-down replacements had almost destroyed the company. He wouldn't commit to the title CEO and worked for a dollar a year for two years.

As you look at how Steve ran Apple, making it the most successful company in the world, you see his style on one extreme. It was autocratic, but creative. One man controlling the furniture picked for the offices, yet departments working together seamlessly. A leader with what was called a "reality distortion field" who got employees to accept the unreality and do the impossible. A leader who had a hundred ideas an hour but would only let the company work on three big projects at a time. A leader who was cruel to waitresses, family, employees, and friends, but still kept key employees who remained loyal and learned to overlook the abuse. A leader who never dressed for business, but was a ruthless negotiator who held grudges forever.

Somewhere in the middle, you have Corporate America. A place where diversity rules, political correctness is king, treating employees with dignity is a must, delegation expected, control is passed down, and decisions are made by teams.

On the other extreme, you have government. No accountability. No real leadership, just a warning: "Don't embarrass me." Departments don't work together, so we have Homeland Security. Billions are spent because the other alphabet soups like CIA, NSA, FBI, etc., can't work together. Committees, rules, and bureaucracy decide everything. No creativity, no initiative, no risk taking, no real passion for any job. I'm excluding the troops from all of this.

Is it possible Steve Jobs gave everyone a new business model for success?

Find a genius who cares and give them free rein to run the show. Ignore the problems unless the results don't come. Find a genius who has passion for the business and wants to control everything and has the energy to do it all. Break the molds, folks. HR will only need mops to clean up the blood from all the damaged feelings, employee turnover, and lawsuits. But, Steve said, "A players like to work with A players." He saw it as his job to get rid of B players. How he did it was not relevant.

Is this a one-time, one-person deal, or are there other Steve Jobses out there who could do what Steve did at Apple. Never in my lifetime have I seen any business or government run with the Jobs style, except Apple and maybe the Maricopa County Sheriff's Department. Will business schools look at this and see a need to change the approach to management they teach? Will other companies do the same? I won't even ask the question about governments.

Was Steve Jobs the only person in history who could make this work?

How Amoco, a Once Great Brand, Died

March 14, 2012

Reading Steve Jobs's biography reminded me of the Amoco brand. Steve was passionate to his dying breath about the Apple brand and what it meant. He believed, and he proved, if you make great products, people will buy them and profits will happen. When he was fired from Apple and the suits took over, they put profit ahead of product. The products suffered and the profits disappeared. When he came back, it was the first thing he fixed.

Amoco, like Apple, once had a great brand name supported by great products. The company outsold all competitors in premium products, a true measure of consumer product perspective for what many considered to be a commodity product. Dealers and jobbers benefited from this. Amoco spent extra money to keep unique products through the years. Everything supported the brand.

I was on a team that worked on a potential merger between Amoco and another major US oil company (not BP). When we evaluated the advantage of the Amoco brand to this competitor's brand and quantified it, it was well over $200 million the competitor would have to throw in the pot to get access to that brand advantage.

But that merger failed and another one came along. I'm glad I left before that happened. I had spent many years protecting the brand in various jobs. I felt a little like Steve Jobs: passionate toward what Amoco had created with the brand and proud of my many jobs that worked to build that brand.

Amoco merged with BP and the rest is history. BP had one of the worst brands in the United States. But, the suits in London decided the BP brand should replace the Amoco brand in the United States. It went from the best brand in the country to the worst. In Steve Jobs's language, the BP brand was sh**.

BP lost millions when they made this decision. The customers did not see the little sign that said Amoco gasoline when the BP logo replaced the Amoco logo. Sales of premium products plummeted. Jobbers changed brands. BP profits went down.

When BP encountered several publicity issues here, a refinery fire, a pipeline leak, and the drilling platform explosion in the Gulf, it just grew worse. They have sold most of their marketing assets in the United States.

It just shows what the wrong suits can do to a valuable brand.

Obama's Budget Vote in the House: 414–0

April 1, 2012

The last time I saw a vote like this it was in the Illinois state house. Blagojevich got a goose egg on a bill he touted as one the Illinois legislators were supporting in large numbers. The large number was zero. This is just before the cuffs went on Blagojevich, and the politicians were already smelling the stench.

This is from the Republican National Committee:

"Do you know what striking out looks like? Look no further than Obama's irresponsible, out-of-control 2013 budget being voted down 414–0 in the House on Wednesday. And it's not the first time that has happened. Last May, the President's 2012 budget received zero votes of support in the Senate. Even staunch liberals like Nancy Pelosi were unable to hold their nose and support the President's harmful policies. What does this tell us?

"It tells us that even members from Obama's own party understand the harm that could come from pushing through his reckless $3.6 trillion budget for next year. It tells us that Obama offers no legitimate direction or guidance to lead us out of this fiscal crisis. It tells us that a real change is needed in November. We cannot afford four more years of Barack Obama's irresponsible behavior. Republicans know it. Democrats know it. And now—you know it."

I can't leave it at that. Perhaps the Democrats are sensing the budget hijinks are over. The public takes the budget and deficit very seriously, and Democrats have not. Obama thinks it's his own piggy bank and he doesn't have to worry about spending. When questioned, just bring up "tax the rich" again. This shows some serious distancing from what is looking like a very lame duck president. Just as the Illinois contingent smelled Blagojevich way before the public did, the Washington crowd may be getting the same whiff from Obama.

Joe Biden Never Wanted a Real Job

April 5, 2012

The gaffe master, Joe Biden, had a good week. First, he called for "global minimum tax." Wouldn't that be great? We could kick in the most, just like the United Nations fiasco, and get the least in return.

But, his classic comment was: "I never had an interest in being a mayor cause that's a real job. You must produce. That's why I was able to be a senator for thirty-six years." Gee, Joe, does the VP not have to produce? And, didn't you run for president twice, in 1988 and 2008? Does the president not have to produce?

This explains a lot. Besides confirming what we already know, Joe is a babbling fool. It explains why few, if any, commitments this administration made have come to pass. Both Joe and his boss don't see producing anything as part of their jobs.

Thanks for clearing this all up for us, Joe. Now we understand.

My Hero Died This Week

May 9, 2012

Most of us go through life with people who are very special to us: parents, spouses, children, grandchildren, and friends. We don't normally label them heroes. I had my personal hero, but God took him this week.

Denny Fitch truly saved my life and the lives of many more in 1989. Denny was a passenger on UA Flight 232. He was a United employee catching a ride home for the weekend. When a turbine rotor sheared and cut all hydraulics, he chose to come forward to the cockpit to help the crew. On his knees in the cockpit, he kept a DC-10 with no controls aloft until it got to the Sioux City airport, and he nearly landed the plane.

I was a passenger on that plane, one of the lucky ones. I flew home that night. Denny Fitch didn't. He was in the hospital for weeks and had many surgeries following his release from the hospital.

Denny later made a career of making speeches for charity. I took my family to hear him speak for a local hospice. One by one, my wife, my two daughters, and my six grandkids went up to Denny and hugged and kissed him and thanked him for his courage. By the time I got to Denny he was in tears. My older daughter had given him a poem she wrote and it was more than he could handle. Denny and I had a long talk that night and decided we needed to spend more time together. We were both going to Arizona that winter and made plans to get together. As the saying goes, "Man plans and God smiles." Denny got sick that winter and our meeting never happened.

He wasn't just my personal hero. He was the personal hero of every survivor and all their families—all their friends, as well.

To you, Denny, I say, blue skies and tailwinds forever in heaven.

This is from *The Daily Herald* in Chicago:

As a trained pilot, Denny Fitch knew instinctively everyone aboard United Flight 232 could die in a matter of minutes.

"I was 46, I had the world ahead of me, I had a beautiful healthy family, and at 4 p.m., I was trying to stay alive," he said in a documentary interview.

As the DC-10 thrashed, he took a second to think of his wife and three kids and what their last words had been that day back in 1989. "My wife said, 'I love you, hurry home.' And with that knowledge and that peace, I was ready to die that day if I had to."

Fitch and 184 others survived, due in large part to his troubleshooting from the cockpit floor, pulling every aeronautical trick out of the book to control the plunging jet.

But the man hailed as a hero couldn't stop the aggressive brain cancer he was diagnosed with in 2010.

The sixty-nine-year-old St. Charles resident died Monday with his family around him.

"Denny had a strong faith, and that helped him in the end," his wife, Rosa, said Tuesday.

My family and I met Denny Fitch (third from left) twenty-tree years after the plane crash

Obama Says Spending is Up 1% Since He Took Office

May 25, 2012

Today, in one of his daily campaign speeches, President Obama declared he has increased government spending only 1% a year on average since he took office. Wow, it seemed like a lot more. He says it's the lowest spending rate for a president in almost sixty years.

Like most data, it all depends on the baseline. His baseline includes all the bailout money, TARP, and, of course, the much-maligned stimulus money. He puts this all on Bush, then measures from there. The GM bailout goes into the Bush era.

This is data published today by *The Wall Street Journal.*

Presidential spending per day:

Reagan $2.5 billion, Clinton $4.1 billion, G. W. Bush $6.8 billion, Obama $9.7 billion.

By every other measure, percentage of spending vs. GDP, growth in deficit, debt growth, etc., Obama has set new spending records.

Will the public let Obama support this claim, or will this backfire? It remains to be seen.

Obama Sets God Straight

June 17, 2012

This goes back to Obama's days in the Illinois State Senate. He stopped a law from being passed that would have prevented doctors from stabbing half-born infants in the neck with scissors.

Of course, like Reverend Wright, Bill Ayers, and all the rest, Obama disclaimed any responsibility for preventing a law that would have stopped this practice.

I'm very sensitive about Obama's position on this. My twin granddaughters were premature. They were born three months early and weighed two pounds each. Today, thanks to the medical staff at Northwestern neo-natal care unit, they are healthy, happy, smart, athletic, eleven-year-old girls.

We have a president who would have terminated them.

His work to prevent this law from being passed reflects his life in politics. He stonewalled it until he was gone. Since he rarely went to work while a state senator, he simply was never there to push the bill to a vote. He left no tracks.

If you are looking for new reasons not to reelect Obama, just put this on the pile.

Pinocchio as President

June 30, 2012

It's going to be fun watching the rest of the 2012 presidential campaign. I will give Obama credit: he didn't spike the ball on the Supreme Court decision with Obamacare. He said, let's just put this behind us. He will be haunted by the following lies for the next few months.

It's not a tax. While Obama refused to call it a tax, John Roberts rewrote the words of the document and made it a tax. I don't know how that works. I didn't realize the Supreme Court could turn into Congress and rewrite a document turning a mandate into a tax, but he did. It's a tax that Congress never would have passed in the first place. Raising taxes when this bill was on the floor would have been a disaster, but a mandate that becomes a tax from a conservative justice won't work, either.

So, it's a tax. Obama is giving the country the biggest tax increase in history. Can't deny it; Roberts says it's a tax. How many times will we see that interview with Obama and George Stephanopoulos where Obama insists it's not a tax? Will we see his nose grow?

Next up, you can keep your doctor. That may be a bigger lie than the tax lie. Doctors are already dumping Medicare patients. The bill cuts $500 billion more out of Medicare. What quacks will be left to treat Medicare patients? Those that bilk billions from the system the government can't run now. Businesses big and small will be dumping medical as a benefit. When these people are left with the government medical plan, will their previous doctor see them? No, their doctors will be seeing the elite who still have fair-paying health insurance: politicians, union employees, public union employees, law firm employees, and those who still have good insurance. Plus, with 30 million more potential new now insured, you might die before you see any doctor. The IRS will decide that under the Obamacare plan. Government employees, like those at the Bureau of Motor Vehicles, will decide which doctor you see. Your old doctor may not be on that list.

And, the biggest lie of all: Obama told his core base he would never raise their taxes. Basically, it's the 50% who pay no taxes. But, he just did. If this 50% doesn't buy insurance, Barack will tax them. They will pay a tax and still have no insurance.

It's tough running for anything as a liar. It's easy proving Obama lied. Hence, he is running uphill this year. Thanks, John Roberts.

Most of us know we need to find a way to provide health care to those who can't afford it or can't get it because of preexisting conditions. They receive treatment now, but it's not easy and some go broke trying to pay the tab. The present system doesn't work.

But, sticking with a 2,400-page bill cobbled together by consultants and unread by those who supported the bill is not the answer. We need a fresh start. Let's all work hard to make that happen.

Reagan's Economic Recovery Plan Recalled

July 2, 2012

F *orbes* recently ran an article showing the Reagan recovery plan. The highlights of this article are shown below.

President Reagan campaigned on an explicitly articulated, four-point economic program to reverse this slow-motion collapse of the American economy:

1. Cut tax rates to restore incentives for economic growth, which was implemented first with a reduction in the top income tax rate of 70% down to 50%, and then a 25% across-the-board reduction in income tax rates for everyone. The 1986 tax reform then reduced tax rates further, leaving just two rates, 28% and 15%.

2. Spending reductions, including a $31 billion cut in spending in 1981, close to 5% of the federal budget then, or the equivalent of about $175 billion in spending cuts for the year today. In constant dollars, nondefense discretionary spending declined by 14.4% from 1981 to 1982, and by 16.8% from 1981 to 1983. Moreover, in constant dollars, this nondefense discretionary spending never returned to its 1981 level for the rest of Reagan's two terms! Even with the Reagan defense buildup, which won the Cold War without firing a shot, total federal spending declined from a high of 23.5% of GDP in 1983 to 21.3% in 1988 and 21.2% in 1989. That's a real reduction in the size of government relative to the economy of 10%.

3. Anti-inflation monetary policy restraining money supply growth compared to demand, to maintain a stronger, more stable dollar value.

4. Deregulation, which saved consumers an estimated $100 billion per year in lower prices. Reagan's first executive order, in fact, eliminated price controls on oil and natural gas. Production soared and aided by a strong dollar, the price of oil declined by more than 50%.

These economic policies amounted to the most successful economic experiment in world history. The Reagan recovery started in official records in November 1982 and lasted ninety-two months without a recession until July 1990, when the tax increases of the 1990 budget deal killed it. This set a new record for the longest peacetime expansion ever; the previous high in peacetime was fifty-eight months.

During this seven-year recovery, the economy grew by almost one-third—the equivalent of adding the entire economy of West Germany, the third-largest in the world at the time, to the US economy. In 1984 alone, real economic growth boomed by 6.8%, the highest in fifty years. Nearly 20 million new jobs were created during the recovery, increasing US civilian employment by almost 20%. Unemployment fell to 5.3% by 1989.

Now, by comparison, let's look at Obamanomics:

1. Raise taxes
2. Print more money
3. More government spending
4. More regulation

It follows what Carter was doing to get us where we were when Reagan stepped in and started fixing things.

If you want to try the Carter/Obama/Western Europe/California/Illinois/Stockton plan for four more years, vote for Obama. If you prefer what worked with Reagan, vote for Romney.

Reagan's Messages About Liberty

July 3, 2012

I am not a collector. But I had two items I kept and cherished through the years.

The first has been lost. It was a golf scorecard from a round I played with Neil Armstrong. I was paired with him at a golf outing in Florida. He signed the scorecard. I showed it to my mother, whom I visited in Florida after the round. Her comment was priceless. She said, "It's like having something signed by Christopher Columbus." I asked her if she wanted it. She said yes, and it was always displayed in her home. When she passed away and her effects were packed up, it was tossed.

The second, which I still have, is a picture of my wife and me with Ronald Reagan, the greatest president in my lifetime. He was a speaker at a business conference we attended. We had the opportunity to not only hear him in person, but to meet him and have a picture taken.

As this Independence Day is here, I think a lot about President Reagan. He talked a lot about liberty and independence, reminding us of the greatness of America and what makes it great.

One of his quotes is, "We are a nation that has a government and not the other way around." It's only been twenty-six years since he said this, but today one wonders if it's more or less true.

Here is an excerpt from his 1981 inaugural address:

"It is not my intention to do away with government. It is rather to make it work—work with us, not over us; stand by our side, not ride on our back. Government can and must provide opportunity, not smother it; foster productivity, not stifle it."

It bothers me a great deal that we have strayed from the path Reagan took us back down. Every day I see government playing a bigger and bigger role in the lives of Americans. Telling us how much we need more government; telling us what size drinks we can drink; and pushing us, our children, and our grandchildren into the path of government dependence.

Who is here today to once again remind us of the lessons of Reagan? Who speaks to us with such conviction? It wasn't just Reagan's words that stirred this nation, but the feeling he was just telling us the truth. Telling us what he really believed, not what some poll told him would get votes.

He was a true leader and it was easy to follow his lead.

We, as a nation, seem to be at a fork in the road. We can go back to feeling good about our country and what made it great, or give up, stick our hand out, and wait for our government to put something in that hand.

The upcoming election will decide what path we take. I pray to God it will be the path of liberty and back to a country that has a government, not a government that has a country.

Then There Was One

July 9, 2012

CHAMPS

was cleaning out my desk over the weekend and came across this old picture. It is from 1959 and depicts three high school athletes. It tells three stories.

The young man on the left, Don Dodge, was working to make the 1964 US Olympic Kayaking Team. He was training in Lake Erie. Don's kayak washed up without him. Gone at age twenty-one.

The man in the middle, arguably the best athlete in our class, attended college on a football scholarship. A pregnant girlfriend ended his football and college careers. He went into the used car business with his father-in-law, divorced, remarried, and became a very successful GM dealer. He died on a golf course on Hilton Head Island about ten years ago.

The third person, yours truly, attended college on a partial scholarship for wrestling. I tore up a knee and hung it up. That injured knee was replaced last fall.

Here were three small-town athletes with big dreams. Two died, both too young, on an athletic field of some type: Don in the water and Terry on a golf course. These were two good friends, a lifetime ago. Don never had a chance, but I'm sure he would have been very successful in life.

There are some days when I sit down and reflect on the direction this country is headed, and I'm almost nauseated. It's hard to think about the differences between the time this picture was taken and today. It's harder to wonder what the future holds for my grandkids, who are fast approaching the age we were when the picture was taken. Some days I can't stand to write about the future and feel more comfortable looking back at the past.

I guess this is one of those days.

Why I Blog

July 14, 2012

I've been blogging for four years. I started blogging because I believed my grandkids would be the first generation in this country to have a lower standard of living than their parents. The absolute lack of common sense in Washington was going to make that happen.

When I started my first blog, *Grandparents of America Awaken*, most people laughed when I posed that possibility. Now you hear it every day. I thought blogging might be a way to get more people concerned about the direction our country was taking.

I would listen to friends and family carp about things, but it was unorganized and general. I wanted to sell my position with facts. Blogging forced me to read and get facts and organize my thoughts. I speak to hundreds of people every day, with new readers coming every day. It's more effective than talking with like-minded people around a lunch table.

I have seen our country get worse since I started blogging.

I don't believe the country can tolerate four more years of Barack Obama. Hence, I will continue to blog until the day comes that Obama and all he stands for is gone.

If, I pray, that happens in November, I will hang it up.

Obama: Government Made You Successful

July 17, 2012

I was given a revelation by my president this past week.

President Obama: "And, you know, there are a lot of wealthy, successful Americans who agree with me. Because they want to give something back. They know they didn't— look, if you've been successful, you didn't get there on your own. You didn't get there on your own. I'm always struck by people who think, well, it must be just because I was so smart. There are a lot of smart people out there. It must be because I worked harder than everybody else. Let me tell you something. There are a whole bunch of hardworking people out there.

"If you were successful, somebody along the line gave you some help. Somebody helped to create this unbelievable American system that we have that allowed you to thrive. Somebody invested in roads and bridges. If you've got a business—you didn't build that. Somebody else made that happen. The internet didn't get invented on its own. Government research created the internet so that all the companies could make money off the internet."

Since you said that, I've given a lot of thought to your comments. I admit I'm one of those people who meet your definition of rich. Here's how I became one of those hated rich people who need to give back to Obama:

My parents were Depression-era parents. They migrated from farms in Missouri to Michigan, looking for work. My uncle supposedly had a job and a place for them to stay. When they got there, they found neither. My uncle and aunt turned them out. My dad found a factory job and my mom found work, also. They spent five years getting enough saved for a small house. I was born less than a month after Pearl Harbor. My dad was drafted into the navy and served in the Pacific. After returning from the war, my dad went back to the factory. He and another war veteran started a small construction business.

When I was fourteen, I bused tables at a Greyhound bus station in the summer. I worked there two summers busing tables and cleaning crappers. In between, I baled hay. When I was sixteen, I started working construction in the summers. I did that through my junior year in college. During my college years, I worked. I had a wrestling scholarship that gave me a field house job. So I washed dishes at a sorority house and worked party service as a waiter. With that, and the little help my folks could give me, I made it through college. No student loans. Only the vets were getting help from the government. I did my mandatory two years in ROTC.

Upon graduation, I went off to sunny California to find work. I got a job as a management trainee at Bank of America. Then, my draft notice arrived. I came back to Michigan to take my physical for the army. I met with a navy recruiter to see what I needed to do to get into OCS and flight school. Because of the knee I tore up wrestling, the army flunked me and declared me unfit for military service.

Starting in the training station pumping gas, selling tires, and changing oil, I worked for what was then Standard Oil of Indiana, later to become Amoco, and now BP. After becoming the manager of the training station, I was given a retail territory. At age twenty-two, I was responsible for thirty dealer-operated service stations in rural Indiana. I married my college sweetheart and moved her to Indiana. In the next fourteen years, we moved ten times as each promotion resulted in a relocation.

I spent the next thirty-four years with Amoco. I continued to move through a series of positions, moving up to the position of VP of Brand Marketing. I always maxed out my contributions to the 401(k). After the plane crash I walked away from in 1989, work took on a different role. Family replaced it and at age fifty-six, I packed it in. I had more than enough to enjoy the rest of my life and give generously to family and charity. I made good investment decisions and lived below my means.

Not once in any job from age fourteen did I receive any help from my government. They took part of my pay even when I had none to give. Because I saved, made solid investment decisions, and lived a frugal life, I have money. When my wife and I die, the government, if Obama has his way, will take 50% of what is left.

I believe I was successful despite government, not because of government.

If you want to kill the ambition it took for my parents and me to succeed in this country, just buy into the Obama plan. We will become a country of Occupy Wall Street. I believe anyone can make it in this country. And do better with less help from the government.

I'm waiting, Barack. You tell me what role government had in my success.

Two Roads Face Voters

August 14, 2012

As I look at the upcoming election, I remember the poem by Robert Frost:

The Road Not Taken

Two roads diverged in a yellow wood,
And sorry I could not travel both
And be one traveler, long I stood
And looked down one as far as I could
To where it bent in the undergrowth;

Then took the other, as just as fair,
And having perhaps the better claim
Because it was grassy and wanted wear,
Though as for that the passing there
Had worn them really about the same,

And both that morning equally lay
In leaves no step had trodden black.
Oh, I marked the first for another day!
Yet knowing how way leads on to way
I doubted if I should ever come back.

I shall be telling this with a sigh
Somewhere ages and ages hence:
Two roads diverged in a wood, and I—
I took the one less traveled by,
And that has made all the difference.
—Robert Frost

Here are the two roads voters face in November:

This road leads to Greece. It's more spending, less energy development, higher taxes, less growth, more entitlements, higher unemployment, debt as far as the eye can see, and more of the same. Keep in mind all the potholes were put there by someone else, according to the man who built this road. Just give him four more years and he will repair the road and make sure it goes somewhere other than Greece.

This road begins with a u-turn from Barack Lane. It's lower taxes, less regulation, huge expense cuts, less government, different entitlements, GDP growth, reversal of the debt trend, and a concern for future generations. This road goes past the next turn and recognizes we are back on the road built by Reagan that turned away from the road Carter had us traveling.

You pick your road in November. Just remember, we have kids and grandkids in the vehicle. At some point in time we get out and turn it over to them. They might not like Barack Lane, which ends in a cul-de-sac for them.

Why Does Arizona Want the Border Protected?

August 21, 2012

Five burned, unidentified bodies were found forty miles north of the Mexican border.

The state of Arizona and the president of the United

States have been at war since Obama was elected. Arizona sees first-hand what illegal immigration means. Violence spills across borders. Obama is indifferent to violence in Arizona. He wants Hispanic votes. That says a lot about Obama.

Not content to try and stop the state from enforcing the laws of the United States regarding immigration, Obama's people are also bringing charges against the man who was sending bad people back through ICE, Sheriff Joe.

Let's see, law-abiding citizens in Arizona are concerned about violence spilling across a border from a country with the most violent cities in the world. Who does the president of the United States protect? He protects the country with the most violent cities in the world.

Perhaps Obama should run for office in Mexico and take Holder with him—and Janet Napolitano for good measure.

I Paid $90 to Fill My Gas Tank Today

August 31, 2012

Obama is really looking after the middle class. Today, it cost me $90 to fill my tank.

Someone put a sticky note on the pump:

"Thanks Barack for killing the Keystone Pipeline. Thanks Barack for keeping the ethanol mandate in place. Thanks Barack for killing offshore drilling. Thanks Barack for slowing the drilling in Alaska. If you think I'm not noticing what you are doing to me you are wrong."

This seems like a good plan. I put a pad of sticky notes in

my car and while I'm waiting for my tank to fill I will paste a little note of my own thanking Obama for all he's done to stick it to me and my fellow Americans at the pump.

How Reagan Fixed Carter's Mess

September 3, 2012

Jimmy Carter created Obama's plan to destroy the US economy in four years. He grew government, increased government spending, added regulations, increased taxes, and initiated a timid foreign policy. Those of us who remember watched the rise of pessimism about the future of America.

Here's the comparison. Only twice since WWII has unemployment gone over 10%: in 1982, under Carter, and in 2009, under Obama. In just over four years, the Reagan recovery added 7.8 million jobs. In just under four years, Obama has lost 4 million jobs. Under Reagan, household income grew by $3,380; under Obama, it dropped by $4,000. Under Reagan, people on food stamps fell by 3 million. Under Obama, that number has grown by 20 million. Under Reagan, Medicaid grew by 535,000. Under Obama, it has grown by 11 million.

How did Reagan turn it around? He just undid what Carter had done. He lowered taxes, reduced regulations, cut government spending (except military, where he added a trillion dollars), and sent a foreign policy message that America was once again serious.

Based on this comparison, can you even envision what four more years of Obama's policies would do to this country?

Romney will follow the Reagan road that fixed the Carter economy. Obama will continue the Carter/Obama path that destroys the economy. We gave Carter only four years to break everything. If we give Obama eight years, it may be broken beyond repair.

Reasons to Reelect Obama

September 5, 2012

If you are on food stamps or would like to be on food stamps, he's your man.

If you ran out your unemployment and got on disability, and have no interest in going back to work, he's your man.

If you came into the country illegally, he's your man.

If you believe he can stop the tides from rising and save the planet, and are willing to pay $5/gallon for gasoline and have your utility bills double, he's your man.

If you are a bear and shorting the stock market, he's your man.

If you are indifferent about Iran nuking Israel, he's your man.

If you want gay marriage, he's your man.

If you believe Catholic institutions should provide birth control free, he's your man.

If you want to see our defense dismantled, he's your man.

If your life is better now than it was four years ago, he's your man.

If you need Medicaid, he's your man.

If you have no kids or grandkids to worry about down the road and want to break the bank getting everything you can get for yourself, he's your man.

If you are more impressed by words than deeds, he's your man.

If having an imbecile for a vice president humors you, he's your man.

If the truth doesn't matter to you, he's your man.

If you belong to any union that will keep taking your dues and gets you great benefits the country can't afford, he's your man.

If you are an incompetent teacher with tenure, he's your man.

If you are a college graduate who can't get a job and has student loans you can't pay back but value cool over competence, he's your man.

Only Two Election Issues Mean Anything

October 2, 2012

First and foremost is the economy: the jobs issue, the debt, and the deficit. We are fast becoming Greece, California, and Illinois. They all have one thing in common: spending more than revenue. Obama has only one solution. Tax the rich. This would only be a trickle in a stream. Promise after promise has been made by this president to improve this over the past four years. His result has been to keep spending more. If spending is not curtailed, our credit rating will keep dropping.

Every American now owes $63,000 toward our debt. We are like a household that takes in $50,000 a year and spends $75,000. Soon, the house will be lost and the family will be homeless. Taxing the rich will bring in $5,000 to that household. This will not change the outcome for the family. Most of the rest of Obama's plan is to keep giving more food stamps, cell phones, and other entitlements.

The second issue is the tinderbox that is the Middle East. If they draw us into another war, we will simply go broke faster.

That's it. Pick the person who can fix these two problems. Reagan did it in 1981. Other red state governors are doing it. Progressive governors in Illinois, California, and New York are digging those states in deeper and hoping for federal help.

Talk is cheap. Emotion should be set aside. This is a critical election.

One More Election

November 7, 2012

Congratulations to President Obama for winning a second term. It was a brilliant campaign, as evidenced by the result. Governor Romney did his best. The people have spoken.

America is changing to a different country than I have known for my seventy years. JFK said, "Ask not what your country can do for you—ask what you can do for your country." That is gone forever. It's now: Ask not what you can do for your country, but what your country can do for you. Sad, but true.

My best wishes go out to the Latino citizens who played a major role in this election. I hope your record unemployment eases; the same for the blacks who supported their president with little deviation. The same for females who choose free contraceptives over a sad economy. Good luck to Chris Christie in your future as a New Jersey dogcatcher. Recent college graduates, current students, and those about to start college, good luck finding jobs and paying off those student loans. Those unemployed, good luck to you. Those about to qualify for Medicare, good luck finding doctors.

The next four years and the foreseeable future will see us mortgage my grandkids' futures as we grab what's available for our own selfish immediate consumption. I can't honestly grieve for my kid's generation, since that generation took a pass on this crisis. You will live to see the consequences of this and watch your own kids pay the price.

My wife and I will be fine. This election will not impact our lives, as we have lived conservative lives and even Obama can't take enough to damage our short futures. Our kids will get less when we die, since Obama will take a big chunk. And it's the same for the grandkids.

I'm Unenlightened

November 10, 2012

I recognize how unenlightened I am after the recent election. I don't give a whit if people of the same sex marry. I worry a lot about the $16 trillion debt. I don't care if pot is legal or not. I care about the financial cliff.

I don't worry about climate change. I do notice wind and solar is not the problem in the aftermath of Superstorm Sandy; it's a shortage of gasoline. To me, a Keystone Pipeline that brings oil for gasoline gets priority over another solar farm in the desert that uses Chinese panels, millions of gallons of water, and produces power at three times the cost of conventional power plants.

I do notice that people who reside where enlightenment is deemed to exist at highest levels are seeing the greatest economic stress in their systems: California, with the Hollywood influence, and New York, with the media presence. Enlightenment must be expensive.

I notice some of the most enlightened citizens seem to have a lot of money. They often travel in private jets, live in multiple mansions, and may be limited in education. Bruce Springsteen and Beyoncé come to mind.

Enlightened people talk a lot about helping others. But it's always my money they want to use to supply this help. I try to help others, but I write checks or donate time to do that. I believe it's between me and those I'm helping, not a public issue or a political one.

I take comfort in being unenlightened. When in the company of one who is very enlightened, I find myself seeking a door. They seem smug and somewhat angry. And, very limited in interests. They have the same look about them that those young people who knock on my door toting bibles have. They see enlightenment as a religion, a ticket to heaven. They want to feel superior, and this seems to do it for them. I feel sorry for them.

Every day, more and more Americans become enlightened.

Every day, I work on becoming less enlightened. I find I just let common sense and good judgment keep me from joining the crowd.

When That Which You Despise Saves Your Bacon

December 7, 2012

It is interesting to watch as the oil industry in this country provides President Obama his greatest gift. Unless Obama and his EPA find a way to stop fracking on private lands, estimates show the United States could out-produce Saudi Arabia in oil production by 2015.

US consumers are benefitting with the lowest natural gas prices in decades. If oil and gas production continues unabated, the United States will be free of all oil dependency outside of North America, meaning Canada and Mexico.

States where production is occurring are benefitting with increased revenue, increased employment, and more spending. Jobs, high-paying union jobs, in oil production are giving the economy a much-needed boost.

It's ironic that a president, who would stop this if he could, may find the very thing he detests lifts the US economy and saves his presidential legacy. If we come out of our economic downturn, it will be Obama who takes credit for what the oil industry did, despite him.

Have You Paid It Forward in 2012?

December 22, 2012

No, I'm not talking about the tax increase you will get from your inept government in 2013.

I'm sharing a story of a young man who died too young. It may make you cry. But it should inspire you to think about the coming holiday. You might be inspired to do something special for someone you don't even know.

This story is personal. For many years, I was involved with something called the American Dream Flight. I was asked to donate the jet fuel for the first flight. I called the marketing VP and made the request. He said I needed to go through the foundation. I pressed him and said they needed an answer quickly. He said go ahead, but for one year only. I wrote it off.

I received an album with pictures and notes from the parents who were on the flight. It was a flight to Orlando for kids with cancer, five days with side trips to Sea World and Universal. One parent came with each child under twelve. I sent the album to the marketing VP's home. He called me and said, "You can have the damned jet fuel forever as far as I'm concerned, just don't send any more books to my house, my wife has been in tears for days." I took him at his word and we did give them the fuel even after my company merged with BP. BP tried to cut it off, but we got several of their employees involved and they kept it going. When I retired, my wife and I signed up as chaperones. We would be responsible for three teen boys (me) and three girls (my wife). On the first trip, one of my boys was named Mike. Mike had a brain tumor. I knew he was hurting, but he never skipped a ride, never missed a wakeup call, and never complained once. The trip was in the spring of 1998. It was the most rewarding, charitable experience of my life. My wife and I weren't sure we would go on the next trip. Then, I received this letter.:

December 8, 1998

Dear Mr. and Mrs. Robertson,
It has been some time since we have written but you have been on our minds and in Mike's conversations quite often. We have dozens of pictures and stories for each one.

The news we have for you is not easy but we felt that since you were such a great part of Mike's life we should let you know that Mike passed away on November 18th, 1998. He went peacefully in his sleep and with no pain.

As we were going through Mike's things, we came across a note Mike wrote in his journal. He spoke of how he was at first scared to travel alone and with strangers but that you and the other guys made it such an enjoyable trip. One he never forgot and told everyone about. His principal spoke at Mike's funeral and brought up the trip and told of how Mike spoke often of the great time he spent with "Bill, a cool and genuine man who treated him like an adult . . . not a kid."

Mike loved Christmas and decorating with lights . . . our house always had to be the brightest on the block... so this holiday season when you drive past homes that are brightly lit . . . think of Mike, because he is sitting above, loving the view and thinking of you.

Thank you, again, for giving your time, thoughtfulness and care for Mike and all the other kids who enjoyed themselves because of your generosity and love.

Hope you and your family have a happy and healthy holiday season.

I'm a pretty tough guy, but I still tear up when I read this letter from Mike's parents. We went on the next trip and five more. This time every year, I go to the Dream Flight file and read the letter and look at the pictures of me riding every ride in every park with my three boys. I remember all of them. I pray they are all okay. I tried to pay it forward every trip by treating each kid like he was an adult and doing everything I could do to make sure he had the time of his life. I learned more from them than any group I've ever been around—about courage, attitude, and never, never feeling sorry for yourself or getting down.

2013

The White House Automated Answering System

January 1, 2013

Today, I tried to reach President Obama to wish him the best for 2013. Also, I had some ideas to cut government spending. As you might expect, I got an automated answering message. Here's the message:

Press 1 if we can cut you a check for any reason.
Press 2 to make a contribution to my eternal campaign fund.
Press 3 to speak to someone about a labor union issue.
Press 4 to speak to someone about an environmental issue.
Press 5 to talk to someone about raising taxes.

Any accredited media, except Fox News, press 6 to speak to David Axelrod directly.

Any Hollywood celebrity may press 7 to speak to Michelle directly (except Oprah, of course).

Any illegal immigrant seeking immediate citizenship, press 8 for the automated green card line.

If you are on the other side of one of our borders, press 9 for an escort across.

Anyone with any idea about cutting government spending, press zero for an operator.

So, I pressed zero. I got a recorded message that said, "The high level of calls is resulting in a long wait time. The estimated wait time is four years and twenty-four days."

What Does "We are made for this moment" Mean?

January 23, 2013

The key statement the media took out of the president's second inaugural address was: "We are made for this moment." I'm sorry, I have no idea what that means.

Does it mean he is the chosen one who will lead us from this mess we are in? Does "we" mean "he"? It sure doesn't mean "me." I'm not made for this moment. I find words like this summarize this president—meaningless words that signify nothing, even to him. They are words that some hack who wrote his speech jotted down for job security. It's a big statement that says zero.

My kids and grandkids are not made for this moment. If we sit down with them and ask if it's all right to use up all the financial resources this country has and mortgage their opportunity to enjoy the life we've enjoyed, do they agree? Mine say no.

What exactly stands out about this moment? Polls show public optimism is at an all-time low. Congress is down to single digits in their approval poll. We have hit the debt ceiling and it appears this isn't worth mentioning in the big speech vs. social goals like gay marriage, gun control, and climate change.

In a word, this moment "sucks." Are we all made to suck with the moment?

People out of work for years, houses under water, almost no GDP growth, printing money that will eventually result in inflation, following California and Greece down the same road and ignoring the danger, medical costs skyrocketing, retirement funds drying up, cities going broke—hell, even states teetering—and I'm supposed to feel like this is some cherished moment in my life?

Sadly, the people who gave him the biggest majority for this moment are suffering the most. Unemployment is up disproportionately with blacks, Hispanics, and young people.

I must be out of touch with something. Will someone please explain what this great statement means?

Thoughts of 2012

January 31, 2013

To me, it was a tough year. For six years, I hoped to see justification for me to stop writing this blog. I don't see any justification. I write it for my grandkids. They are the ones I believe will suffer for our actions today.

A new year and another birthday makes one reflective.

Yes, the financial markets did well in 2012. Those of us with investments in the markets enjoyed paper asset increases. Paper is the operative word. Many of us had nice paper asset values when the recession hit. We watched how fast they dissolved, along with the equity in our houses and other means of financial security.

Very few of us in America seem to feel good about how things are going for the country. It's reflected in polls.

When we realize the financial markets are propped up by a Federal Reserve that prints billions of dollars to buy our own treasury bills, we know something isn't right. When we borrow from the Chinese to pay extended unemployment benefits, it makes us nervous. When $17 trillion in debt isn't enough for most politicians in Washington, we worry.

We don't like the idea of our government spying on us. And, it makes it worse when one federal judge says it's okay.

We don't care for the idea that the IRS was used to help one party do well in an election by refusing to let grass-roots organizations that support the other party get a tax status. A president who lies to us with no compunction is not reassuring. A government that can't run anything regardless of which party is in the majority now wants to run everything. Every day some new regulation limits our freedoms.

The Federal Reserve does what is described above to keep inflation down. Yet large numbers of politicians, including the president, want to raise the minimum wage. A city in the state of Washington has raised it to $15 an hour. There is no faster way to jump-start inflation than doing that. Any of us who ever worked for the minimum wage or ran a company manned by minimum wage employees knows how that works. The people who have those minimum wage jobs in that city with the $15 wage will all be out of work, replaced by college grads. The prices of everything will go up and people will shop in adjoining cities. The businesses will close and the economy in that city will go south. It's a simple act with complex consequences. I was in Poland when capitalism was getting its start there after years of communism. Every cab driver had a graduate degree in something.

What happened to Detroit is not going to stop with Detroit. Cities and states across the country have made pension commitments that can't possibly be met. Most are putting Band-Aids on the problem. Only in places like Wisconsin are real corrections being made. Remember how that went down with the unions and the media.

Obamacare is a disaster. But, it will get worse until Americans get so upset that anyone who supports it will be looking for a new job. We did have prohibition in this country once. Remember? Now we have legal marijuana.

Those of us who lived through Jimmy Carter can sense that when it gets critically bad, we Americans get it fixed. When I sense that is starting, when it's "morning again in America," as Ronald Reagan said as he began to repair what Carter had broken, I'll be able to stop this project and relax. Until that happens, I will type on, hoping to change a few minds and energize a few more fellow countrymen. In 2013, a half-million read this drivel. Maybe in 2014 it will be a million.

Disincentives to Work

February 22, 2013

Here are the numbers. A single mother of two will receive $45,000 in government benefits each year. This is food stamps, childcare, and Medicaid.

If she gets a job, she keeps gaining up to $9,000 in annual wages. The next $5,000 costs her some benefits. If she gets a better job that pays $29,000, her income plus benefits goes up to $57,000. So, she gained $12,000 by working full time. This $57,000 number pretty much maxes her out. If she goes above that, she begins to lose benefits. She must go to $69,000 to get back to the $57,000 taking lost benefits into consideration. Between $29,000 and $69,000 she pays 100% taxes if you equate lost benefits to a tax.

This points out the problem with freebies. To get freebies you must be poor. When you get less poor, you lose freebies. If you work, you begin to see the disincentive to that work and question whether you are better off just taking the freebies.

I'm for helping people who need help. But, I also sense we are creating a larger population base who are doing the math. No one wants to work if you can do better financially by not working. Or, better yet, work and get paid in cash and have the best of both worlds.

A Fish Story

March 7, 2013

Sometimes it takes years to measure the wisdom of government.

Ninety-three years ago, the National Park Service packed fertilized trout eggs onto mules and took them into the Grand Canyon to create a recreational fishery. Last week, a crew of workers waded the stream with backpack shockers killing hundreds of Brown Trout, many generations removed from those long-ago fertilized eggs.

In the passing ninety-nine years, hundreds of American sportsmen have enjoyed the thrill of catching brown trout in the shadows of the Grand Canyon. If you've never caught a brownie on a fly, it's as good as it gets. Why would the same government that created such a great free pleasure for American fishermen decide it's time to take it away?

Brown trout eat humpback chubs, that's why. In 1920, the government didn't know humpback chubs existed. They weren't a classified species. Now they are declared an endangered species. When the dam was built and Lake Powell created, built by the government, it cooled the river. Trout favor cool water; fat-assed chub minnows don't. The government panders to the folks who look after the spotted owls and the humpback chubs. So, the poor brown trout, not a native species, must go to protect the worthless chubs. Anyone who has fished has used chubs for bait. Brown trout really like them.

You fishermen who have enjoyed catching brown trout in Bright Angel Creek, go elsewhere. You don't get a vote. Environmental groups rule today and they want to protect the chubs.

The same government that spent your tax dollars to make this creek a fun place to go will now spend some more of your tax dollars to stop the fun. You really want more of this?

Reality Checks

April 10, 2013

First, let's start with border security. It's a hot issue now that some form of immigration reform is about to be passed on a bipartisan basis. Look at your map of the United States. The border is over 650 miles long. So far, we have spent $105 billion trying to secure it. This doesn't count the annual costs of patrolling the border. The Soviets couldn't keep East Berliners from going into West Berlin. They had a huge wall, barbed wire, dogs, and machine guns, and shot to kill. So, don't accept any noise out of Washington, D.C., that we will have a secure border. It will never happen.

So, the real solution is what? It's simple; send them home. Sure, try to cut down on the flow, but realize it will never stop. The only answer is to accept that crossing the border is where the law is broken. But, no date stamp magically appears on the crosser's forehead. There will be no way of knowing whether it's a pre-immigration reform crosser or post-immigration reform crosser. If immigration reform doesn't send people home, immigration reform will be like the last version under Reagan, a "Welcome to the USA all of Latin America" plan.

There is only one solution: send home those who broke the law. As often as they break that law, send them home. That's the reality. Delude yourself all you want, but that's the law.

Next reality, unemployment. Eighty million Americans who were once in the work force have quit looking for work. Only 63.3% of the "participation rate," the government term for working age adults, are working. It's the lowest level since 1979. And, only 69.6% of those 25–29 years of age are working, the lowest level in forty-one years. This doesn't include old coots like me who are retired and past the government "participation age" category.

Got this reality? It's bad—real bad. But it's less bad than it would be if all those who quit working weren't on unemployment and/or food stamps. Are we raising a new generation of young people who may be enjoying retirement at ages 25–29? How does that 63% who are working support the 80 million who quit looking for work? Supposedly, like the 1% supports everyone for everything. But the math won't work.

Here's the reality. If some of those 8 million don't get off their asses and look for jobs, this country will go broke. It's as simple as that.

Finally, another hot topic: gun control. There is a simple answer to gun control. And, it's the only solution. Where it's been tried, it works. Violent crime from guns goes down and crime in general goes down. All other ideas, including all from Obama and Biden, have been tried and don't work.

Here's the reality. Drunk driving is much less a problem now than it was twenty years ago. Why? The penalties for drunk driving are much harsher. In Arizona, you know you will go to tent city if you get caught driving drunk. Ask Charles Barkley or Mark Grace, who resides there every night now for four more months. The same solution will work for gun control.

If you get caught with an illegal firearm, you go to jail for two years. It doesn't matter if you are an NBA superstar or a Hollywood idol. Two years.

That's the reality. Yes, it will require more jails. But, it will be cheaper in the long run than the ideas from Biden or Obama. And those costs will fix nothing. This solution works and it will keep thousands alive that will otherwise die with the Biden plan. That's the reality.

Amazing Grace

May 6, 2013

Sometimes we work too hard to find things that are not working right. In today's cynical world, negatives outweigh positives far too much.

The media is all up in arms because some funeral home in Boston agreed to bury the dead terrorist. What do they want to do with his body? Why is this an issue? Why must a small businessman in Boston be dragged through the mud because he agreed to do business? When has it ever been an issue who buries a killer? Who buried the shooter from Newtown?

I'm getting off the cynical train today and bringing you a nice story. My city in Illinois has enjoyed success with their high school football teams. In the past ten years, they've won several state championships.

Last week, I was in a local sub shop buying sandwiches to go. Four young men were in front of me in line. They had their shirts and hats identifying them as high school football players. I recognized one as last year's starting quarterback, who will be back next year. They were big young men who looked typical. One had a hat on backwards and another had a full beard.

As I waited for a to-go order, the waitress brought their dine-in orders. They were at the table next to me. As I watched, they joined hands and the quarterback led them in a prayer. I was stunned. I've seen families do this. I've seen couples do this. But I've never seen four tough-looking teens, who will probably play college football, do this. Sure, the teams do it on the sidelines before and after games, mostly for the crowds. Here there were no crowds, no cameras, and only me and three employees who were too busy to watch.

There may be many things wrong with our country today, but there are many things right, as well. I was truly moved by the four young men who chose to pray in public in a local sub shop. To me, it ranks right up there with watching a half plane load of military men and women deplane at O'Hare to a standing ovation by those of us waiting to board. You could tell the troops were truly moved by the spontaneous applause.

It's a great country populated by great people. It's good to remember that.

Decoration Day in My Day

May 26, 2013

When I was a kid, it was called Decoration Day. My small town was full of vets coming home from WWII, or not coming home. Some came home wounded for life, physically and mentally. In those days, the mental issues were called shell shock. It was easier to know who hadn't been to war than those who had served. Those who didn't serve were talked about a lot and those who did serve never talked about the war, but they did point out the dodgers with more than a little resentment.

The purpose of Decoration Day was clear and no one needed a history class or civics class to understand why we were taking time to recognize the sacrifices made. Kids my age were without dads. Dad didn't come home. Or Dad couldn't work because he was disabled from the war. We got it. We understood how much our town and everyone in it gave to the war. We heard whispers about men in town who had been decorated for bravery in combat. It was always the little guys, never the John Wayne types, and kids looked at them and courage differently. Size didn't matter. It was strange how we knew who received all the medals.

I never felt the parades or attention meant much to the vets. It was all too fresh and didn't seem adequate for the sacrifices most had made. I know it didn't for my dad, who served in the navy in the Pacific. It was another workday for him, with a little time off to listen to the Indy 500 on the radio.

Besides, Korea was heating up and a new group of dads were leaving. Some of the dads who just got home were probably thinking they might get called back. Mine did worry about that. I marched in the parade as both a Cub and Boy Scout. As I remember, most of the town turned out. It was embarrassing the first time. It seemed like everyone on the curb was staring right at us, and some of my friends would yell out something inappropriate as I passed.

A lot of years have passed since then; a lot of wars, a lot of sacrifice, and many parades. My generation got to experience Vietnam. I flunked my army physical and was happy to do so. Some of my friends didn't come back. Some who did are just now getting the respect they deserve. It was the beginning of how inappropriate behavior by a few thousand people can influence the entire country. It showed how liberal colleges and universities with strong encouragement from the faculty could get a lot of things wrong. It was a wrong war, but those who fought the war deserved the same respect as those who came home from prior wars. They didn't get it. Now, a country still feeling guilty is trying to give them respect and thanks, but it's far too late. They suffered too much from those who got it wrong and took it out on them. It was a very sad time in our history.

It's a good thing we learned from that. Many think Iraq and Afghanistan are bad wars, but few seem to be taking it out on the brave young men and women who went and those who continue to fight those wars. Everyone in uniform today seems to get a lot of positive, special attention. As they should. We hear a lot of good people step up and say "Thank you for your service." These wars have lasted longer than WWII. Thousands of veterans from those wars are back home today.

Memorial Day is reminder to set aside time to think about all those who have served in all the wars this country has fought. I have six grandkids and I'm guessing not a one will give one thought to those veterans this weekend. There probably won't be a thought from my kids, either, although one goes to the parade almost every year. When you do that, it is hard not to give it some thought. Especially if you go to the cemetery where the parade ends. I hope I'm wrong.

When I do think back on the days when it was called Decoration Day, it reminds me that it was the Greatest Generation that fought that war. Most didn't wait to be drafted. They literally ran to the recruiting office days after Pearl Harbor. Today's military is all volunteer. That speaks volumes about today's generation. Maybe we don't give them enough credit for that. They might be just as great.

Whatever you do this weekend, try to reflect on why we have this holiday. Think about someone you know who's in the military. Think of someone you know who lost someone in a war. Think of someone who came back wounded. Write a check to Wounded Warriors. Think about a relative of yours who died fighting for our country. Think about that small town where I grew up; for many years, there were few young men in town.

Explosion in Quebec and the Keystone Pipeline

July 9, 2013

President Obama will not approve the Keystone Pipeline. He says it's not safe because Canadian sand crude oil is corrosive and could create pipeline leaks to environmentally sensitive areas in Nebraska. That's possible in a hundred years or so. The aging pipeline system seldom leaks, despite some being in the ground over a hundred years. Some of which have been carrying that Canadian crude to US refineries for years.

The real reason is not pipeline leaks; it's due to environmental groups who don't approve of tar sand extraction. No matter that it's in Canada. In one of her first missions as Secretary of State, Hillary Clinton traveled to Canada to tell them to stop the process. That went well, since Canada was enjoying a healthy economy while Obama was busy blaming Bush for sinking our economy. Canada was smart enough to understand how important their oil was to their economic growth. Obama never will, even though fracking is saving his bacon here at home.

So, whether you believe Obama cut a deal with Warren Buffet or not, Buffet's railroad, Burlington, carries crude oil to US refineries that would be carried by Keystone Pipelines. Oil industry experts have warned that it's far safer to move crude by pipe than by rail. Common sense is all that's needed for that judgment.

It happened. Rail cars carrying crude from Canada to

Maine derailed on the Canadian side of the border. The explosion wiped out most of the town. At least one is dead, with sixty missing.

Will the media connect these dots for you? Probably not. Media in the United States, with few exceptions, do not support building pipelines.

Environmentalists contribute to Obama. Buffet helps Obama with the "tax the rich" election campaign. Obama halts the pipeline. Canada is upset with us and begins planning a pipeline to their west coast to ship the oil to China. Buffet makes more money by hauling the oil to the United States by rail.

Detroit Will Never Recover

August 1, 2013

I was there when it all began. Just transferred to a new position in Detroit, I watched the city burn from a motel room in Southfield. It was 1967 and the riots had broken out. I was trying to convince my wife with a new baby that moving to Detroit was a good idea. The result of the riot was forty-three dead, 1,189 injured, over 7,200 arrests, and more than 2,000 buildings destroyed. It all began at a speakeasy at 12th Street and Claremont.

My job took me to the war zone, where three of our Standard Oil of Indiana stations had burned to the ground. I was on a team to assess damage to our retail businesses. It was like a combat zone. We were nervous with good reason. The curfew was on and there was still occasional gunfire. The Michigan National Guard and US Army Reserves patrolled the city.

The riot was the beginning of the end for a once-great city. Detroit has never recovered and never will. Many of those 2,000 buildings destroyed were never rebuilt. This left nesting places for mischief and eyesores.

My second stay in the Detroit suburbs began in 1971. My job took me to the inner city several times a month. I didn't go to meetings but to the street. The streets where our retail service stations and our dealers were at war with the criminals every day. Sometimes the dealer or an employee was shot trying to run his business. Sometimes a dealer shot a crook trying to take his money and his life. Crack cocaine had come to Detroit and no one was safe. Crime is what added to the damage done by the riots. Detroit became the murder capital of the world (harken, Chicago). It was too dangerous to live south of Eight Mile Road, and whites left in droves for the suburbs. Followed by middle-class blacks.

Coleman Young was running the city and he was interested in only two things: getting rich and getting reelected. To do both, he needed the unions, and he got them by pouring money into their coffers and cutting good deals for union employees. The private sector jobs were leaving and 60% of the people who worked were working in the public sector. Taxes had to be raised, but there were no people to pay the taxes. The greater the percentage of blacks, the higher the vote count for Coleman. Running whites out of Detroit worked in his favor.

I read articles with great optimism that the city will come back. I ask how? No one has a job and the public services are unacceptable. It takes one hour to get a cop to a 911 call.

There is twice the geography needed for the population. The crime is still bad and there are no cops to keep it from getting worse. You can't sell a house for a buck. There are no assets and no jobs.

Money doesn't solve everything, and money won't fix Detroit. The city needs a "do not resuscitate" form.

Detroit is the endgame for America if the Democrats keep getting elected. The Obama game plan is identical to the Coleman Young plan. Grow the government employment and pay them better than the private sector. Give the unions what they need. Pander to the environmentalists, even though jobs are lost and energy costs go higher. And make speech after speech about inequality. In Detroit, it was inequality against those who tried to stay and support the city vs. those who stole and killed them. It was serious inequality. But those who left won, and those who stayed to pilfer what was left of their neighbors and the city are mostly all that are left.

Today, symptoms of Detroit are everywhere in America. States that have the Detroit virus are New York, California, and Illinois. Cities have it worse, like Chicago and Washington, D.C. People are leaving those states just like they began to leave Detroit. Chicago is now the murder capitol of America. And it's moving to the Loop. When it's not safe to shop in the Loop, the exodus of residents in Chicago will begin. It's comforting to believe it can't happen here. But, I can tell you from my experience in Detroit, it can happen anywhere.

We have a president today who seems to want to see it happen. With his new buzzword, "inequality," and second favorite, "racial unrest," he's beginning to sound like Coleman Young. He's using Trayvon Martin to stir up the minority community.

This week in Park Ridge, Illinois, cops claimed a ninety-five-year-old man attacked them with his cane and they had to use force to subdue him. He died en route to the hospital. For we elderly, isn't this as bad as the Trayvon Martin situation. Taking on a ninety-five-year-old makes less sense than the age difference between Zimmerman and Martin.

There is no Jesse Jackson or Al Sharpton or Barack Obama to speak for the elderly. Unfortunately, there is no one to speak for the kids of America, either. The ones who will inherit a country much like Detroit because we watched while it happened.

Obama's Plan to Reduce College Tuition

September 13, 2013

The man who wants to do selective bombing in Syria for dubious reasons with high-risk consequences shows the down side of having a community organizer as commander in chief. Flawed logic shows up everywhere when a leader with that background tries to solve big problems.

His solution to high tuition is a two-pronged approach. He controls the $150 billion in grants the feds dole out to colleges and universities. He suggests a merit system to allocate the grant money based on graduation rates and grades. He would then have student loan repayments tied to income. The more a graduate makes the faster the loan must be repaid.

This is how a left-wing community organizer approaches all problems.

Here's how a business executive (retired) would address this issue.

First, eliminate the entire $150 billion in federal grants. Force the universities to cut all the bloat they have created with all this extra free cash. Lay off layers of useless administrators, make professors return to the classrooms, and cut activities the new budget won't accommodate.

Next, put onto student loans the measurement Obama wants to apply to grants. If the student doesn't maintain a certain grade point and isn't on a path to graduate in a reasonable time frame, the loan is pulled. No more loan. This will result in fewer students and fewer universities competing for those smaller numbers of students. Price becomes a competitive factor.

Universities may need to dip into those trillion-dollar endowment funds to offset your missing tax dollars. Some universities that refuse to get lean will go away.

Here are two examples. Mitch Daniels, the former Indiana governor who balanced the state budget, is running Purdue. He is cutting costs dramatically, just as he did as governor. Janet Napolitano, the former governor of Arizona and Director of Homeland Security, will take over the University of California system. She almost bankrupted the state of Arizona. She was incompetent as Director of Homeland Security. Why let her run the University of California system? In my opinion, so she can siphon off maximum grant dollars with her contacts in Washington, D.C. Which system will cut tuition in the next five years, and which will increase tuition? Purdue will cut tuition and UC schools will increase tuition.

The business of educating students for jobs and careers will become a business. Well-run institutions will prosper and the inefficient will fail, just like in the real world. Students who go there to learn, take courses that lead to a well-paying job, and maintain grades will get a loan to help them get the degree to do this. They won't be punished for their success.

Others will get loan funds cut off and go to trade schools, the military, or enter the job market. Just as they do now, but without the billions in student loans they accumulated.

There aren't enough jobs that require a degree in this country to support the number of students pursuing degrees. We need fewer students, fewer universities to serve fewer students, more competition between fewer universities for fewer students, more efficient universities, and zero tax dollars pouring into the system causing all the problems.

It's Econ 101, which Obama skipped for Soc 101. Not social studies, like I took, but Marxist studies, in his case.

Things America Must Do

September 27, 2013

To help make the United States as great as Cuba, here is what we must continue:
1. Borrowing money to meet our spending requirements. Just as a junkie must steal to support a habit, we must steal from our grandkids to support our spending. If a politician votes to stop or lower spending, we fire him or her.

2. Fighting all the world's wars. We did in the last century and it made us king of the hill. To stay king of the hill we must keep doing it. There is a bit of a problem—see 1, above.

3. Let the government run everything. To do this, we become Cuba or Detroit, but it makes politicians more powerful and they decide how much government we need. Government can't run anything—see post office, Freddie and Fannie, the FHA, Amtrak, Medicare (fraud), the TSA, etc. But you will get more (Obamacare) whether you want it or not—see 1 above, makes politicians more powerful.

4. Add more to food stamp rolls—see 1 and 3 above.

5. Refrain from drilling, stop fracking, and keep the hold on the Keystone Pipeline. Eliminate coal-fired power plants, etc. Fracking has added $1,200 to every household in this country. Europe has started burning coal because wind, solar, and cap and trade haven't worked. But there is that little fable about climate change and that environmental lobby, so we must comply, regardless of 1 and 3 above. Oh yes, let's keep ethanol in the mix while we are managing energy for the masses.

6. Have everything above spun by a complicit media so it all sounds so great.

7. Have all the above taught in our schools by our union teachers and far left professors, so we raise another generation that buys this plan.

8. Continue to hire the worst possible people to run things at all levels of government. People who have law degrees but seldom practiced law or spent their entire lives in jobs other than running something. He

who has the biggest war chest gets the job. And, can keep it until he dies. Pay them too much and give them better benefits than those who hired them. Have zero accountability so we have no measure of their performance, except how much they gave us personally.

9. Run this whole program on the backs of those who choose to work and succeed, despite the incentive to do neither. As they end each year with less, add more burden to them next year to see how much they can take. Let them watch their neighbors who do nothing get more with no effort, until they quit and join the neighbors.

There you have it. It's the plan that made Cuba great. It's being brought to every nook and cranny of America by the great leader, Obama. Take your next vacation to Cuba while you can still afford a vacation, and see how great it is there. It's like going to an antique car show seeing all those 1950 Chevys, with all that rust, still running.

Oh! What a Tangled Web We Weave When at First We Practice to Deceive

November 12, 2013

Sadly, our president is a serial liar. His latest example will long be remembered, but he has learned nothing from the pain he's feeling as the country turns against him.

The latest 39% approval rating has to smart.

I'll keep this brief, something our president can't do.

Over and over again, to sell his bogus health care program, he lied to 300 million Americans. It's illegal to lie to the 500 liars in Congress, but not to lie to 300 million Americans.

Fifteen Democrats came to the White House to ask the president to save their bacon by fixing the Obamacare mess. His first effort: blame the insurance companies. Someone, probably Valerie Jarrett, the real president, told him to stop doing this. They need help from the insurance companies to try to fix the unfixable.

Then he said he was sorry. Sorry that he must cancel the insurance for the 5% of the Americans who are too stupid to buy the right kind of health insurance and needed his help to do it. That's an outright lie. Many of the citizens being canceled are not being canceled for insufficient insurance. And, Duke University says it will be 130 million who will get their insurance canceled. Another lie.

Trying to change the subject in his speech in Louisiana, he shifted to the economy. He said the economy would be much stronger if the Republicans had not shut down the government. This, at the same time his own economic team reported that the shutdown had no appreciable impact on the economy and the positive jobs report caused the stock market to set a new record.

On the day after you apologize for being a liar, you tell another whopper. Now we can all tell when you are lying—when you open your mouth, which has far exceeded any previous president's need to talk. Love thyself, Obama; the country is going in the opposite direction.

Energy Independence in America at Last

November 21, 2013

Every president since Nixon has pledged energy independence for America. Jimmy Carter established the Department of Energy to get that done. The DOE has blown billions of your tax dollars and accomplished nothing. Those presidents who made that pledge, especially the current one, have done everything they can possibly do to keep their pledge from becoming reality.

They have made it nearly impossible to drill on your land. Your land, not theirs—federal land. They have piled regulation on regulation on any form of oil and gas production. They have taxed domestic production to make it less attractive. They have tried their best to keep energy independence from happening. Politicians and liberal media have demonized the oil industry since Teddy Roosevelt's time.

That very evil industry, the one that will gouge you at every opportunity, made independence happen without a dime of your tax money. Last month, for the first time in decades, the United States produced more crude oil than it imported. The technology developed by the oil companies made that happen. And, they made it happen primarily on private land.

Meanwhile, Mexico watches their oil production dwindle. See, Mexico has the Obamacare version of an oil industry. Run by the government. A government that has no technology to find and develop replacement oil to replace oil from wells with diminished production.

Still want your government to run health care? Still believe big oil is the bad guy with energy prices? Still buy the propaganda about big oil? Which is worse, big oil that has put an estimated $2,400 dollars per year in every household in America in energy savings, or big government that blows billions with a worthless DOE? We could be Mexico, and will be, if Obama has his way. He would stop fracking and slow domestic oil production, if he could. If asked, he would lie about that, but we know how well he lies, don't we?

The Youth of America are Getting the Shaft

December 16, 2013

For those of you who are between eighteen and twenty-five years of age, here's a little message. Your love for President Obama may be misplaced. It may be time to sit down and evaluate what he is doing for you.

His biggest and latest gift to you is bad health insurance. You get to buy his insurance whether you want it or not. And, it's not the type of insurance you would be directed to buy. It's very high deductible and very expensive. Why expensive? Because you are subsidizing the insurance provided to older and sicker Americans. Why is the insurance inappropriate? A good advisor would suggest you need insurance for big health issues that has low deductibles for those types of illness. But, you pay out-of-pocket for normal doctor's visits.

Unemployment is highest for the young these days. He's just about wiped out jobs for you with his economic policies.

College tuition is at record levels. Student test scores are falling despite more and more money pouring into secondary education. This has created nearly a trillion dollars of student loan debt held by your government.

Debt for the country keeps piling up. This is debt you will pay for some day. Ask the few residents of Detroit who are still left. They are paying in numerous ways for profligate spending by Democratic mayors for fifty years. Try forty minutes for emergency response, with most street lights out, to see how much you like what spending by previous generations has done. This is what is coming to other cities in the country soon, and sometime in your lifetime—not mine—the whole country.

As I look out my window and watch the beautiful falling snow, I wonder how you might feel about the global warming scam in twenty-five years. There has been no increase in global temperature for the past fifteen years, but you are told it's coming. Academics who support this cause have been granted billions in research money. Politicians who support this have been given more political power, and some have gotten incredibly wealthy peddling this program (Gore). In the 1970s, both groups got the same benefits selling global cooling.

I could go on and on, but hey, it's your life, not mine. Most of you are smart enough to make your own judgments. Many of you are already feeling the pain in some way, shape, or form. I can only feel abject sorrow that you are supporting what you consider cool and not supporting what is best for you. Just remember: Detroiters supported Coleman Young because he was black, not because he was competent and honest. Coleman is long dead, but Detroit is still dying. My advice: vote with your head; don't vote along the lines of your fellow youth. Ignore your teachers and professors, ignore your friends, and spend a little time assessing your current plight in American. You are being screwed by those you believe are looking out for you. It's time to look elsewhere for options.

Try This at Work

December 31, 2013

The next time your boss calls you in because something under your direction has gone terribly wrong, look the boss square in the eye and say, "No one is more frustrated about this than me."

Be sure and let me know how this works out for you. Remember, "No one you work for wants you fired" over this mess. That will give you the necessary courage to tell the boss about your frustration.

If, God forbid, you misjudged your boss on this, don't worry. The man who invented this approach, President Obama, will look out for you in your time of need. He will give you a year and a half in unemployment pay. He will furnish you with a free cell phone. He will help you with your mortgage payments. He will provide you with medical care. He will give you a food stamp card. See, the old stamps were so humiliating we had to discontinue them. Now, you can whip out a card just like everyone else and no one will know you're on the dole.

After a couple of years living just as well as you did when you worked, you decide, why work—ever again? Or, if an opportunity should present itself, why not work a few hours a week for cash. Just to supplement your comfortable lifestyle.

Once the majority of Americans get comfortable with this program, two things happen. No one who doesn't support this program will ever be elected to any office. And, the growth of nonworking Americans will continue as it has for the past five years. Then we can stop crowing about America being the best country on earth. It won't be.

2014

Turning the Page on a New Year

January 1, 2014

Every year I do soul searching about the wisdom of continuing this blog. The determinant remains: Is the country on the right track to provide a reasonable future for my grandkids? Will they be the first generation in this country's history to have a poorer standard of living than their parents?

The answer: the blog goes on.

Things We Are Told Make America a Better Country

January 9, 2014

In California, illegal aliens can practice law. Better or worse? Lawyers are officers of the court. Felons can't practice law. Lawyers who have violated a federal law can practice law?

In Colorado, pot is legal. Better or worse? The state will reap tax benefits. Growers will make a profit. It will reduce pot coming in from Mexico. It will make it easier for those who didn't want to break the law to try pot. There will be more Coloradans addicted to pot. Obamacare is the law of the land. But, the majority of Americans don't want Obamacare. We have always said majority rules in this country. This decision was made by one Supreme Court justice. Better or worse?

The NSA is spying on us. One federal judge says they can't do that. Another says it's perfectly okay. Obama says nothing. Democrats say it's keeping us safe. The Constitution says they can't do this. Better or worse?

Hundreds of brave Americans fought and died or were injured in Iraq and Afghanistan. Obama didn't like the Iraqi war that was won. He pulled all the troops. Now the bad guys have taken over the country and are doing the same things Saddam Hussein was doing. The same will happen in Afghanistan. We have learned to respect those who fought those wars, unlike Vietnam, but one man, the president, decided to forego the gains those troops made for their sacrifices. Better or worse?

Windmills have gone up all across America to produce power. They kill hundreds of birds. Evidently, members of the Audubon Society and PETA all belong to the Sierra Club, and must overlook dead birds, including endangered species. Better or worse?

Ugly solar panels are going up all over the desert in Arizona to produce power. They produce steam, which then produces power. Lake Mead is supposed to be at historic low levels and water shortages are just down the road, like climate change. Is it a good trade-off to produce very expensive electricity using scarce water? Better or worse?

For my entire lifetime, politicians have said they would simplify the tax code. For my entire lifetime, they have made it more complex adding pages of regulations every year. Yet, we put them back in office every year overlooking their broken promises. Better or worse?

Over half the population pays no taxes. They could care less about the tax code. The very rich like complexity and have lobbied for most of the complexity. The remaining 40% pay billions to get their taxes filed. Better or worse?

The federal government is always deciding what every American is entitled to as part of their lucky geographical good fortune. For a while Clinton and Barney Frank decided it was home ownership. That didn't work out so well with the housing bubble. But they got Bush blamed for it so it worked well politically. Now it's health insurance. Obamacare may turn out to be worse than the housing bubble from a cost standpoint. Lurking back there is student loans. Obama said in his first inaugural speech that every American is entitled to a college education. We, the people, have over $1 trillion in student loans that are growing. Many are bad loans. Better or worse?

The big debate this week is about unemployment insurance. For my lifetime, it was twenty-six weeks. In recent times, that wasn't good enough. Some of it may be due to the answers to the questions posed above. We have been told we are in economic recovery and have been for four years. But we can't leave those who have used up their unemployment insurance without financial help. Better or worse?

Our student test scores keep going down versus the rest of the world. But we love our teachers. We can't hold them accountable for this. It's a money thing, even though we spend more per student than the rest of the world. The unions won't let us get rid of marginal teachers. When we try to hold teachers accountable, they dummy up the test scores (Atlanta, Georgia). Is it time to get real on education? Better or worse?

I've barely scratched the surface here. Comparisons are much greater than this list. But it's an exercise that makes one think. Maybe it all comes down to a simple solution, like more people voting or term limits. But it seems there is work to be done.

Income Redistribution at Universities

January 15, 2014

I just learned that something I have long expected is true. Universities are practicing income redistribution and doing it without telling anyone. A big part of the tuition increase at colleges and universities is through something they call set-asides. Basically, they tap students who can afford tuition by having them pay into a fund that is used for students the institution deems needy. According to a *Wall Street Journal* article, this amount has jumped 174% in real dollars in just eight years. It is estimated to be $512 million in the past academic year.

I have six grandkids. According to *The Wall Street Journal* formula, they will pay $40,000 into set-asides in their total four years in college. Or, they will educate several strangers. Because their grandmother and I decided to set up college trust funds for them when they were born and their parents set up 529 Plan educational funds, we will be punished. We could have spent that money, like those parents whose kids get the set-aside money. What happens to the kids who don't have the benefit our grandkids have, but don't qualify for the set-aside money? They just get it added to their student loans. So, the kids who receive the set-aside money get free tuition or smaller student loans.

The rationale for all this is to educate more poor kids. Does it work? Does any government program work? Students from the wealthiest 25% of US households are nearly nine times more likely to earn a bachelor's degree by the age of twenty-four. So, the answer is no, it doesn't work. This percentage has remained constant for thirty years.

And, this doesn't take into consideration the billions in scholarships. That number is $33 billion in 2011–2012, up from $23 billion in 2006–2007. Most of this goes to students who can present need. Is it any wonder that the very universities who inundate students with liberal philosophy practice as much socialism as they can? To those in academia, this is the right way to do business. Take billions in funding from the federal and state governments, steal a few dollars in a little hidden scam called set-aside, and still increase tuition to waste on more perks and frills and salaries. Jump student loans to what is now $1.2 trillion, held by you, the taxpayer, and produce less-educated graduates.

Much of that money went into climbing walls and elaborate architecture or bloated bureaucracy or salary and benefit increases for staff. The percentage of jobs requiring a college degree has remained fairly constant, especially in the Obama economy, while the percentage of college graduates has increased significantly. Hence, the gap in pay between college degree jobs and non-college jobs has shrunk. So, the incentive to go to college has diminished while the cost to go has skyrocketed. The cost to attend has doubled but the quality of the education at most US colleges has gone down.

In summary, you borrow money from the government to go to a college the government already gives millions to in grants; the college gouges you to go there, takes money to give to other students, spends recklessly, and provides a lesser education that is worth less in the job market.

We do put up with a lot in this great country, don't we?

The 2014 President Obama State of the Union Address: My Version

January 23, 2014

Hello, Fellow Americans. As I embark on the sixth year as our president, I would like to reflect on my accomplishments. But, sadly there are none. True, I have spent trillions of your tax dollars, but the economy remains stagnant and jobs are scarce, especially for minorities and young people. Yes, I have my signature piece of legislation, Obamacare, but the efforts I'm making to drop that name reflect the problems this program is encountering. A mouthful of ashes for me.

I got the troops out of Iraq. Sure, we still have thousands of troops in Japan, Germany, and Korea, but I, the wisest of all past presidents, decided to take a different tactic. I pulled them all. Now, the hard-fought victory we got in Iraq is gone and the enemy has retaken the country. I will try my best to get the same result in Afghanistan. Foreign relations have never been worse. I have managed to mismanage the entire Middle East. Our friends are mad at us (the Saudis and the Israelis) and our enemies have grown stronger. With help from John Kerry, we are telling you we will broker deals with Syria and Iran that will lead to a more peaceful Middle East. Basically, the Syrian deal was brokered by the Russians after my line in the sand fiasco, and the Iranians are pulling the wool over our eyes once again.

I'm continuing to stop the Keystone Pipeline project. Rail accidents now total four with almost one hundred innocent people killed, but a pipeline is a scary thing. This country is moving to energy independence, despite my efforts to stop that progress. This year, I will do more to stop domestic production. I will invest more in companies that fail, like Solyndra, to keep the environmental vote in our camp. I will give more to unions for the same reason. I will close more coal power plants and replace them with plans to produce more clean energy (see Solyndra, above). This will increase electric bills to the poor.

I will continue what I do best. I will raise money for me. I will heighten my class warfare programs. I will find more and more scapegoats to blame for my incompetence. I will improve my golf game. I will spend more time in Hawaii.

If you are expecting much from me in 2014, forget it. I hate this job. I know nothing of leadership. I am a campaigner and a fundraiser. I will fire no one regardless of performance. I will meet less often with Republicans; I hate those guys. I will spend every dime I can spend and find more programs where money can be spent. My goal is to get the debt to $20 trillion when I leave office, and I've got to step up my game.

Whatever good happens to this country in 2014 will happen despite me. Maybe those I love to blame will get some things done that help the economy, like sequester did last year. When it is clear that we will lose the Senate in 2014 and more seats in the House, I plan to shut it down completely. I didn't sign on to deal with a mess like that. I will show them how well I can make that veto power work. I'll rule by resolution, unless the Supreme Court says no.

So, in summary, expect more of the same from me. I'll spin a few more tales (if you like your doctor, you can keep your doctor, period), keep my head down, blame the world, play a lot of golf, and take a lot of nice trips. One change: don't expect me to take any more selfies of me with a hot chick, since Michelle is still upset about that.

God Bless You, and God Bless America.

Another Case for Tax Reform

February 7, 2014

Real tax reform can't and won't happen in this country. It's a sad example of how those we elect trash us.

Those of us who pay taxes spend billions to have our taxes prepared. The more complex the tax code, the bigger the bills we pay. The people who sift through the complexity and collect the billions own our elected officials. We don't have a say in what kind of tax code we have. It's as simple as that. Lobbyists and campaign donations decide that.

Not only do we pay billions to have our taxes prepared,

we pay billions more to employees of the IRS to process our taxes. Here's what we get for those billions. Only 61% of the more than 100 million phone calls made last year to the IRS were answered. For the 61% of callers who were lucky enough to get someone to answer, the average wait time was seventeen minutes.

Like everything else in politics, it is a money issue. If we increased the budget, they could do a better job. Just like the educational system. We already spend more than any other country to educate our children, but they don't get a quality education. We all know why, but can't face up to fixing the problems.

Want to fix the IRS call problem? It's simple. Put the income tax return on a one-page form, no other requirements needed. The 100 million calls go to 1 million. This is mostly for forms. Thousands of IRS agents, who don't really care about the people who try to call them and can't get through, have to get a real job. Thousands of CPAs have to find other types of work. H&R Block and the others go out of business. See why we can't fix the problem? There is pain involved and we are pain avoiders. We can't get rid of bad teachers and improve education and we can't get rid of bad IRS employees.

Why can't we accept pain? Because the media will feed you hours of sob stories every day. You are the problem. This country has become a soap opera. Someone sobs and we buy the tears. Somewhere down the road there are big pains waiting. Our kids and grandkids will learn about the pain we are accumulating by watching the soap opera and not dealing with reality.

Here's some reality. We don't have to have a complex tax code. We choose to live with what we have. We don't have to pay government employees not to answer the phone. We choose to tolerate that. We don't have to have undereducated kids. We accept that.

Here's an example: In Illinois, the worst-run state in the country, there are four gentlemen running for the Republican nomination for governor. Three are career politicians up to their eyeballs in connections and the substance that put the state where it is today. The fourth is a billionaire, who has no reason to steal anything, owes no favors, and has proven he can run a business. The billionaire wasn't invited to the first debate. In the second, he was attacked for his lack of political experience. There are voters, probably the majority of them, who bought that criticism. We don't get many people who want to fix what's broken and when we do, we listen to those who break things and elect the same thieves we have now.

It's all on us.

Analyzing Inequality in America

March 13, 2014

When I was in school, there were three options for young men who graduated from high school. One, go to the plant or back to the farm. Two, join the military. Three, go to college.

From memory, in 1959, it seems like it was about one-third of each. Factories were hiring and family farms could always use an extra hand. The military was happy to get high school graduates. College tuition was cheap by today's standards and you could work in the summer and part-time at school and pay the freight.

Fast forward to today. Let's examine options and see what has changed and why.

The family farm is a corporate farm and farm hands are replaced by equipment or migrant workers. Very limited employment options there.

The plant is gone. In my hometown, there were several options for high school graduates in manufacturing. There was Tyler Refrigeration, National Standard, Bendix, Simplicity Pattern, and Kawneer. Studebaker had already closed in South Bend ten miles away. None of these plants exist today. What happened?

First, it was the Japanese who took our manufacturing—cheap goods at low prices. Then, higher quality goods at lower prices. The labor unions here fought quality and cost progress. Hence, GM and Chrysler almost fell. They haven't quit. The UAW tried to unionize a plant in Chattanooga, Tennessee, and lost. But, they are coming back and Obama's NLRB will let them. Then it was electronics, shoes, steel, and everything else. The Chinese replaced the Japanese with questionable quality at even lower prices. And, the cycle repeats.

Besides the labor unions, what else contributed to our manufacturing demise in this country? The Green Movement. No manufacturing is the goal. Just enough fuel to fuel their private jets and Teslas.

What party supports the labor unions and the environmentalists while preaching against income inequality? The Democratic Party. The party of the people, except when it comes to high-paying manufacturing jobs like building a pipeline. The same party that announced they will cut jobs in the military back to pre-WWII levels. Wow, there goes another option for the high school graduate.

Well, there's always college. Before the Democrats pushed equal opportunity in college admissions, 7% of minorities graduated from college. Now, far more enter college but only 7% of graduates are minorities.

Obama, even after his party preached home ownership in America as a basic right, began preaching a college education as a basic right. Doesn't that sound great? What a country. A place where everyone graduates from college. Except, Mr. President, only 18% of the jobs in this country require a college degree. Makes for a lot of degreed taxi drivers like they had in Poland when the Russians were through. And, it's just not possible to get everyone through college. See, some are too lazy to study or even go to class. And, some just can't cut it academically. Or, do we give them five strikes like we do in kid's sports today? Lower the requirements to get a degree so all degrees are devalued? What kind of naïve person even suggests that everyone should have a degree today in America?

The liberal Democrats run the college system in this country and have for years. Just as they run the EL-HI system. How's that going? Just like manufacturing is going in the United States. To hell in a hand basket. We continue to drop in test scores vs. other countries. The tuition at colleges keeps going up at twice the rate of inflation. The student loan debt owned by you, the taxpayer, is over a trillion and climbing with no collateral to back it. The average graduation rate is 40%; a lot of those who owe us money are flipping burgers since there are no high-paying manufacturing jobs to fall back on to cover that debt. Get the picture?

When I got out of college, my high school classmates

were making far more than I did for several years working in the plants with four years of seniority. When today's college graduate gets that first job, if they do get one, they will make far more than their high school graduate peers right from the jump.

Let's go back to my hometown where all those plants have closed. When I graduated from high school, it was a large class A school. When my brother graduated, they built a second high school, a class B school. Today, they are back to one high school, the one I attended, and it's a class B school. That's what the Democrats have done to my hometown with the labor unions, the environmental craziness, educational mess, and the military reductions that are coming. No jobs, no people. It's a microcosm of Detroit in southwestern Michigan.

Tell me again—who's for the little guy?

The Hillary/Barack Foreign Policy Scorecard

April 17, 2014

Let's see, right off the jump, Hillary trucks off to Canada to tell them we don't like them extracting oil from tar sands. That was brilliant, and Obama continues to refuse to approve the Keystone Pipeline to receive their oil that they threaten to ship to China.

Let's stick a finger in the eye of our best neighbor. The one who produces oil for us so we don't have to buy it from the Middle East. The one who isn't shipping their people here since their economy is so much better than ours. Because of their oil, of course. Then Obama embarks on his "World Apology" tour. Remember, the one where he told the world we were sorry we had spent so much blood and treasure to try to keep the rest of the world safe. The one where he bowed to the Saudi prince. The one that won him the Nobel Peace Prize. Obama then took his prize to the IOC to get the Olympics for Chicago. Sorry, Obama, it goes to Rio.

Then they announce the threat of terrorism was over. The word terrorism could no longer be used. It was to be replaced by "man-caused disaster." When the first Ft. Hood massacre occurred, it was declared a workplace accident, thus preventing the military families from getting wartime benefits. It let our troops know what to expect from this president. He announced we would pull all troops from Iraq, hence turning a victory into a great opportunity to let the enemy retake a country where so many Americans had died and so much had been spent. An isolated, friendly democratic country in a sea of hatred. Gone. All to further embarrass an ex-president.

Then he reduces the air defense presence in Eastern Europe to appease Putin. Now, Putin is paying him back by retaking the Ukraine.

Then he faced the situation in Benghazi. He had to lie big time on this one, both he and Hillary. The election was coming up and it was again obvious terrorism was not over, as he had repeatedly promised. Still lying about that one.

Then the line in the sand with Syria. He announced we were going to retaliate, then looked to Congress for an out, and finally turned it over to his buddy Putin to resolve. Meanwhile, watching while Iran puts the finishing touches on their nuclear weapons program and waiting to see if they blow Israel off the map as they promise.

These are just some highlights. But, the biggest issue is yet to come. He is turning America into a socialist democratic country, like Europe. It brings up the core issue with that plan: Europe has spent almost nothing on defense, allowing them to put it all back into social programs. If we do the same, who is the world's defender? Europe could do that because they had us to back them up. Who will back us up if we can't protect ourselves? China, who is stepping up their defense spending?

Meanwhile, Gitmo, the first thing Obama pledged to do, remains open for business. Some cartoonist just published a cartoon showing George W. Bush in a tub being waterboarded with the caption "art critics." W. has been showing some of his paintings, which is a hobby he has pursued in retirement. Obama has been sitting in a room deciding who gets zapped by a drone for five years, and the left is still trying to bring back Bush and waterboarding.

It would not be fair and balanced if I didn't mention that Obama killed Osama. Some say it was the intelligence gleaned from waterboarding that allowed it to happen. So, score one for Barack and Hillary.

But in every other example, they were wrong. It's a terrible record and one that will haunt Hillary and her "It doesn't matter" comment over Benghazi and this dismal foreign policy record on her watch. She put a lot of miles in the air, like George Clooney did in the movie *Up in the Air*, but it's results that count. She was like a sales rep who piled up frequent flier miles with almost no sales. Sorry—thanks for your dedication to travel, but this is about results.

Think about it. How can an administration be wrong about so many things?

We Can't Handle the Truth

May 28, 2014

Memorial Day for me has become a day of deep thought. My country turned me down for service. I flunked my physical due to a knee I torn up wrestling in college. That knee has since been replaced, but every Memorial Day I feel some guilt for not serving my country.

This year, I have thought a great deal about the veterans our government is failing in veterans hospitals across this country. I had occasion to sit with one a couple of years ago and hear his story. He served in Vietnam, a place I might have been, and was exposed to Agent Orange. He developed Parkinson's at an early age. The government recently put Parkinson's on the list of illnesses one can receive disability benefits for if the veteran was exposed to the poison. This man was.

A 2013 report by the Congressional Research Service found it took an average of 1,094 days for the Board of Veterans' Appeals to decide on a veteran's claim. According to this man, it was this long or longer. The man was an executive at a large fast food chain before he retired. He knew how to gather data and talk to bureaucrats. It didn't help.

According to him, he was exposed to the worst of the worst government employees. He went back and forth between

Arizona in the winter and Illinois in the summer, so he was dealing with two VA hospitals. He was told he needed this list of documents to complete his claim. He gathered the documents and set up a meeting with the appropriate individual at the local hospital to have the claim reviewed. Every time, he waited up to an hour to see the person. Then the person, never the same person, would say, "Who told you to bring this stuff? I don't need any of this. I need this instead." They would refuse to make copies of what they could accept or give him written acknowledgement of what they said they needed. He would go back and the process would be repeated. The VA was trying to get veterans to give up and stop filing.

It's not just the time and incompetence the VA is exposing our veterans to. It's the frustration and humiliation from uncaring VA employees who are not trained or criticized for poor treatment they render. They treat the vets like they treat you at the license bureau or the post office. You know the drill. Morbidly obese employees who can barely get off a chair dragging their huge carcasses over to yawn and tell you to go back to the end of the line. At the post office, six places and one filled with a bored employee. Like the bears at the zoo that never come out when you are there with the kids or grandkids, they disappear into those back doors and rarely make an appearance.

We have a president who could care less about this except for the political fallout. We have senators and congressmen who are the same. We, too, care less because we never get the truth. It's because we can't handle the truth. Remember this.

Your Government and My Twin Granddaughters

June 12, 2014

My twin granddaughters just graduated from eighth grade. They are healthy, beautiful, sweet, athletic, and bright. At birth, one was just under two pounds and the other just over. They were in neonatal care for three months, and God bless Northwestern Memorial Hospital. They received the kind of treatment that enabled them to be the healthy young ladies they are today.

Do you want to support a government and a health care system that will knowingly refuse to allow early birth babies to have the same chance in life these young ladies had? Or, you for that matter, if you are too old to get Obamacare cancer care? See, with Obamacare you may be asked to die if you are born too soon or live too long.

Twenty-Five Years Ago Today, I Had Forty Minutes to Live

July 19, 2014

Twenty-five years ago today, I was aboard United Airlines Flight 232 with my headphones on listening to music when there was what seemed like an explosion in the rear of the plane. I switched my channel to the one that allowed you to listen to the cockpit conversation. I heard the captain tell the tower we had lost all hydraulics. I'm not a pilot but I knew that meant we were pretty much doomed. You can't keep a DC-10 in the air without hydraulics.

Captain Al Haynes and a pilot passenger, Denny Fitch, and the rest of the men in the cockpit did, and tried to land us on a runway in Sioux City, Iowa. For forty- minutes we flew in circles with only the engine thrusters, and they lined us up with the runway. They almost got us down. But, we stalled and the right wing dug in and we cartwheeled onto our back and broke in five pieces.

Over one hundred of my fellow passengers died that day. Another one hundred suffered terrible injuries. Some of us walked away physically unscathed, but mentally never the same.

I have awakened every day for twenty-five years and thought I was somehow spared by God and thanked him for giving me this time. I try hard never to find any reason to let the first negative thought cross my mind. I try to leave that to those who don't know that today could be their last day on this earth. Aches and pains—at my age I have many. Sadness—I've lost family and friends over this time. But for me, every day is a bonus.

Work was a big priority for me. Not so much after that day in 1989. Family became number one. Being a better person was a mission. Smiling more and being angry less was high on the list.

As the anniversary approached, the media began to seek survivors to interview on TV or for print media. I don't choose to participate, but I don't begrudge those who do. It's my personal choice that the families of those who didn't survive don't need to see me talking about my good fortune. I write this to you, the reader. Maybe I can give you something without you having to suffer through my ordeal. Life is short, delicate, and precious. Treat it accordingly.

Government and Selective Inflation

August 5, 2014

If you wanted to create a housing bubble, what would you do? First, have a president like Bill Clinton say, "Owning your own home is a basic right in America." Then, you put in place lending organizations that will make it happen, like Freddie, Fannie, and the FHA—government-run institutions that will buy any bogus mortgage from any private lender. Then, you force all lenders to have a certain percentage of minority loans. After your little system gives mortgages to millions who can't afford to own their own homes, the bubble bursts. Sorry, Mr. Clinton, but it's a reality that owning your own home requires you to actually pay a monthly mortgage amount. Millions of mortgages not paid pushes down the price of houses, and millions go underwater. Then, you rush in and bail out most of the banks that own bad paper. In 2013 and 2014, you extort payments from some of those banks for playing the game you established with your rules.

Now, you turn your attention to colleges and universities. President Obama, in one of his serial rants, says, "Getting a college education is a basic right in America." You take over the student loan business and stop banks from making student loans. Next, you increase the government aid for students, increasing demand for a college education. Schools raise prices. Students who can't cut it go to college flunking out and defaulting on student loans. Next, you get in the business of rating colleges. Obama now plans to introduce a system to do just that, based on variables like their numbers of financially needy students, average age, tuition costs, loan debts, graduation rates, alumni earnings, and percentage of graduates who go on to get advanced degrees. Let the lying begin just as it has in high schools on student tests that determine teachers' pay.

Here's the real issue. The easy money has allowed colleges and universities to bloat. Administrative costs at every college and university have doubled, on average, in the past ten years. Mitch Daniels, the former governor of Indiana, who cut the fat from the state and balanced the state budget, is now the president of Purdue University. He has frozen tuition and begun to cut the fat. But, most efforts meet with faculty and student protests. Our students today are so influenced by far-left faculty that they will protest when someone is trying to reduce their student loans. Would you hire one of these fools?

Paul Robinson, a former president of the faculty senate, said Mr. Daniels's worth as a leader will be tied to his ability to prune that administrative bloat. "Let me put it this way," Mr. Robinson said. "A blind man on a galloping horse at midnight with sunglasses on can see the problem. The question is, what can he do about it?"

The tuition bubble, so similar to the housing bubble, marches on and will do so until it bursts, and the country will face a trillion dollars of bogus student loans that can't be repaid.

Obama, like Clinton on the housing bubble, will be long gone when that happens. If your kids pay for college or repay their student loans, they will be really unhappy when those who don't get forgiveness. Just like the ones who walked away from houses they lived in or trashed and then stayed for eighteen months after they stopped paying the mortgage. See, we punish those who do the right thing in this country today and reward those who skate. It's the new American way.

Righteous Indignation

August 26, 2014

Ferguson, Missouri, has been at the top of the news for days now as protests break out over the shooting of an unarmed teen by a white policeman. This is a perceived injustice. A white policeman in a predominantly African-American community shoots a black teen in the street. Injustice or not, it's always sad to see a young man die before his life really begins. It brings to mind the song by Elvis from years ago.

This injustice, sad as it is, seems yet to be fully explained. A grand jury has been called together to do just that. Injustice does not justify greater injustice. Greater injustice as described by rioting, looting, shooting at police, throwing Molotov cocktails, burning, cursing police, throwing urine at police, etc.

Reverend Al Sharpton must think it does, since he always appears at any tinder box like this and adds the spark it

takes to light the fire. A civil rights leader? Not by my standards. Ferguson is settling down as the media loses interest
and moves on to New York, where the young man died from
a choke hold. The funeral was announced and Reverend Al
declared he will go back to Ferguson and the media will rejoin
him there to see if they can rev it up again.

While all of this went on, there was a clear-cut injustice in
Chicago. A nine-year-old boy got mad at his mom when she
wouldn't let him have a muffin. Mom was trying to follow
the first lady's advice on sweets. He stormed out of the house
barefoot. Ten minutes later, the police knocked on her door
and advised her she needed to accompany them to the hospital. Her son had been shot four times execution style and
was dead. There is no policeman in this story. Nor is there
an Al Sharpton. Nor will there be an Al Sharpton. You see,
this young man died at the hands of a gang-banger in the
neighborhood and if one protests here, they may be putting
themselves or their family in jeopardy.

Two opportunities for righteous indignation. A police
shooting, where there may or may not have been a policeman who was being threatened by a young man with marijuana in his system, and a simple case where someone just
killed an innocent nine-year-old who may have been in the
wrong place at the wrong time. In the first case, the media
can't get enough and a town is under siege. In the second, end
of story. You decide.

Fall Is Here

September 7, 2014

Fall is a season you either love or hate. It's a time when nature sends a message: We're shutting down for a while. The leaves are turning color and falling, not to return until spring. The days grow shorter, with less sunshine.

Those of us who have grown older feel the seasons and equate them to our lives. We sense we are shutting down like the seasons. Grandkids are off to college and we're off to the doctor for some new ailment. Our energy level is like the sunshine. In the fall of our lives, we have less and less.

Today, I was tempted to drive around the neighborhood and take pictures of all the front porches that were installed right after 9/11. Nearly every house, including mine, added something like a porch in front of the house. It was a big trend, bigger than the ice bucket challenge. People wanted to be more neighborly. If we just went back to that, maybe it would solve some of our problems. Sit in front of the house and talk to the neighbors who walked by. Get to know those dog walkers.

I was in and out of the neighborhood a lot over Labor Day. Not once, in dozens of houses, did I see a single person sitting on their front porch. Like most fads, it came and went. We spend our lives indoors.

So, fall changes nothing in the neighborhood. Kids will still sit in front of the TV or the computer or on the couch with the iPhone. The only change is the grill in the back of the house will be covered for the season.

We are back to our lives as isolationists. This is a season that has overtaken the country. It puts a chill on society. President Reagan once said, "It's morning in America," in his political commercial that goes around the internet every election season. Maybe it's time to say, "It's fall in America," for a multitude of reasons.

Teacher Absenteeism

September 24, 2014

Here we go. It's wrong to criticize teachers in America. Especially when your sister was a career teacher. And, when many of your friends spent their careers in the classroom.

US student test scores keep dropping vs. the rest of the world. When politicians approach this problem, it's always money. We spend more per student than the rest of the world, so how do we reconcile that? Charter schools do well in inner cities, but they aren't union so we can't have more of those.

Okay, let's test students and pay and fire teachers based on test scores. Most of us agree this is a good plan. It's accountability in a union workplace, right? Whoa, scores were bad. What happens? Teachers just go back and change the test scores so everyone can get paid and keep their jobs. The teacher of the year in Wisconsin was let go a few years ago because she had no union seniority when the cutbacks came. Teachers in New York City with serious discipline problems, including sexual abuse, sit in rooms and do nothing and get paid because they can't be fired.

Let's look at another problem everyone sweeps under the

rug. The school year for students and teachers is a breath-taking 186 days. A burger flipper at McDonald's puts in 250 days. That 186 is far too rigorous. The average teacher in America misses eleven days a year. Chronic slackers miss eighteen days or more and they comprise 28% of the national teaching population. Every day a teacher doesn't show up, a substitute gets paid, and kids aren't taught anything.

Put this on the pile of educational reform issues facing this country. Just keep cruising along and say, "Teachers in America are great," and wonder why so many young people are unemployable in this country.

Denial is not a river in Egypt. It's the educational system in this country not being reformed from top to bottom.

Uniforms That Count

October 4, 2014

Every day for the past month, we have been inundated with stories about the retirement of Derek Jeter and Paul Konerko. Two great athletes who stuck with their respective teams and showed loyalty to their cities despite offers to go elsewhere for more money. It's unusual today. I have no issue with these stories. I admire both men for their class and athletic records.

But, I do have issue with the absence of stories about true heroes. We have been at war for over a decade. We do see stories about our military men and women who come home and surprise their kids at a school. We see stories about a local reserve unit shipping out. We see Obama pinning a medal of honor on someone who should have gotten that medal fifty years ago. We see where a former governor sues and wins in court to get money from the widow of a Navy Seal who was killed at a shooting range by a fellow veteran suffering from PTSD. Shame on you, Jessie Ventura.

I was born a month after Pearl Harbor. When we were kids, we played war games. We used sticks as guns and rocks as hand grenades. We fought the same people our dads were fighting. Then we fought the Koreans when our neighbors went off to war again and some never came back.

Some of this is due to the way our country treated and presented the men who were protecting our country. Hollywood stars then did go off to war. Pick one now who would do that. Ted Williams was an ace in WWII and lost baseball time to shoot down enemy planes. Neither Jeter nor Konerko come close to Ted's statistics, despite his military service.

Isn't it time we put our true heroes above those who play a kid's game? Shouldn't we see stories of those who fought for our country in the past decade? We tend to cover up the real work of war unless Obama, the worst commander in chief in my lifetime, wants a photo op.

We don't trash them like we did my generation who fought in Vietnam, the most embarrassing thing this country has ever done, but we don't recognize them either. We honor them at sporting events holding flags, but is that enough? Can't we have both? Sports heroes like Derek and Paul, and military heroes, with the latter taking priority over the former.

Thanks for Your Readership

December 27, 2014

The NSB blog hit new records in all categories for 2014. I thank you for taking your valuable time to read my amateur thoughts. This work is still dedicated to my grandkids, who will have a lower standard of living in this great country than my kids enjoyed. We have been on a very bad path and the next election will determine whether we get off that path or auger deeper into becoming a lesser country.

Small businesses make mistakes and go out of business. Large corporations do the same. Huge countries do, as well. The Roman, Dutch, and British Empires have shown that. The USSR, more recently, broke up because their economic model failed. In my humble opinion, this country still has the people, the resources, the energy, and the determination to remain a job-creating economic engine with the political model that makes all that work.

That political model was not socialism, the model we have tried for the past six years and will continue to utilize if many have their way. Most Americans agree the government can't run anything. But many want to see that happen. If they win, my grandkids lose, simple as that. It isn't just the Democratic party, it's the media, Hollywood, and the educational system, from grade school through graduate school; it's the labor unions, those who don't want to work, those who came here illegally, over-the-top environmentalists, most lawyers, and most of several big states (you know them well). That's a lot of opposition. It's a tipping point and I fear we will tip. We all need to work harder to try and keep this country great.

At my age, I'm unelectable, can't put on the uniform, can only contribute in financial ways, volunteer, and write this blog. Hopefully, I can influence a few people to do more than I'm able to do at this point in my life. I can look back and have regrets that I didn't do more. I see Bruce Rauner, a billionaire who was just elected governor of Illinois, and I fervently hope he's doing that for the same reason I'm writing this blog: to save a state that is the dysfunctional poster child for the rest of America.

2015

Time Moves On

January 1, 2015

Time moves on. I now have two granddaughters in college, one at University of Indiana and the second at University of Texas. Every day I am thankful that I was given this extra time after the plane crash in 1989 to enjoy the achievements of my beautiful, nice, smart grandkids. I feel it is an obligation to keep adding whatever effort these blog thoughts might produce to help make this country offer them the same opportunities offered to my kids and me.

So we write on, hoping it might make a difference. Last year was another record year for readers, so new people keep coming here and that is encouraging.

Statistics for College Tuition

January 5, 2015

Elizabeth Warren and the academics in this world are looting college students and putting the stiff wind to their faces for the rest of their lives. Here are a few statistics to support my charges.

College tuition has gone up 1,100% since the late 1970s, while inflation in the same period is up 240%.

In 2010, a study was done. It compared time in the classroom for professors to twenty years earlier. Their teaching load is shrinking from twelve to fifteen hours a week to six to nine hours a week, yet 75% of a college budget is spent on personnel expense. The B.S. put out by colleges says professors must do increased research, more extensive classroom prep time, and committee work, plus administrative and counseling time. Translation: your kid's tuition pays their salaries, but they double-dip with research and consulting time. And, like most bureaucracies, they keep adding administrators, and that means more meetings to keep the non-teaching executives busy. Result: you pay a professor $200K to teach two to three classes a week for twenty-eight weeks a year.

To the bureaucracy issue, the number of college administrators has increased 50% faster than professors in the past fifteen years. Now, it's one per 3.5 students. Can you believe that? That's a lot of babysitters for the professors and the students. What are all these clerks doing? Building the college president's empire, that's what. Remember, it's free money with zero accountability. Who cares? Do college presidents care they are destroying the futures of their students with student loans that may never be able to be repaid?

Maybe one in the entire country cares.

Mitch Daniels, the former governor of Indiana, is the president of Purdue. He's been attacking the system and making some progress. But the state universities of California hired none other than Janet Napolitano, former governor of Arizona, to run their numerous state colleges. She almost bankrupted Arizona, while Daniels balanced the budget in Indiana. Old habits are hard to break.

Over the past twenty years, the building spree at colleges has doubled. Not for classrooms, but for all sorts of prestigious frills like climbing walls, luxury dorms, student centers that rival the Four Seasons, and other such nonsense. A few university presidents need to go to prison and share cells with those hated Wall Street people. Lock up Napolitano with Bernie Madoff—a perfect marriage. Except Bernie stole from the rich and Janet is stealing from the kids who borrow money to go to college. Elizabeth Warren doesn't like Bernie, but she and Janet are friends.

Here's a thought. Perhaps parents who have young kids in elementary to high school need to worry less about whether your favorite college team is going to make the playoffs and spend more time trying to figure out where the $250K is coming from for each of your rug rat's college tuition. Less about whether that pro coach will take the $8 million a year to coach the football team and more about how to fire the jerk who is mishandling the entire institution. Believe me, this is serious. With the single exception of Mitch Daniels, there is not one college president anywhere in this country who cares about fixing this problem. There may not be one idiot in Washington, D.C., who thinks about it more than once a year. There may not be a parent with children younger than fifteen who cares. But, there are one hell of a lot of young people between sixteen and thirty who are worried sick. Try to pay back a $60,000 student loan when you are driving a cab with that degree in humanities and living in the parents' basement.

Wake up, folks. You slept through the housing bubble. You watched while our federal government let the money flow through Freddie and Fannie and the FHA and forced banks to make bad loans in the name of diversity. When it destroyed the economy, the culprits got off scot-free. Now, it's flowing again to colleges through grants and to kids in the form of bad loans. People paid the price when houses and jobs were lost. Markets went to hell and banks were bailed out. If you want to stop the train wreck this time, you better act now, or just watch in a few years as the cars pile up.

The Differences Between a Leader and an Obama

February 27, 2015

Respect and trust, in equal parts, are necessary to be a great leader. Both must be earned; they can't be requested. Respect comes from getting results. Trust comes from getting the results the right way.

Communication is critical to both. Not just communications in front of large audiences delivered with a teleprompter, but day-to-day communications. Selling one idea is as important as selling ten because that's how you get to ten. Bringing people along with big plans is how results happen. Leaving multitudes behind is how distrust happens.

Leaders must speak the truth as they believe it in their hearts. Ask Brian Williams. He was considered a leader by his organization. Not by me, since like another prominent leader, he just read a teleprompter and appeared on late night talk shows and cracked wise. You only get one chance to tell a lie. Many, including Brian Williams, said George W. Bush lied about the WMDs in Iraq. That includes those who saw the same set of intelligence and voted to invade Iraq (can you say Hillary Clinton?). Leaders do make mistakes. The batting average will determine the success of the leader.

From the CEO of a major corporation to the owner of a small business, decisions can't be short term. Neither business can run on feedback from today. You can't run a state or a country based on polling. You must believe in what you are doing and that it will work in the long run. Dig in and keep bringing employees and voters along with you. Therein lies the rub with President Obama.

In his heart, he believes in socialism. He wants to make this country a socialist country. But, he can't say that. He can't tell us what he really wants for America. It goes all the way back to the conversation with Joe the Plumber. To tell the truth will not only destroy him, but the Democratic Party, as well. So, he lives a lie and tries to bring this country to a place where a majority of the country does not want to go. It is a recipe for failure, as we are seeing.

Look to places like Canada and the United Kingdom, and you know how socialized medicine works. You don't get to keep your doctor; your government assigns you a doctor. In this country, to get to socialized medicine, you must do it in steps. Step one, Obamacare, moving toward the system. To attain the ultimate goal, you must lie every step of the way, as the professor who was outed telling fellow professors, "You must lie to a gullible public to get what you want." Obama greets the sunrise every day knowing he must lie his way through the day. He can't just call a news conference and say: "A socialist system is best for this country, and I will take you there." It's his only goal, his only hope, his only plan. He cares not about the rest of it. Foreign policy, ISIS, etc.—doesn't care.

Here's his latest example: a plan deceivingly referred to as "Net Neutrality" involves declaring the internet a public utility and gives the FCC the power to decide what internet service providers can charge and how they operate. This is not only a direct attack on the free market, but it will also result in an increase in internet access fees for millions of consumers in America. It's a massive tax on the middle class, plain and simple.

So, he fails as a leader. He replaces Jimmy Carter as the worst president of all time and takes his party down with him. His vision does not fit the country's vision. When the majority of the public get it, despite his lies, he is sunk. Fewer and fewer are following him, including much of his party who see their fate.

Obama Lecture Series #4,975

March 2, 2015

Once again, our esteemed president finds it necessary to take a group to the woodshed. This time, it's the entire international community. He wants to puff out his chest and tell them why we have had no terrorist attacks since he's been president and what they need to do to stop any in their countries.

In the fight against violent extremism, President Barack Obama has argued the United States has one thing going for it that Europe doesn't: a long tradition of warmly embracing its immigrants, including Muslims.

With the Islamic State group spreading and terrorists gaining strength in the Middle East and Africa, Obama has sought to use this week's White House Summit on Countering Violent Extremism to urge the world to broaden its response far beyond military interventions. US airstrikes have managed to blunt some of the militants' gains in Iraq and Syria, but they don't address the extreme ideologies that underpin deadly groups such as ISIS, al-Shabaab, and Boko Haram.

"If we're going to prevent people from being susceptible to the false promises of extremism, then the international community has to offer something better—and the United States intends to do its part," Obama told the summit Wednesday. He planned to speak again Thursday when delegates from about sixty-five countries gather for the summit's closing session at the state department.

His state department people have been delivering the latest Obama message regarding the roots of Islamic terrorism. This message seems to be received rather poorly by whatever audience is receiving the message. The new spin: "Islamic terrorism is the outgrowth of economic hardship. If those young people only had good jobs, they wouldn't be joining ISIS or whatever group they join."

There you have it. America does it right again. Largely due to a great leader who sees things other leaders never see. Or is it the opposite? Do you know how much countries like the United Kingdom and France, which have huge Muslim populations relative to the United States, will enjoy this speech? Or the wealthy family in Minnesota whose son has run off to Syria will applaud this logic of Obama? Or the dreamers who just had the Obama rug pulled out from under them by a judge in Texas who said Obama is not a king?

Thank God for the remote on the TV. I stopped at lecture

number two. My dad told me as a young lad if you blow your own horn too much, someone will use it for a funnel. The world is pouring water into Obama's horn so fast, he's being waterboarded.

A Question My Grandkids Will Ask

March 23, 2015

Someday, long after I'm gone, my grandkids will ask their parents this question: "Mom/Dad, we think it's great that your generation and the prior generation put such emphasis on diversity, but couldn't you find a competent minority and an honest, qualified female president?"

C'mon folks, Hillary Clinton is a dishonest, incompetent, senile female. She answers her latest scandal with the question, "Isn't it time we had a female president?"

There are over 300 million people in this country, and more than half are female. A large majority of those are well educated, honest, and have done some very remarkable things in their young lives. Is Hillary the best we have? Was Barack the best minority? An unqualified man with no intention of doing anything but campaigning for eight years, since that's all he ever did.

If you watched Hillary lie about her email illegality, you knew it was a lie—a blatant lie. Go ahead; elect her. I won't have to answer the questions from my grandkids. You will.

Fixing Obamacare

April 6, 2015

All the costs and taxes used to support Obamacare should be totaled and published for the world to see. All this so 8 million people can have insurance who didn't or couldn't get insurance before. It is not cost-effective.

If you are retired, like me, you have watched the insurance deductions from your Social Security and that of your spouse, if married, go up and your net benefit go down. Remember, you paid for both, or at least, paid into both. Soon, Medicare will be all you will get from Social Security. The rest will go to support Obamacare. Keep in mind: AARP did this to you.

Businesses are paying billions to comply with the paperwork requirements of Obamacare. I just read where a medium-sized business showed it will cost them $100,000 to comply. They hired two people just to do the compliance with the law. The National Small Business Association estimates it will cost $15,000 for small businesses to comply. That will kick in next January when all businesses with fifty or more employees must comply. This doesn't include the premium increases that have kicked in to cover the insurance for the high-risk who get coverage from the plan.

Here's the solution. Today, you and I pay for the folks who have a house in a high-risk flood area. They can't get insurance and it's for good reason. The floods come and the damage follows and they take the insurance and rebuild on the same lot. The hurricanes and floods come again and the money you and I pay into the fund covers the repair again and again.

Obamacare would be much cheaper if handled the same way. Create a fund for people who can't get, or won't buy, health insurance. Pay their health care out of the fund. It would be far cheaper than hiring hundreds of new government workers in the IRS to monitor Obamacare, businesses paying millions for compliance of the paperwork, and people paying more and more for their existing insurance so 8 million people are covered.

Let's do the right thing the right way for a change. Hopefully, the Supreme Court will help the brain-dead Republican Party figure this out by eliminating Obamacare and forcing a do-over.

Hillary Clinton's Scandal in Terms Even I Can Understand

April 30, 2015

If it isn't a sound bite today, no one listens. Complex scandals are too much unless it involves a Hollywood star.

Here's my sound bite: Hillary was involved in brokering a deal that turned over one-fifth of our precious uranium production to the Russians on a long-term contract. Uranium is the stuff that is used in nuclear bombs. It could grow to 50% over time.

Immediately thereafter, Billy gets a $500,000 speaking gig in Moscow. Then the Clintons get a $2 million donation to their so-called foundation. But, they don't report the donation. Some Canadian reporter finds the transaction. Then, and only then, is it reported, along with several other amended tax filings for said foundation.

So, the Russians can now resell our precious uranium to the Iranians for a profit that more than covers the pittance they gave the Clintons. How do you feel about this deal, Israel?

This is just one deal the traveling salesman, Ms. Secretary of State, was peddling as she traveled the world. So many countries, so much money to reel in, so little time. When this breaks, she resigns from the board of the family foundation.

Go ahead, vote for this despicable person; demonstrate your ignorance once again when it comes to this family. Just remember—if you don't believe the money issues, who would ever broker a deal to give our uranium to Russia?

Is Anyone's Word Good Anymore?

June 18, 2015

A long, long time ago, my dad taught me about giving and keeping my word. I made a commitment to the wrestling coach at CMU to go there to wrestle. He helped me get an academic scholarship, a field-house job, and a couple of other things to help pay the bills. Then, the University of Michigan wrestling team stopped by on a trip and our high school coach set up a scrimmage. I did well in a match with my counterpart at U of M and received a letter from the U of M coach offering me a place on his team. I was very excited. When I got home and told my folks, my dad took me aside and said, "Son, what part of commitment don't you understand? You told the CMU coach you were coming and that's what you are going to do. End of conversation." At school the next day, I told my wrestling coach about the offer from U of M. He said, "You are committed to CMU, aren't you?"

Funny thing about those two men, my dad and my coach. Dad served in the navy in the Pacific in WWII and my coach was a marine on Iwo Jima. Guess they knew about commitment. I admired them, and today, I admire them even more. They're part of the Greatest Generation for good reason.

I am reading today's sports page in *The Chicago Tribune*. One article addresses Russell Wilson's purchase of injury insurance, since he is on the fourth year of his $1.5 million-a-year rookie contract. He wants to protect the big contract that's coming down the road.

The other article addresses the contract dispute Martellus Bennett is having with the Chicago Bears. He has two years left on the four-year contract he signed for $20 million. He didn't attend any of the informal team activities. He did show up for mini-camp out of shape and out of sorts. He doesn't know if he will play this year for the measly $5 million. He says an NFL contract is no different than a cell phone contract—people break them all the time. Or a lease on an apartment. You see an apartment you like better, just pick up and move.

My coach died last year, and there were literally hundreds of notes sent to the online obituary. He touched so many with his character and humanity. He was a true tough guy, a decorated marine, a college football player and wrestler, and a stern disciplinarian. But one lady said it all in his obituary. She worked in his office. He asked who she was going to the prom with that month. She said she didn't have a date. That night, five boys called and asked her to the prom. She said she turned them all down because she knew coach had twisted arms. But, she never forgot coach for caring.

It's all going away. The men and women of the Greatest Generation, and even the lessons they taught us. Somewhere along the way, Russell Wilson had a parent or a coach or a mentor who taught him the meaning of his word. But far too many, like Mr. Bennett, didn't. Sadly, it seems, most of them reside in pro sports and politics.

Lectures from Obama

June 28, 2015

It can't be over soon enough. The entire world is very tired of the weekly lectures from Professor Obama. The great orator does not make speeches; he lectures. The tragic shooting in the church in Charleston is the latest. He even slipped in the "n" word to spice up the lecture. I will say right up front that I'm going to criticize the man, so, in his eyes and those of his supporters, this will be a racist blog. There will not be one memorable speech in his eight years as president. Not even one sound bite. The closest thing might be, "If you like your doctor, you can keep your doctor." Sad.

His lectures have a common theme. There is a villain and he's the victim or the savior. Guns are the villains in the aforementioned example. For years, it was George W. Bush. It's been Fox News.

I remember when we had a leader as president. Ronald Reagan spoke about a vision. Or, if seeking approval for something, he explained why we needed to do what he was suggesting. It's called getting the country on board. It's called leadership.

This Professor Obama is a one-trick pony. He sets up a straw man, then he throws rocks at the poor straw man. He even threw rocks at the Supreme Court in a State of the Union Address, a definite faux pas. He's thrown rocks at the Republican Party for six and a half years. Even when he had the majority in both houses, he threw his rocks.

See, professors don't live in the real world. But as one professor's wife I know often says, "My husband is seldom right, but never in doubt." Professors have a captive audience. They have all the power. They are not leaders; that's why they are professors. Many of us learned from professors but in most cases, we could have learned the same from a book. After all, that's where the professor learned what he professes.

So, we grow tired of the lectures and the professor grows boring. We sleep in the class or skip the class and read the text. If we disagree with the professor, woe to us.

I will close with a "What goes around, comes around" story. I was working on an MBA at night. I had a professor for a class, Law in the Business Society. A paper was required at the end of the semester. I wrote mine on no-fault divorce. Even then, I had a distaste for professors, and the professor, David Jones, was a divorce attorney who was teaching the night class. This is before no-fault divorce, and to get a divorce, one had to prove a wrong. I wrote the paper making the case for the elimination of the "fault" in divorce law. I was a visionary, even then. I got a B on the paper with comments, "Solid piece of work, but faulty logic." I went to see Professor Jones to argue my case for an A. I lost the argument.

Several years later, I was in the real estate department of my company. Someone brought me a proposal to hire part-time counsel to do some routine real estate law for us. The attorney was none other than David Jones. I made the phone call personally to Mr. Jones, Esq., to tell him we wouldn't be using his services. I started the conversation by saying, "I see by your resume that you were primarily a divorce attorney. Why are you doing real estate?" His answer: "No-fault divorce has cut way back on the time required in the divorce area, so I needed to diversify." That took us back to my paper and when we got there, Mr. Jones said, "I think I'm not going to get this job, right?"

See, even professors have a lick of common sense now and then.

Fix the Food Stamp Problem

July 9, 2015

It's another step on the way to Greece. Obama has expanded the food stamp program 70% since he took office in 2009, with a record 50 million Americans on the program.

One state, Maine, found a way to cut the food stamp population. The number of food stamp recipients in the state was

12,000. Then the governor, Paul R. LePage, a Republican, imposed a requirement that recipients work at least six hours a week in a volunteer program. Guess what? The number receiving food stamps dropped to 2,530. Where did they go now? To the food pantries. Rather than put in a rigorous six-hour week as a volunteer, they opted to drop out of the stamp program.

The governor calls this group the ABAWDS: able-bodied adults without minor dependents. Unless they work twenty hours per week, take state job-training courses, or volunteer for the six hours a week, they get a three-month limit on food stamps every three years.

Let's see, if a president who cared about the $18 trillion-plus debt and this country becoming Greece initiated the same plan at the national level, it would cut the national program from 50 million to 10 million. Plus, all those volunteer hours would be beneficial to the country. The 10 million who weren't too lazy to volunteer six hours a week could do a lot of good around the country.

If the intent is to increase the numbers of voters on the program, not eliminate the cost, then that's a bad idea.

If we want to leave a decent country for our kids and grandkids, this is the type of thing we need to consider.

Style vs. Substance

July 25, 2015

I detest the arrogance of Donald Trump; his look, his walk, his superior attitude. But I'm not voting for style. We just did style for six years. A president who is twenty miles wide, fifty miles long, and one inch deep. Here's what I want you to consider.

Trump has attacked two issues so far with a vengeance. One, the porous border, and two, the VA issues. I have posted dozens of blogs about these two issues. In the first, he said illegals coming across the border commit crimes. For that, he's skewered. In the second, he went after John McCain. Let's address the border. Yes, many drugs, guns, and criminals come across that border. He says he will fix the problem.

Now, the second issue. The VA problem is not fixed by putting Bob McDonald in charge. It may be worse. It was discovered in John McCain's back yard in Phoenix. John was heroic for what he lived through in Vietnam. But, for that we need not hire him to fix problems like the VA in Phoenix. John is senile and needs to retire to the wife's beer business in Arizona.

Now, tick off the list of candidates running for president from both parties. Name one who can fix either problem. They are all blah, blah, blah, just like Obama. All will name a committee, initiate a new department like Homeland Security, or hire a Bob McDonald, who failed at Procter & Gamble and is failing again in this job.

Trump would approach both issues the way all business people would go after them. He wouldn't hire a political hack like Janet Napolitano, who has failed at everything to fix any problem. He would hire someone from his own organization, someone who has succeeded at large jobs. Then, he would hold that person accountable for getting the job done. He would have regular reviews with that person. He might fail, but progress would be made and improvements would happen. It's the old "skins on the wall" question. If you have a multitude of successes and have a system that works, you have some right to be a bit arrogant.

We, as a country, have skins on the wall. We are the big winner. Trump won't bow to a Saudi Prince. He won't fail to mention what he doesn't like about a Mexico or a China to a leader of either country. He's a sausage maker. Not pretty to watch, but he makes good sausage. We just hired a billionaire, Bruce Rauner, to fix Illinois. He's making sausage. Not pretty to watch, but it's the last hope for Illinois before bankruptcy. He took the job for one reason: to fix the state. He's beholden to no one. He's trying, despite daily wars with the Democratic politicians who broke the state and want to finish the job. I'm not sold on the idea that I can tolerate Trump as president. But, I do believe he is the type of president we need to save our bacon. The rest are all blah, blah, blah.

A Week Without TV

August 9, 2015

Last week was spent in northern Michigan on beautiful Walloon Lake with eleven family members. We rented a place with three TVs. Not once did anyone turn on a single TV. Only once did I glance at a newspaper. That was a *USA Today* my wife bought, which is a left-wing version of a McDonald's drive-through.

Occasionally someone who was checking their phone would mention a piece of news from the outside world, like the latest Patrick Kane (Blackhawk hockey star) shenanigan—the rape investigation in his home in New York state.

We spent our time at the lake on a speedboat, pontoon boat, or wave runner. Skiing, tubing, fishing, or just enjoying the multimillion-dollar cottages on the lake that go back many generations. The air was fresh and the conversation around the firepit at night was never too serious. It was like a trip back in time. All the way back to when I was a kid on a family vacation at nearby Burt Lake. The occasion was our fiftieth wedding anniversary celebration, and the family did us proud with a surprise renewal of the vows, with them conducting the ceremony. It was a beautiful week.

Ernest Hemmingway grew up on Walloon Lake and his family cottage is still there. He claimed the fishing was good, but you can't prove it by me.

Never once did I feel I was missing anything from the outside world. That includes the Republican presidential debates. It was detox at its finest.

So, this blog reflects all the news I can report about the state of the country and the world this week.

Obama: Seldom Right, but Never in Doubt

October 10, 2015

Let's give the man the benefit of the doubt. Maybe our president is not explicitly trying to destroy the country. He's just not very good at the job, simple as that. It's no more complex than an imperfect human who's wrong most of the time.

His background for the job was sketchy to start. He never really had a job. Whatever job he had, he was always spending most of his time working toward the next one. As a lawyer, he never spent any time in court. As a professor, he never went to work. As a community organizer, he was working toward being a politician. As a state senator, he was working toward a bigger role, voting present when he was present, which was seldom. As a US senator, he was voting present, fundraising, and campaigning for president. Perhaps in all these jobs he was wrong all the time, too.

Now, he's got the big job and there's no bigger job to work toward. He's forced to make decisions. His batting average is not different from what it's been on every job he's ever had— near zero, wrong all the time—but with real consequences now. Scary, isn't it? We put a man in office twice who can't make good decisions.

Now, we're interviewing for his replacement. Will we do it again? Very possibly. Let's just look at Hillary as an example. She married Bill, which was questionable decision. A womanizer who is still a womanizer. She was involved in the Whitewater decision. She tried to push through health care reform as first lady and got Bill in trouble right away.

She did nothing as a US senator to keep from having any record, except she did vote to invade Iraq. She was running for president. Her run against Obama was so bad, we got Obama. The foreign policy she implemented has us in trouble all over the world. Let's say she had no ulterior motive for having all her emails on a personal server (right); that means she makes bad decisions. Now all of those decisions add up to Bernie Sanders ahead of her in the polls in New Hampshire and closing in Iowa.

I guess all of this is as depressing for you as it is for me. Takes me to a place where I must look at Trump whose decisions add up to a net worth of $10 billion. That's a lot of hits and few whiffs. It means he has hired the right people to work for him, picked the right things to invest in, and juggled a lot of balls—and few have dropped. When it comes time to make the big decisions for the country, I like his odds vs. the others on the slate from both parties.

I'm not looking for someone who can read a teleprompter and can play the political game. I can bring you thousands of those. All Obama ever did was study to be a president. All Hillary has ever done is wait to take the job she believes is rightfully hers. I'm looking for someone who can step up to the plate and pick the right pitch to hit most of the time. A doctor can heal the batters' injuries, but he's not a hitter. A businesswoman who struck out most of the time is a bad choice. A vice president who has been hit in the head with pitches too often, no. An eighty-year-old who mostly worries that everyone should have the same batting average and fans should get to play, no. Then the rest are career politicians who should be in the booth describing the game since they are all talk, no.

Guess we have only one hitter in this game, and we can

only hope he's not like the Mighty Casey from Mudville and doesn't strike out. I'm sending the Donald up to bat.

Obama Energy, Inc.

November 9, 2015

No president in history has gotten it wrong on energy more than Obama. He's betting the farm on unproven alternative energy, and if he's wrong, the farm will be up for grabs.

He blew billions on bad ideas like Solyndra. His failure to make this work does not deter him from trying to curtail hydrocarbon production in any form. Hence, the Keystone Pipeline is dead. Cheap crude from Canada coming to Nebraska for redistribution to Gulf Coast refineries is a bad idea, why? Obama and his progressives are against Canadian tar sand production. Will not building the pipeline change anything? No, but the environmental lobby will keep donating to the Democrats. Canadian oil will go to China.

He has closed coal mines in West Virginia. No Democrat will be elected dog catcher in that state again. He has closed coal-fired power plants using executive privilege through the EPA. Does he care if there is replacement power? No, doesn't matter. Does it matter to the poor and working people who have higher electricity bills? Of course.

He knows one thing for sure. He and the Democrats will never be blamed for any of these bad decisions. Want proof? Here it is.

In the summer of 2014 when oil prices were going up, Obama made this speech: "I have unleashed my law enforcers to make sure that acts of manipulation, fraud, or other illegal activity are not behind increases the price that consumers pay at the pump." See, the politicians who create the problems have a compliant media to point the finger at others when the problem occurs. It's been that way since 1974. Why are the speculators who Obama sent the law enforcers after not driving oil prices back up? They didn't drive them down and they can't drive them back up.

Despite Obama, the oil industry has used technology they developed to generate production on private lands. This has driven prices down and created a recession in the oil patch, curtailing new drilling.

Every decision Obama and his progressives have made and will make will lead to higher energy prices in the future. He wants to set an example for the world that we are doing more than any other nation for climate change. That's tantamount to having the nicest lawn in the ghetto. Your house is a wreck, shots are fired at you weekly, neighbor's dogs and kids run wild over your lawn, but it looks really good.

There is precious little common sense in Washington, D.C., and virtually none in Obama Energy, INC.

Syrian Refugees

November 17, 2015

The decision to bring in some number of Syrian refugees (10,000 to 180,000—numbers seem to range between these two) is a hot debate topic. When it was discovered that a refugee was involved in the Paris attacks, the debate escalated.

The Obama position revolves around dogma. He says we need to be true to our values. Sounds nice, like so many things his speechwriters put on his teleprompter, but what does it mean? I think it revolves around two statements we are hearing a lot these days. One, "We are a nation of immigrants." That's a lot like "true to our values." This gets used a lot with the 11 million illegals here, as well. Two, "Give me your tired, your poor"—the inscription on the Statue of Liberty, a gift from France.

If I understand all of this, I'm supposed to set aside all common sense and salute whatever crazy idea any leader puts forth. "We are a country of laws" is also being used. This doesn't require a lot of interpretation, since we can read laws—like immigration laws. These laws say those who snuck in go back. My friend has a daughter-in-law who came here illegally. She and his son have four kids. She went back and it took well over a year for her to fulfill the laws to return to this country. That's how it should work for the remaining 11 million as well. But, I'm supposed to buy the baloney that we owe them something for committing a crime and it's based on us being a nation of immigrants. Excuse me, those seeing that inscription did not see it on a rock by the Rio Grande. They came through the front door.

Now, Obama has done another "line in the sand" deal. For political reasons only, he wants to import Syrian refugees. Again, it's based on "who we are" and "our values." My values don't include importing terrorism. My values don't ask me to set aside all common sense for dogma. Obama dogma. Some say our invasion of Iraq is the reason for the terrorism. Really, do you remember "freedom fries"? That came about because the French refused to support us in Iraq. If ISIS is an outgrowth of Iraq, why did they attack the country that refused to invade Iraq?

Let's examine all the illogical dogma distributed by this president. He said he wanted to close Gitmo because it was a factor in our being hated by Islamic followers. He wanted to try them in civil courts. He wanted to apologize for the enhanced interrogation tactics. He called Ft. Hood a workplace incident. He put some dumb label on terrorism that no one can remember. He has never once uttered the words "radical Islam." He bowed to the Saudi prince. Despite all of this, ISIS, or ISIL as he alone calls them, are on my TV telling me they are coming here. And, I'm supposed to believe the man who always gets it wrong will get it right and vet the refugees so no bad guys slip in. And, it is bad guys, because few women or elderly men are coming.

Here's why we have ISIS or ISIL, Mr. President. After every war in our history, we left troops behind. We still have them in Japan, Germany, and South Korea. But no, you, Mr. Genius, knew we didn't have to do that in Iraq. And, you didn't. We left behind a weak group of Iraqi troops with a lot of US weapons, and guess what? Radical Islam, which has declared war on all non-Muslims, scooped them up, took over, and moved into other parts of the Middle East.

Now, based on that judgment of yours and a few pithy

comments, I'm supposed to accept a few boatloads of young men from Syria? When your own CIA, FBI, and Department of Homeland Security people are saying there is no way they can keep an eye on them? No dice. No way, no how.

Government and Golf

December 22, 2015

There's an old saying in the Middle East: "My grandfather rode a camel, my father drove a Model T, I drive a Mercedes, my son has his own jet, and my grandson will ride a camel." Many of us think this is looking like it might apply in this country.

The modern game of golf is thought to have begun in Scotland in 1457. There were 267 clubs in the United States in 1910. My house is less than a mile from one of the oldest, Chicago Golf Club, which was established in 1880. By 2013, there were 10,600 clubs.

When I started this blog, it was because I felt my grandkids will be the first generation to have a lower standard of living than their parents. The country seemed to be going in the wrong direction, and I felt Obama would accelerate that demise. At the same time, golf began to lose popularity and the sport was struggling. The only correlation was poor leadership.

The country was veering away from the foundations that made it great. From capitalism to socialism. It didn't make any sense, since there was not one example of a successful socialist country. But our leaders were being elected to do that job and the public was buying the idea. It's self-destruction by willfully eliminating manufacturing due to climate issues and hence a stagnant economy with fewer people finding jobs or choosing to work. Over a trillion dollars in student loans that will not be repaid. Trillions more in promised retirement pay that can't be paid. Eighteen trillion in debt that is growing. For reasons that no one can explain, none of this destruction can be halted. The good times were gone and the music stopped, but the crowd danced on.

The sport of golf had experienced growth from 1910 to the early 2000s and no one thought it would stop. But, it has. There are 643 closed courses since 2006. With 4 million fewer golfers today than in 2005 and a 5% drop in players between the ages of 15–24, there will be more courses closing—between 130–160 next year. The economy has made millennials tentative about commitment; they are glued to phones and have short attention spans. Golfers are dying or becoming too old to play the game. They are not being replaced by younger golfers. The leadership of the golf business, the USGA, the Royal and Ancients, and the PGA are mostly ancients. They see it, but they have no clue how to fix it. Hence, it won't get fixed.

Here's an example why. The Waste Management Phoenix Open in Arizona draws over 500,000 fans. The sixteenth hole has 20,000 fans, and there are 155 skyboxes around the 162-yard par 3 hole. The caddies used to race to the green, but the PGA stopped that for fear a caddie might get hurt. The golfers used to throw token gifts to the fans, but the PGA thought it might be unsafe. Get the picture? A PGA event does not publicize attendance, but most would be lucky to draw in a week what the Waste Management draws in a day. The

PGA had nothing to do with how this was created. It was done by a group of volunteers called the Thunderbirds. But the PGA, and some pros who don't like the atmosphere, will try their best to destroy it and make sure it's not duplicated anywhere else. It's called fun. The millennials love it and turn out in droves.

So, in both cases, the country and the sport, there is ample evidence of problems. In the country, there is time to fix the problems, but not much. This election will decide whether we get four more years of socialism. In the sport, it's too late. You can't replace a generation of people who don't play the sport. So it's more courses closing, fewer players, and continued bad leadership watching the train wreck until the first responders are called.

Want to watch your country follow the sport of golf down the tubes? Then vote for Hillary or Bernie or another attorney who talks a good game but can't run anything. It's a pivotal election. You see it as well as the leaders of golf see it, but they didn't see it when it was fixable. Care about your grandkids? Better act.

2016

Trump May Win in 2016

January 1, 2016

Happy New Year.

The pundits and the establishment tell us it can't happen. Trump is not "presidential," they say. He attacks, he has no filter between the brain and the mouth, and he's not professional.

What does being presidential mean? Does it mean spending years attacking Bush, then the entire Republican party for your failures? Does it mean never speaking without a teleprompter and when you do, stuttering and muttering like a kid giving his first speech? Does it mean engaging in buffoonery like a First Lady doing a rap video, being on a Bear Grylls special, or driving Jerry Seinfeld around the White House in a Corvette?

Here's the real kicker. Those pundits and establishment hot shots are not respected by the voters. Karl Rove doesn't understand that Trump was right calling him an idiot and pointing out his little trip down the hall with Megyn Kelly on election night when he refused to believe Romney was going to lose to Obama. Karl epitomizes the Republican establishment still touting Jeb Bush. Debbie Wasserman Schultz, the wicked witch from the South, the Democrats. *The New York Times*, *The Washington Post*, and the big three TV networks represent the media that still believes it will call the shots in 2016.

Here's reality. The voting public despises the elected officials in Washington, D.C., right now. But, just behind them is the media. Both richly deserve what they have earned.

With a consummate narcissist as president leading the parade, preening and finger-pointing at everyone else, things are not going well. Around the world and here at home. A Republican majority didn't help. Boehner quits; Ryan makes them beg to elect him and immediately he gets in bed with Obama on a trillion-dollar spending bill. The media are spinning us to get the world's greatest liar elected. She says it's time for a woman president. But some of us remember Paula Jones and James Carville speaking for the Clintons, saying in Bill's defense, "Drag a hundred dollar bill through a trailer park, you never know what you'll find." Okay, feminists who think it's more important to have any woman president than one who really represents women, respond to this. Put yourself in Paula Jones's place. There is no difference between Bill Cosby and Bill Clinton. Bill is a serial sexual predator. Which Bill? You pick.

So, here's the bottom line. People who think they are hurting Trump are really helping Trump. The past is not the present. The country is done with lawyers for politicians, career politicians, media people selling their agendas, and the so-called establishment. The people want change, and it's not going to make one iota of difference what non-change says about change.

Trump standing before huge crowds with no teleprompter and no notes is radical change. The alternative is Hillary, who can't utter one unrehearsed word without her handlers going berserk. Tightly scripted and fully rehearsed is the way we've grown accustomed to professional politicians. That's what they call presidential.

The times, they are a-changing, and Trump may be the change.

Obama: The Blue-Serge-Suit President

January 5, 2016

We are getting yet another example of our president making a production of something that will create zero results. I once worked for a man who called these actions "wetting your pants in a blue serge suit—a nice warm feeling, but nothing to show for it."

Seven years without a legacy and the man is getting desperate. He knows that Obamacare is just another blue serge suit. Fewer and fewer people sign up every year and states continue to opt out. Young people are mostly out. As the cost for them goes up and the deductions rise with the cost, they will pay the fine. The most onerous parts keep getting shoved back, like the Cadillac tax and the fifty-employee rule. Most, if not all, will be repealed over time.

Gitmo, the first big wetting of the suit, is still just that—a big wet suit.

The Iran nuclear deal. We now have Saudi Arabia and Iran mixing it up and Iran violating the truce with the missile tests. The blue suit is heading to the cleaners. Does this really surprise anyone?

Getting out of Iran with all troops. What a big mistake that was. For war after war, we have kept troops behind. We still have them in Germany, Japan, and South Korea. Not this genius president, who is smarter than any on earth or in the grave. Gave us ISIS, eh Barack? But, terrorism isn't a big concern according to you and John Kerry, another suit wetter. It's climate change. The red line in the sand in Syria—pissed backwards on that one. Really splotched up the pants, eh?

Now we are getting another executive action on gun control. Better take this whiz to keep everyone's mind off the Iran treaty unraveling. But, the result will be the same. Loonies, terrorists, and Chicagoans in the neighborhoods where he will build his presidential library will still have all the guns they need to wreak their havoc. Just another pair of wet pants with a lot of press coverage. The media seem to always overlook the reek of urine when it comes to Obama.

When he isn't just fooling around and doing things that matter, it is not good. He has increased the number of illegals in the country, closed power plants and coal mines, destroyed the economy, and ruined teleprompters for every president to follow. He has emasculated America with his mom jeans and little bicycle with the basket and bell and his ballerina moves on the golf course. Ask Putin, who looks at him like he's the wimp he is. I guess if you wet yourself all the time it's hard to play John Wayne.

Hillary, don't play the gender card, we've already had a female president.

47-Cent Gasoline in Michigan

January 19, 2016

A station in Houghton Lake, Michigan was posting 47.9 cents a gallon for regular gasoline this week. Whom do we thank for this and is it a good deal?

First, let's thank the Saudis. Second, let's thank the United States oil industry. For the most part, it's the most hated industry in the past century.

Let's address the second thank you first. Despite the government, despite the media, and despite the environmentalists, free enterprise did prevail once again in this country. Oil companies hiring the brightest petroleum engineers from US universities developed technologies to extract oil and gas from pockets deep under rock that could not be penetrated by previous technology. Combining high-pressure water and chemicals, they drove through that rock and extracted the gas and oil. Then by horizontal drilling they could reach other pockets.

It's an expensive process, costing $30–$40 a barrel. But a necessary process, since our own government put cheaper oil and gas off limits on public land. Public land, as not owned by Barack Obama and his environmental friends and supporters, but by you and me. We don't count in a democracy that counts votes by dollars contributed and media support. This all took place on private land and without one ounce of technology from the Department of Energy, which has consumed billions of taxpayer dollars with zero contribution toward that 47-cent gasoline price.

Now, back to the Saudis. When this country became the world's largest oil producer, it was unacceptable to the Saudis. The United States was determining the price of crude oil, not the Saudis. With the US government now allowing oil companies in the United States to export oil, it was a big problem for the Saudis. So they start pumping the hell out of their oil. It costs $15–$20 a barrel to produce oil there. They have one goal in mind: stop the US oil production by keeping the price below the cost of fracking. Why? The US oil companies stop fracking, lay off people, lose money, and regress. When prices go back up above the cost of fracking, it will take a long time to get back to where the business was before the Saudis shut it down.

Every decision the government of the United States has made in the field of energy has been wrong, from the days of Jimmy Carter. The government in concert with the media has created an illusion that the government is the answer and the oil industry is the enemy. If you want to see how that works, just look south to Mexico. That government has run the oil business for decades. Supply is drying up and the Mexican government is begging the oil industry to come in and solve their problems by producing new wells. But they don't want to share fairly. So, it hasn't happened.

Just think about this. If, God forbid, this country elects a Hillary or a Bernie, what happens to energy here? Like 47-cent gasoline, how about $10 gasoline? Hillary's first job as Secretary of State was to go to our friend and neighbor, Canada, to tell them we don't approve of their extraction of oil from tar sands. Who are we? Hollywood, environmental zealots, and libtards who still believe energy comes from magic and a country can have an economy with $10 gasoline. If you believe that, vote for one of them. If you don't, and want to see us get back on track with our dominance in the energy production business, vote for Trump. He gets it.

Obama's Comments on the Death of Justice Scalia

February 16, 2016

There is a lot of talk about political correctness these days. It was even a question in the Republican debate. No one ever says much about class. I'm not talking about Bernie Sanders class war in a sense of socialism. I'm just talking class. You can't describe it, but you know it when you see it.

Peyton Manning has it; Cam Newton doesn't. Laura Bush has it; Michele Obama doesn't. Jordan Spieth has it; Tiger Woods doesn't. It's an individual thing.

I play a lot of golf and have played with hundreds of people through the years. From Neil Armstrong, the first man on the moon, to John Doe, the common blue collar guy who loves golf. I can tell in the first six holes whether the person has class.

I played in a LPGA member-guest years ago in Toledo, Ohio. It's a two-day event. The first day, I played with Catriona Matthew, the Scottish golfer. It was her rookie year on the tour. She has enjoyed a stellar career with eleven wins, including the Women's British Open. She was in her early twenties and had amazing class and maturity. The next day we played with Sandra Palmer. She was heading on the downside of her career and wasn't happy about her game. She wanted to be somewhere else and spent most of the time going off to the side to try to repair her broken game. My host was a sponsor of the event since Kroger had pulled out and they were desperate for a sponsor. At the end of our round he took her aside and told her he was writing a letter to the LPGA about her conduct. He suggested she skip the event the next year if he was still the sponsor. No class, Sandra.

You see it in tough situations. Those with class show composure, while others go viral. It used to be the only version of what we now call political correctness.

Let me give you the latest example of no class: President Obama. The classless, tacky, narcissistic antagonist uses a televised tribute to an esteemed deceased Supreme Court justice to declare war on Republicans should they deprive him of a court nomination.

Politicians Destroying Our Youth's Futures

March 24, 2016

Yeah, we all saw the movie, *The Big Short*. The greed of Wall Street sets our teeth on edge. Two small facts were left out of the movie.

First, without Freddie, Fannie, and the FHA, none of those questionable mortgages would have been made by the banks to begin with. Second, beginning with Bill Clinton, the idea that every American should be able to own a house pushed banks to make a percentage of minority loans or face punishment by Washington. Since it was no-risk loans guaranteed by that same Washington, why not?

Hence, we all saw the carnage. People losing the houses

they couldn't afford, the entire economy hitting the skids and the bailouts, etc. The very instigators of the problem, Dodd and Frank, sponsored a law regulating Wall Street. Meanwhile, Freddie, Fannie, and the FHA go on their merry way, insuring mortgages.

The very same thing now exists with student loans. Over a trillion dollars and growing, student loans provide free money to the colleges and universities, just as insured mortgages did to the lending institutions. Kids who can't get through college are getting loans to try. Kids who can are leaving college with degrees that make it hard to pay back the loans.

But the sick part, the truly sick part, lies in the educational institutions. There is zero accountability to keep tuition costs down. In fact, Obama has stepped in and ensured they will go up even more. His proposed overtime pay rule will hit colleges hard. The University of California school system faces a $39-million-a-year tab for raises to avoid paying overtime to thousand of postdoctoral scholars, librarians, and specialists. This system is being run by Janet Napolitano, who nearly bankrupted both the state of Arizona and the Department of Homeland Security. The entire higher educational system is run by nonbusiness types who never saw a budget they couldn't increase.

The community college near my home in Illinois, College of DuPage, had a scandal. The board woke up one day and found the administration was having a grand old party with college funds. But they just fired the head guy without due diligence. Why not? They were people who never ran anything, trying to do civic duty. The legal tab is now $3.9 million and growing. To be paid by higher tuition.

In Arizona, my second home, the Maricopa Country Community College District students have been hit with three tuition hikes since 2012. Investigations show it's the same deal as the aforementioned COD situation. The administrators are giving themselves huge raises and big perks. See, no one is watching the store. Not at MCCCD, not at COD, not at the California system. They are institutions run by boards that like the football or basketball tickets and the prestige but are clueless about cost control. Politicians like those who created the $18 trillion debt at the national level.

See, no one stops coming to their schools, because the same governments just gives bigger student loans. Sound familiar? No one will care until the young people really suffer like the people who lost their homes. Many are already. They won't own anything for 10–15 years, until they pay back the $100,000 in student loans. Then you get the real idiots who say free college. Can you imagine what those administrators will do with that? Unlimited demand for the product.

It's sad and no one cares. I do and I hope you do, since it's a terrible injustice to our youth.

The Republican Establishment

March 28, 2016

Who is the Republican establishment that is telling voters who favor Trump they can't have Trump? Here it is folks, the Republican establishment:

Mr. Denny Hastert. A man who went from high school wrestling coach to the House to Speaker and on to retirement. A man who never made more than $150,000 a year but could still pay a blackmailer $3 million in cash to keep from being exposed as a pedophile who molested one or more of his wrestlers when he coached.

This is what the establishment wants to keep. The secret formula that allows a congressman or a senator to have a job for life and retire a multimillionaire. If you don't play ball, you don't get the support.

As a voter, this is enough for me. I don't care if Trump is arrogant. All politicians are arrogant, especially Obama. I don't care if he can't take criticism. None of these egotistical maniacs can, especially Obama.

Does it bother me that the "establishment" can put together polls that show Trump losing to Hillary? No, I believe Democrats dislike Hillary so much they will find Trump a better option. John Kerry calls Trump an embarrassment. What is Kerry, if not a huge embarrassment? Only Hillary could screw that job up more.

McCain, the bottom of his class at Annapolis. Ditched two planes in flight training. Married money and wants to be wheeled into the senate ala Strom Thurmond. Romney, a titular head of a successful venture capital company who made a ton of money by putting his establishment name on the door. Got stomped into the ground by Obama, a man short on *cojones*. Hillary, the evil one, who would do anything to get this job and has no resume to make it work. John (Casper Milquetoast) Kasich, the consummate RINO, made millions the same way Hastert did. Bernie, sure, let's become a banana republic. Ted Cruz, the most hated man in the Senate. A hypocrite posing as a Christian who spends quality time with prostitutes.

One candidate who reminds me of the same criticisms directed toward Ronald Reagan. A man who knows how to manage 22,500 people and do business around the world. A leader who starts with a vision and gets the team behind him and gets complex jobs done on time on budget. Most importantly, a man who can't be bought.

Will he destroy the Republican Party? No, he will fix an almost-destroyed party. The Denny Hasterts will have to go off to be lobbyists to Democrats. Fitting work for those who know how to be bought and can find others who are for sale.

The Cupcake Generation

April 4, 2016

It's doubly bad that our grandkids will inherit a country in trouble. One, because we let it happen and it's on us. Two, because they are less prepared to deal with it than any generation in American history.

Everything offends them. A student at a prestigious university filed a complaint that his roommate had an American flag on the wall and it was offensive to him. This is what you get when you have seven years of this. We are on the very brink of making a decision that will either save the country or finish it off. Four or eight more years of liberal philosophy and politics will ensure this generation is emasculated to the point where they will not be able to survive the legacy we left them.

The Cupcake Generation is the result of helicopter parenting (no explanation needed). The result of everyone getting a trophy and no one losing. Parents paying hundreds to get mediocre students good enough test scores to get into good colleges. But, not good enough for technical degrees or into the top business schools. All of that explains this.

In 2009, American colleges handed out more business degrees than engineering, computer, and biology degrees combined. We graduated about the same number of engineers as we did "visual and performance arts" grads.

What the crybabies of Generation Cupcake want—a good-paying, white-collar job right out of college—is available, if you're willing to do the hard work necessary to earn a valuable degree. But because these little snowflakes can't do calculus, they end up burying themselves under $50,000 in college debt for a degree in Women's Studies. Half of current college kids are mediocre students who will earn meaningless degrees and wind up working as the assistant manager at a TGI Fridays.

Who ends up getting screwed? The rest of the students who qualify to be in college.

Because demand is artificially high, so are college costs— up 8.3% in just the past year at public colleges.

And because there are so many more degree holders, each degree is worth less.

And it's a generation not prepared to deal with the future they will face.

The Greatest Generation Is Dying

April 20, 2016

My dad's generation: They fought the Great Depression and survived the Big War, and they were tough. Oh so tough, mentally and physically. The world knew not to mess with this bunch. They built things and grew things, and raised kids who could do the same.

My generation: They pushed us to go off to college. Most of us helped pay for that college by working summers and at school. College was a reasonable price because the government was not subsidizing colleges and students and passing out free loans. Free, until you must pay them back. If you ever intend to do so.

My generation took those degrees and went to work. Many of us worked for the same companies our entire career. We raised our kids and sent them off to college. Life got easier for every successive generation. And we as a country got softer.

The world knows we are soft and getting softer. Hence, we have the snowflake generation. They require safe zones and are offended by almost everything. If life gets tough and we have an economic crisis, a major war, or tough times, the snowflakes will surely melt.

Had Enough Political Correctness?

May 7, 2016

The justice department wants to discontinue using the term "criminal" and replace it with "justice-involved individual." Why does this sound familiar? In 2010, Janet Napolitano, then head of Homeland Security, introduced us to "manmade disaster" as a substitute for terrorism. Janet coined that phrase to avoid saying terrorism.

And you wonder why so much of the population is sick of all this. Hence, we have Trump, God bless him. He tells it like it is.

The media in this country have declared themselves judge and jury regarding political correctness. They honestly believe they can destroy individuals and institutions if they deem one has crossed their lines on what is acceptable.

Remember Rachael Ray? They got her. Before her, Jimmy the Greek. Something offends someone, they run to a lawyer or the media and get publicity. Whoever the offending party is gets trashed. I'm tired of all of it. Mostly, I'm tired of the media that created the problem. But, they are self-destructing in their ignorance and will soon be gone.

The two younger generations no longer read newspapers. Network news is losing viewers for good reason. Local news, the same thing. Cable news is mostly fighting for the same audience, and the outlier Fox just lost viewers for their anti-Trump position. Before long, everyone will get their news on the net.

Soon, Obama and his propaganda will be gone. The ACLU will be around, finding liberal courts to get everything they find offensive out of society. But the ACLJ (American Center for Law and Justice—the conservative counterpart to the ACLU) will be taking them on and stopping some of the nonsense. God is gone; transgender is in. Cops are bad, "justice-involved individuals" need protection. You can mistreat our flag, but not the Mexican flag. Immigrants are part of being American, and when they kill us they are manmade disasters. The death penalty is wrong, but killers need compassion. Guns cause most murders and need control, especially in Chicago, where there will be 1,000 murders, many of them young kids. But they have gun control in Chicago.

See, there is one thing always lacking in PC: common sense. Take common sense out of the equation and you get ignorance. Ignorance is the media's best friend. They prey on it, they use it, and they all have more than their share of it personally. Remember Brian Williams?

Why Trump?

June 23, 2016

Reason #1. The security of the country is foremost in the minds of the people. The Orlando tragedy brought it home again. The president made his normal gun control speech and Hillary jumped on board. The Democrats in Congress are trying to get gun laws passed to help the president and the nominee. Republicans may play ball. Why not? You have far too many RINOs in Congress. But no logical American believes this will do one thing to protect us from ISIS and radical Islam. Trump's proposal to stop Muslim immigration until we have a handle on background checks does resonate with voters.

Reason #2. The economy. Voters know the economy is not good and the prospects for it getting better are not good. Too many out of work, too few good jobs, too much debt, too many on food stamps, too few investment options, and a crumbling infrastructure. Nothing is really working right. I can prove this with one click.

It's the National Debt Clock. Our eyes go to the debt number and we click off. Yes, the debt ticks toward $19 trillion. But please take a moment and look at the other key numbers. Like state debt, local debt, the workforce (today and in 2000), those not in labor force, the number of government employees, manufacturing jobs (today and in 2000), food stamp recipients, and those without insurance (despite Obamacare). There is zero good news here. All Trump has to do is hammer away at this, because it tells the story of the Obama years and what career politicians have done to the country.

Reason #3. The country is tired of career politicians. We can't get term limits because those we elect are benefitting far too much from staying in office. Trump won the Republican nomination for this reason alone. He will be elected president for this reason, as well.

Reason #4. Obamacare. It isn't working and the debt clock proves its not working. There are still 40 million uninsured. Those insured are being hit with huge premium increases. Insurance companies are dropping out of Obamacare coverage. This will be more of a factor during the campaign.

Reason #5. Hillary is a sleaze. Simple as that. Zero trust for the serial liar.

So, that's my list and I'm sticking with it. This is why Trump will take office in January of 2017.

Brexit: Power to the People

June 25, 2016

An impact heard around the globe. The people of the United Kingdom have spoken. They have had enough. Enough what?

Little bureaucrats in Brussels deciding what British citizens want. Like little bureaucrats in D.C. deciding what Americans want. Brussels bureaucrats decided the United Kingdom wanted more Muslim immigrants, and they were forced to take them by the rules of the EU. Americans have been told we need to do the same, plus have a porous border to the south where millions come through to live at the public trough that is empty. Common sense prevailed in the United Kingdom and it will prevail here, too.

Minorities ruled in the United Kingdom. Described as Greeks, Italians, Swedes, etc. Minorities rule here. Described as those who want to use the wrong restroom or locker room, those who believe Orlando was a gun control problem, those who want to run up the $20 trillion debt, and those who decide what is and isn't politically correct.

Who are those minorities? First and foremost, the media. The same media who told the voters in the United Kingdom they had to stay in the EU. The BBC and *The Times of London* there and the networks and *The New York*

Times here. Then the corrupt politicians who the voters in the United Kingdom now reject. The elitists who said anyone who wanted out was stupid. The celebrities who said the same. The same people who are telling you here that anyone who supports Trump is the same: stupid, politically incorrect, and out of sync with society. The media there blasted Brexit for months. The media here does the same with Trump. *The Chicago Tribune* is relentless. But, *The Tribune* gave us Chicago and Illinois, both broke and beyond repair. The paper has backed all of the poor decisions that have led the state to the precipice of bankruptcy.

The winds of change swept the United Kingdom, and they blow here and in other countries in Europe. We've had enough. Enough bad ideas that don't work. Enough politicians who don't work. Enough of media who peddle bad ideas. Enough brainless celebrities who think we need to listen. Professors, climate scientists, career politicians, corrupt politicians, talking heads, and minorities who can't get enough of everything.

In the United Kingdom, the polls said Brexit would fail. In the United States, polls say Hillary will win. Now it's said in the United Kingdom, pollsters don't poll the true voters. Who are all those supporters who turn out at Trump rallies? Where are the supporters who don't turn out at a Hillary rally?

The collective majority in the United Kingdom have common sense. They showed it at the polls. The collective majority in the United States have common sense. They will show it in November when our version of Brexit will prevail.

The Death of Investigative Journalism

July 7, 2016

Remember these guys, Bernstein and Woodward? Woodward grew up in my adopted hometown, Wheaton, Illinois, where I've lived for thirty-seven years. Their work brought down a president. They uncovered the infamous Watergate break in that caused Nixon to resign. Take a good, hard look at this picture. That kind of reporting went the way of the passenger pigeon.

That beautiful bird is extinct. Done in by humankind. A stark reminder of what we can do to nature. Investigative journalism is extinct here in America, as well, also done in by humankind. Not shot into extinction, but by design. Maybe it already started before Watergate; I can't really say. If Nixon had been a Democrat, perhaps the bosses at *The Washington Post* would have killed the story. Whenever the heads of all media in this country became part of the Hollywood and academia liberal movement, all objectivity ended.

Some of the greatest investigative opportunities of all time are lying dormant due to the death of objective reporting. Where would I begin?

1. The factual background of one Barack Obama. Why does no one remember him in undergraduate school? How did he get there; what are his academic records? How did he get into Harvard Law School?

2. The IRS scandal. Lois Lerner takes the fifth. Did all of Nixon's men get away with that?

3. Benghazi. Did Bernstein and Woodward trust a Trey Gowdy to get to the truth?

4. The Justice Department was culling reporters' phone records. They can't even protect themselves when it's the Democrats doing them wrong. Add the James Rosen criminal charges to that. Then monitoring his phones and emails.

5. Holder then perjured himself by lying about approving the Rosen investigation.

6. Fast and Furious. The guns to the Mexican drug lords program. Holder then lied about when he knew about this great idea.

7. Kathleen Sebelius demanded payment donations from companies the HHS might regulate to help ring up uninsured Americans for Obamacare. That's never happened, the signing of uninsured Americans, but is it a story? Is the failure to get uninsured on insurance a story? Is the stupendous increase in health care premiums a story?

8. Reckless spending by agencies. The GSA blowout in Vegas that cost $823,000; the Veterans Affairs $6 million on two conferences in Orlando.

9. The Clinton Foundation. The FBI supposedly has 150 agents working on this. Zero investigative reporters report.

10. The Secret Service goes nuts. The administration fires IGs who poke into things they don't like. Examples: they paid millions to Axelrod to promote Obamacare; the Pigford scandal paying several billion dollars in cash to thousands of minority and female farmers who weren't discriminated against by the Agricultural Department, Solyndra and all the Solyndras, and on and on.

11. Illegals who commit crimes freed from prisons by Obama.

12. Muslim immigrants who have committed crimes.
13. Pouring through the Hillary emails released by WikiLeaks to see if the FBI blew the investigation. Showing a slight indignation over the FBI and Justice Department decisions on those emails.

There are a dozen Watergates in this pile of trash, but not one Bernstein or Woodward stepping forward to expose the truth. Why not? They would be fired in a heartbeat. See, their job is to elect Hillary, not get her indicted. Simple as that. They investigate Republicans and promote Democrats.

They rank just above Congress on the trust meter, and Congress is just above Hillary. If the voters know Hillary is distrustful, why doesn't the media? Love is a wonderful thing. We can forgive those we love, but woe to our enemies. That explains why Jeff Bezos hired a bunch of new reporters at *The Washington Post* to find a Watergate on Trump but ignore the Watergate that exists on the Clintons and the Clinton Foundation, the biggest money-laundering crime in history.

Gun Control

July 11, 2016

Every mass shooting that has occurred since 2008 has brought the same response from President Obama and his followers. Gun control. Everyone who doesn't buy his simple ridiculous solution has scoffed. We know the government has failed when they have tried things like this.

Prohibition for the alcohol problem. Jimmy Carter trying to run the oil business from the White House and creating lines around the block. I'm in the latter camp, but I am willing to try something.

See, in the business world, they have what they call market testing. You have a big new idea, but you don't roll it out across all markets. You test it in a market to see if it works. You establish a set of quantitative expectations and then measure against those goals. So, Obama, Hillary, most Democrats, a few so-called Republicans who hate guns period, and the rest of you who hate gun owners, the NRA, and the Second Amendment, let's give your ideas a try.

Here's your test program:

1. Establish your gun control program here. Not one of you has ever put any proposal in writing. Put it down on paper and spell it all out. What guns are prohibited, what is the criteria for owning a gun, what is the penalty for an illegal gun, etc. Draw the border around the area in the above document that shows where the shootings occur. Or, just say the city limits of Chicago. That's your test market where you implement this high-minded gun control plan.

2. Set the improvement parameters and qualify the goals. Establish the time frame to measure progress—one year, two years, etc.

That's it. Shut the hell up about gun control until you can prove in this test market that it makes a difference. Should be like fishing with dynamite. It's a war zone. If black lives truly matter, make it matter here when so many die every week. Women and kids and innocent bystanders die every week. Far more than the police kill each year. Let Father Pfleger, Jesse Jackson, Reverend Al, the new Black Panthers, the Black Lives Matter Organization, and other interested parties who have hollered for gun control help design the plan.

Probably every gun in those record number of shootings for 2016 was illegal, so you just gather up those and you've got some gun control. Unless, of course, some leak in from other parts of the country. Or, from other countries, like Mexico. How you get around the profiling is up to you, since most of the areas where the shootings occur are predominantly black. But, law-abiding black neighbors are asking for something like this.

Go about it and prove to skeptics like me that you can make any gun control program work. No more talk—just do it.

See, if I have a problem, I would address it this way: (1) Call the police. I have the utmost respect for their training and ability to help me. I have never had a problem with a cop. Of course, I am polite and don't tell the cop to kiss my ass when he asks me to do something. Maybe that is a factor. (2) I would grab my Model 12 Winchester pump with a polychoke. It appears to me that those of you who will be running the market test in Chicago want the good people of Chicago to give up both those options. You hate the cops and you want to take the guns from the peaceful people in the war zone who need them. Then, you will protect them, right? No thanks, folks.

But, I could be wrong. So, prove it. Go make it work in Chicago.

Killing Cops

July 18, 2016

Time to stop tiptoeing around this issue. Angry blacks have declared war on policemen in this country. There is plenty of blame to go around on this, but I have my perspective.

Really, it began with the Harvard University professor Henry Louis Gates Jr. and Sgt. James Crowley and President Obama on July 16, 2009, merely six months into the Obama presidency. Then it moved to Trayvon Martin. "If I had a son, he'd look like Trayvon." In these cases, the president spoke before the courts spoke.

Then on to Ferguson, "Hands up don't shoot," burning and looting and riots. On to Baltimore with Freddie Gray and the indictment of the cops. Then Sandra Bland, the lady who purportedly kicked the cop, was arrested, and then committed suicide in her jail cell.

It's the frequency of visits to the White House of Reverend Al Sharpton, present at all of these situations. Whipping up the emotions of his fellow blacks. It's the media declaring cops guilty before any investigation. The media that seems to want to make the news rather than report the news. There is no balance to this issue with the media. Whip it up, keep it whipped, and cover it daily, weekly, and even on an anniversary, as local Chicago stations did on the one-year anniversary of the Sandra Bland suicide. Cover the protests, cover the riots, cover the violence, and skew it against the police.

Focus on the blue on black issue. When the president went

to Dallas he denigrated a solemn memorial ceremony by endorsing Black Lives Matter and dragging out the tired old gun control issue.

This explains why we have a new homegrown terrorist group in America. One directed toward cops. As Sheriff Clarke so aptly said, the police are the only protection those hardworking black citizens in Chicago have from those who are killing them and their children in record numbers.

If more people don't set aside political correctness and come forward with solid solutions like Sheriff Clarke, we will lose more and more policemen to this movement. CNN could start by firing Mr. Lemon. He personifies the media involvement in this crime spree.

Trump's Immigration Policy

September 4, 2016

Now all I ask is that you be objective here. Trump went to Mexico and met with the president of Mexico. The media were unanimous that he pulled a coup and looked very presidential on the stage with the Mexican president.

He went from there to Arizona, where he gave his scripted speech on his immigration policy. This was blasted by the media. He was labeled as bombastic and a liar and the normal media vitriol.

What changed?

The media doesn't like his position on immigration.

Here is his position. He will collect and send home all illegals who have committed crimes. He will build a wall and reinforce the border. Having done that, he will look at the remaining illegal residents and divine a fair and reasonable plan to give them a possible path to citizenship. That might include them going back and returning legally, depending on their circumstances.

Do you have a problem with this plan? If not, do you have a problem with the media that is against the plan? If that's the case, I suggest you just stop listening to them.

Trump's Business Experience Is Winning

September 7, 2016

Trump, per Reuters, has pulled even with Clinton. No one is happy except the American public.

We are witnessing what really happens when a very intelligent businessman runs against a career politician.

He is offering insights we have never been offered by career politicians in my lifetime. He is ignoring the media and responding to the public.

The vast majority of voters are tired of someone else telling us what we should support. For example, do you support the illegal immigration of poor people who require government aid from another country? Do you support criminals coming across our borders, and when sent back, coming back again? Do you believe we should make it easy for the Mexican drug cartels to ship drugs, guns, and crime across our borders? If no to the above, why have you put up with it for years?

Do you think the big cities run by Democratic mayors for fifty years are hopeless and there is no answer? Is there a link between over zealous environmentalists and this problem? Environmentalists don't want manufacturing in this country. Once, there were manufacturing plants and jobs in these cities. They want $10 gasoline. Who can't afford high energy prices? The working poor. Is there a connection between too much environmental attention and high energy prices? Who suffers most?

Do you like the idea of Obama freeing felons so they can vote?

Do you believe pay for play is always going to be a part of the scene in Washington, D.C.?

Do you believe we should continue to let our military deteriorate? To abuse our veterans? To have government waste? To support the United Nations when they vote against us on every key issue? To give foreign aid to those who hate us? To let college tuition costs go through the roof? To annex all government land to parks so we can't touch any resources there? To run up the debt at the rate Obama has done for the past seven years? To have a GDP less than 3% forever? To have zero interest rates?

This is a once-in-a-lifetime opportunity to elect someone who might just fix some or all of the above.

Are you going to let the media sell you on the other candidate who supports business as usual or worse?

Hispanic Vote

September 9, 2016

Before I retired, I was on the National Hispanic Corporate Council Board of Directors. I was a keynote speaker at a national convention. My subject was "How business was missing the mark by not recognizing the power of the Hispanic consumer, and how to find and capitalize on that opportunity." My company had over 50% of the Hispanic market in the three key markets where we operated: Miami, New York City, and Chicago.

How did we do that? We advertised on the Spanish-speaking TV stations for years before our competition ever noticed. We became experts on the buying habits of that consumer base. I learned many things and I believe most still apply today.

First and foremost, there is no "Hispanic or Latino" market. Cubans do not relate to Mexicans and Mexicans do not relate to Puerto Ricans. Language is all they have in common. So, our three markets were very different. Chicago was mostly Mexican, NYC was Puerto Rican, and Miami was Cuban. Each required a different approach.

Communications needed to be in Spanish and family oriented. Our normal advertising messages did not always appeal to this segment. In some cases, it was offensive. We used a Latino advertising agency to sort all this out, not our normal agency.

What's my point? I don't believe the brain-dead media in this country have a clue as to how this group will vote in November. Nor do I believe they will vote as a block, like the media is telling us.

Like most political knowledge, the media gets it wrong. They are sure the Trump message on immigration will offend this group and Hillary will get all the votes.

I'm not so sure. Stay tuned.

Clinton or Trump: Here's the Answer

October 13, 2016

I worked for a great corporation that is now gone. It's a crossword puzzle clue. A Fortune 50 global organization that is no more. What happened? HR (human resources) took over the company.

Employees spent all their time on issues the HR department deemed critical. Diversity, safety, and those interactions that fall very closely into the political correctness category.

As I observe the pending election, I see the same thing happening to this country. The mainstream media in this country has become *The National Inquirer*, informing the voters hourly on the personal habits of one candidate. WikiLeaks has become the mainstream media, reporting daily on the abhorrent behind-the-scenes behavior and dirty tricks of the other party—the work *The Washington Post* once did on Nixon when they were practicing true journalism. Voters are getting a lot of improper past behavior of the one candidate and dabs of the dirty tricks, since media is trying to drag the old gal across the finish line.

This country is in serious trouble. We have had eight years

of HR running the country and no one focused on the priorities. This is what happens when leaders abandon the job of prioritizing resources. When the media runs the country, its like having HR run a company. Neither is equipped to run anything. Good intentions are nice, but they need to be mixed with good practices.

So, if you weigh the bad behaviors of two bad actors and find Trump's worse than Hillary's (hard to fathom, but the media says you do), then for the good of my kids and grandkids take a peek at the scoreboard. With Hillary, you get four more years of those trends or worse. That's her platform. With Trump, you get a chance to dig out of the mess we are in and the worse mess we are headed into.

By the way, the CEO of that fine company walked away with a boatload of cash, just like Obama will. The employees, not so good.

Media and Polls Say It's Over— Hillary Wins

October 21, 2016

It's been quite a week. Trump started the conversation about the election being rigged. He wasn't just referring to the process of voting, but the entire campaign. The billions of dollars in free negative campaign air and print time given to Ms. Clinton by a media that still tries to pretend they aren't doing what we all see them doing. If you had a food fight with the media and the rules said, "We can throw food, but you can't," would that be rigged? It's bad enough they are doing it, but worse that they are denying it.

Let's just look at WikiLeaks vs. the Trump tape. The emails show all sorts of improper behavior that should be part of a fair election decision. Suppression was applied and the public was spared the gruesome details of the inner workings of the Clinton campaign.

Now, we see she came up with the idea of hitting up Morocco for a few million for her slush fund. This was after, not before, she announced she was running for president. She says she visited 110 countries as Secretary of State. Probably passed the hat for cash at every one. That may have been the point of the visits, since she did nothing of consequence. Now, she's doubling back to get the stragglers. No reason to stop this when she's president; she can send Bill and Chelsea to Morocco. Still, the bimbo thing was front and center and no mention of the Clinton corruption. Here's the classic example.

The after-debate analysis on Fox News was handled by Brett Baier and Megyn Kelly. It was a good debate and Chris Wallace did a fine job. Megyn went off for several minutes about Trump's alleged groping of women. It was embarrassing. I checked in with Twitter/Fox News. It was ugly—calling her names, suggesting she go to CNN, and viewers turning off the program.

So, Fox News, the last bastion of so-called fairness is now aligned with the left.

It was a good debate. By most accounts Trump won, until the media seized on the "No, I will contest if I lose," comment. Ignoring all the rest—the absence of any economic plan by Clinton, the Foundation issue, the failures of all her foreign policy work, the email scandal, etc. Really. The media are handing the election to Hillary.

Let's go back to 1980, Carter vs. Reagan. For weeks before the presidential election, the gurus of public opinion polling were nearly unanimous in their findings. In survey after survey, they agreed that the choice between President Jimmy Carter and challenger Ronald Reagan was "too close to call." A few points at most, they said, separated the two major contenders.

But when the votes were counted, the former California governor had defeated Carter by a margin of 51% to 41% in the popular vote—a rout for a US presidential race. In the Electoral College, the Reagan victory was a 10:1 avalanche that left the president holding only six states and the District of Columbia.

One of Reagan's quotes before the election: "Professional politicians like to talk about the value of experience in government. Nuts! The only experience you gain in politics is how to be political."

The media, wrong at every step, the pollsters, wrong at every step, the cowardly Republican establishment, wrong at whatever little they have done since we gave them the House and Senate, all of them are sure Hillary has it in the bag. Poster boy for that is Karl Rove—remember him from the last election, making a fool of himself?

The American public was fed up with Jimmy Carter in 1980. The American public is fed up with Obama in 2016, and Clinton is just more Obama. Who knows, maybe voters will address the issues and not the shiny things the media is attracted to and pushes like drugs to the public.

Hey, who can argue with term limits?

Who Will Be Our New President?

November 2, 2016

Four years back I was wrong about Romney. The day before the election, I was pretty sure this country had learned that Obama was not the answer.

This time I run the risk of being wrong again. It's hard to imagine that Trump can win against the long odds he is fighting. After all, he's fighting the Clintons, the Democratic Party, the mainstream media, Hollywood, the Justice Department, the Republican Party, and women who will put a personal taped discussion with Billy Bush eleven years ago above a criminal enterprise. That's one hell of a lot to overcome. How many individuals do you know who would hang in there against all that?

I believe he will prevail. Why?

First, 75% of my fellow Americans believe the country is not going in a good direction. Second, the country is sick to death of all politicians in Washington, D.C., in their statehouse, and in their local courthouse. Third, the Clintons may have worn out their welcome. One public disgrace too many. Fourth, the voters get it with the mainstream media. When CNN is feeding questions to Hillary before a debate, ist's just confirmation.

So, we will see. It's beyond me to accept a Clinton win. She is a confirmed serial liar, a criminal, incompetent, unwell, and has a creepy clown for a running mate who can't draw one hundred people to a rally. Since she's a potential indicted criminal or a physically or mentally incapacitated elected president, he's the guy.

It will be 1980 all over again, with Trump playing the Reagan role and running away with the election, or it will be 2012 again, with Clinton beating Trump like Obama did with Romney. The outcome will be significant for the future of this country. If she's elected and indicted, it will tear this country apart. I do believe she will be indicted. Not for email issues but for the Clinton Foundation, which is a criminal enterprise on a grander scale than Madoff. Huma is going to sing and it's going to get ugly.

Good luck, America. Mic down. I'm outta here until this is settled.

I Am Proud to be an American

November 10, 2016

I will not gloat. I promised on my Facebook page I wouldn't gloat if Trump was elected. I went out on a limb there and predicted he would be our new president like I did here.

But if I had been wrong, this would be the last blog entry. I started this in 2008 because I felt my country was headed in a bad direction.

Now I feel vindicated. The voting public agreed and we have a pivotal change in direction coming. None too soon. I believe Trump's win kept us from sliding into full-blown socialism.

How Trump Became President-Elect

November 16, 2016

He ignored all conventional wisdom. Used the advice of those he trusted to be smart, talented people combined with his years of good business judgment and sailed on that ship. First on the list of those he ignored were the media. He recognized the media for what they are: a tool. Used them like a hoe.

Then came his fellow Republicans. Losers of the last two elections. Detested by many for their lack of performance after being given the House, then the Senate. He picked a few who recognized that he was a smart guy and had a plan, but many were cast aside. Right, Messrs. Ryan, McCain, Graham, and all named Bush.

He forged ahead into the stiff winds and emerged Trump, the Conqueror, slayer of the evil Clintons. I have written this blog for over eight years waiting for this hope. Now, as he makes his plans and puts his staff in place, the same wise people are coming forth and critiquing his decisions. It won't end. The ignorant losers patch their wounds and long for the days when they were wrecking this country.

Here's the classic example. Mayor Emanuel, who barely won a runoff against a man named Chuy Garcia, is front and center. Sees his last chance to be our president. Why not, presiding over the worst-run city in the country is better than being a community organizer. He challenges Trump's immigration policy by telling the illegal immigrant criminals Trump proposes to deport to come to Chicago; they are welcome here.

Sure, what Chicago needs is more gangbangers, more drugs, and more guns. Just think about that. The media are all over this. It fits their ideology. And further explains why Trump is president-elect. The sea of stupidity in this country has shrunk to a pond replaced by an ocean of common sense.

Everything these progressive elitists wish for is not in the best interest of the majority of Americans. They have used positions of power to sell bad political policy for the past eight years, and the public isn't buying anymore.

Trump recognized that and sold common sense to the multitude of voters who still possess some. I don't know what will happened to the media, but I suspect there will be alternatives to the ones we have. When US carmakers stopped making quality cars, the Japanese took over and forced quality on the domestic manufacturers. There will be new media to replace the existing train wrecks, and they will do very well. Someone like the Koch brothers, who also misjudged Trump, will buy a failing CNN, for example, and make it a common-sense newscaster. It will happen rather quickly since Trump supporters have stopped watching, listening, and reading the left-wing propaganda we have now.

As someone said, when the tide goes out we can see who is swimming naked, and it's those who believe America appreciates naked swimmers or unisex bathrooms.

Snowflake Protests

November 19, 2016

It's inconceivable to me that we have a generation of young people who can't deal with an election that doesn't go their way. Further, I don't understand who would spend millions paying people to protest to create unrest in this country. If it happens as advertised, I worry about a clash of cultures if the snowflakes show up by the thousands at the Trump inauguration to blend with the thousands of bikers who plan to show up to support Trump. What has Obama done to my country? Kids who are afraid of their shadows and bikers who support Republicans?

The media is going crazy over this election. I can't read a paper or watch a TV news show. The very people who got it all wrong during the election are now telling us who Trump's staff will be and what's wrong with every choice, and warn us of unrest in the transition team. They get upset when Trump goes off to dinner with the family because they need to know where he is and what he's doing every second. Yet they still can't tell us where Obama was the night of Benghazi. *USA Today*, which I subscribe to for the sports page and the puzzles, now has two female writers putting politics on the sports pages. Bye bye, subscription. I am so lazy I keep my AOL address. I would have to notify so many about an address change, I just hang with them. When I click on, I get a barrage of *The Huffington Post* propaganda. It's so inane, I must laugh.

I can't relate to the snowflakes because I was busing tables at a Greyhound bus terminal cafeteria at age fourteen and meeting the salt of the earth. Then working construction with the greatest men I ever met, all WWII vets. But I can relate to this. Those of us who backed Trump and are happy with the election have options.

Idiots can march around with signs, skip classes, and require puppies and safe places, but the Trump people aren't idiots. We can protest in our own quiet ways. I will not tolerate four years of the media trashing everything Trump does, so I will be part and parcel of the consumers who put them out of business. Replacements will be available just like Coke is for Pepsi, and I will get my news and products from the replacements.

Putin's Election Hacking

December 18, 2016

Mr. Obama, during what is his version of a press conference, directly accused the Russian president of influencing the US election by hacking the DNC. Then, he said the US media tilted the election in Trump's favor by utilizing the information and blasting Hillary with the news.

First, let me address what "his version" of a press conference means to me. Selected reporters who are fawning over Obama are asked a question. Then, Obama makes a speech often lasting ten to fifteen minutes. Hence, in a one hour and forty- minute press conference, ten questions get asked. None of the ten have anything to do with huge relevant issues that might shed a negative light on Obama. After eight years, we have grown weary of this.

He is simply using the purported Putin hacking as his excuse for his role in Hillary losing the election and Democrats having the fewest people in office since Reconstruction in the 1800s. Simple as that. Look no further for any explanation. It's the Obama out.

Polls showed that 75% of the voters thought the country was headed in the wrong direction. That's why Trump is the president-elect. The country is headed that way because the man pointing the finger at Putin took us there.

A narcissist can never take responsibility for any failure. There will always be a convenient list of excuses to explain away even the most obvious mistakes. This man is very good at this. He has practiced it all his life.

Sadly, he will use this to the detriment of fragile relationships with the Russians that are the result of his administration's failures. His, Hillary Clinton's and John Kerry's. No matter, not his problem, pass this on to Trump. And, take a few cheap shots at Trump on the way out the door.

Yes, over 40% of the public will buy your blather, that's still your approval rating. That included the press groveling at your feet, both coasts, Hollywood, educators at every level, and those who have enjoyed the largess of your generous run-up of the debt to $20 trillion. The problems your fictions cause will damage the Democratic Party for years to come as you replace Jimmy Carter as the worst president in our recent history.

Blog of the Year—2016
Trump Wins

November 8, 2016

You will wake tomorrow to this headline.

I have faith in my fellow Americans to do the right thing. Underneath all the noise, there is a fundamental groundswell that sees the corruption in D.C. This country has been through many rough patches and always came through.

If I am wrong and you are happy, I know we will survive another Clinton takeover. If I am right and you are unhappy, I hope we can make you happy by doing things that will make millions happier.

I have an old hat and a saltshaker standing by.

November 8th can't come fast enough.

New Beginnings

December 31, 2016

Here it is, published before the election. As the blogs will show if you go back and look, I was a Trump man from the get go. Never wavered. I have great positive vibes for 2017. The swamp will be drained and the snakes deposed. The media will attack Trump on a daily basis but the media has lost clout and is seen for what it is: a wing of the left. And the attacks will be offset by poorly reported successes. Strap it on; it will be a wild ride.

Happy New Year, and thanks for your readership.

2017 and Beyond

For those who would like to continue reading, the author will continue to post entries to the blog at nosmokeblown.com.

Addendum

The Story of United Airlines Flight 232

I t was a beautiful day. I had been to Casper, Wyoming, on
business. A business associate and I were flying back to
Chicago and connecting in Denver.

We tried twice to upgrade to first class. We were denied
both times.

It was a beautiful day to fly. The DC-10 was full. The skies
were clear with puffy white cumulus clouds. I had my headphones on and was listening to music.

Suddenly, out of nowhere, it was like we hit a big bump in
the sky. I switched the headphones over to the cockpit trans-
mission and heard, "We have lost all hydraulics." I'm not a
pilot but I have flown enough to know that no hydraulics
means no control. I had to decide whether to tell my business
associate that piece of news. He looked at the flight attendant's face and said, "What's going on? She look like she's
about to faint."

I told him, and we both concluded best case we would
overrun a runway with no brakes and no flaps. Worst case,
we didn't discuss. We had about forty minutes to observe the
flight of the plane. It was obvious they were flying in big circles, locked into whatever configuration they had.

The captain told us we were going to Sioux City, Iowa, and would land there. We knew it was a military base and had long runways. When we approached, he said he wasn't going to sugar coat it—it might be bad. Follow the directions of the flight attendants to the letter. They instructed us in the crash position. We crashed.

It seemed like we rolled forever. When we stopped, it took a second or more to realize we were upside down in the seat. We could smell fuel and smoke. There was light at one end of the tube.

For the most part, passengers were quiet. There were sobs and some panic. We helped some out of their seats and kept one man from panicking and creating a human stampede and pile up at the opening. When I jumped down, I heard someone calling for help. We found a Catholic nun trapped in the wreckage and helped her out. She was an invalid and we carried her out of the cornfield. When we got her to safety, I went back to see if anyone else needed help and to look for my traveling companion.

I encountered a young woman screaming at our flight attendant. She said she put her baby on the floor and when we crashed she lost the baby and it was the flight attendant's fault. I did not encounter my traveling associate. A piece of the plane was on fire with flames going thirty feet in the air.

They put us in buses and hauled us to the armory. The route they took was through the main carnage. It was then we realized how bad it really was and saw what no one should see. After an hour, I was reunited with Tom, my business associate, at the armory. He had walked to the airport terminal and had a few beers. Someone called the authorities, they came and got him and hauled him to the armory. A video of the crash was on at the armory. It was the first time we saw what really happened. I was able to call my daughter, Beth, who was at work. My wife, Sue, was in downtown Chicago shopping with a friend. Beth and her boss came to the house to meet Sue and tell her I was in a plane crash.

We were then taken to the hospital. I had torn the sleeve off my shirt since it was caught in the wreckage. They gave me a scrub shirt to wear. I had a cut on that arm and a lump on the shoulder the size of an egg. After an exam, I was taken to a cafeteria and waiting area.

We were told a plane would be available for any of us who chose to fly to Chicago that night. Tom and I opted in, volunteering immediately. I called Sue to let her know I was flying home. Then, she saw the video and went into full-blown panic. The next thing Sue saw was me on TV, coming through the airport at O'Hare. I was interviewed at the airport that night and the interview was carried the next day on all the network morning shows.

My street was full of media vehicles when we pulled in. I skirted them and found Sue, Beth, and Beth's boyfriend. We had a tearful reunion.

Oprah called and invited me to be on her show the next day. I opted out. We did one photograph the next day of Sue and me on the back patio and it was on the front page of *The Chicago Sun Times*. I did one TV interview with Elizabeth Vargas and one interview with a local reporter for *The Daily Herald*. I've turned down all other requests.

Several years later, I was flying on a United flight from Denver to Chicago. A flight attendant came to my seat and asked if I knew who Jan was. Jan was the flight attendant who told the mother to put the baby on the floor. The baby was lost. When I said I knew Jan, the flight attendant asked if wanted to talk to her. Jan was a training instructor on this flight and was in the galley. Jan recognized me when I walked on the plane. We talked for several minutes. She couldn't work as a flight attendant and had spent endless hours in Washington, D.C., lobbying for child seats on planes.

You can let an incident like this define you or you can work to move on.

My family got me through it. We spent more time together and had more hugs. Without them, I would have needed more help.

Acknowledgements

Thank you to the thousands of blog readers over the years who kept me going with their comments and encouragement.

A special thank you to the kids on the American Dream Flight, who taught me so much about courage and reaffirmed my decision to retire and my dedication to this blog.

To my wife, who gave up our time together allowing me to research and write the blog.

To my kids and grandkids, who make me so proud and to whom I used as sounding boards about my thoughts.

To my parents, who brought me up in a blue-collar world and never gave me reason to fear anything in that world. This is all about the common sense one gains from the street combined with solid education and business experience. What a boss once labeled street sense and business judgment—a great combination.

To Kim Bookless, Gwyn Snider, and Joann Dobbie, who helped and guided me through the publishing process.

Finally, to the cockpit crew of United Airlines Flight 232, who saved so many of us in a wounded airplane that can't be flown.

About the Author

Bill Robertson is a successful marketing executive who has been married fifty-two years and has two daughters and six grandkids.

He was born and raised in Niles, Michigan, and graduated from Niles High School. He received a BS in Business from Central Michigan University.

Bill started his career in California with Bank of America in a management training program. When he received his draft notice, he returned to the Midwest for his army physical. A knee injury that had shortened his wrestling career at CMU caused him to be rejected by the army.

His professional career then took him to Standard Oil, where he was hired as a sales trainee. Due to his success in sales, he was promoted to sales manager. This began a series of management positions, including Merchandising Manager, Manager of Marketing and Strategy, Lubricants Business Unit Manager, and Manager of Operations, Planning and Transportation. He was then promoted to VP of Commercial Sales, with his final position as VP of Brand Marketing. After thirty-five years with the company, Bill chose to retire in 1997.

In 1989, Bill was a passenger on United Airlines Flight 232 that crashed on a runway in Sioux City, Iowa. This experience changed his perspective on many parts of his life, including his career, and prompted his decision to retire.

Bill served on the boards of Children's Memorial Hospital, The National Hispanic Corporation Council, and Canmax (a Dallas Corporation).

Bill feels blessed to be here twenty-eight years after the tragic crash of UA Flight 232. His survival is considered an aviation miracle. Because of this, he values every day and equates it to a quote from Lou Gehrig: "Fans, for the past two weeks you have been reading about a bad break I got. Yet today, I consider myself the luckiest man on the face of the earth."

Bill lives in Chicago, Illinois, and Phoenix, Arizona, with his wife, Susan. He enjoys playing golf and spending time with his grandkids.

Made in the USA
Coppell, TX
04 April 2022

76020889R00201